EXCUSE ME,
YOUR JOB
IS WAITING

EXCUSE ME, YOUR JOB IS WAITING

Attract
The Work
You Want

laura george

HAMPTON ROADS
PUBLISHING COMPANY, INC.

Cover design by Bookwrights Design

Hampton Roads Publishing Company, Inc.
1125 Stoney Ridge Road
Charlottesville, VA 22902

434-296-2772
fax: 434-296-5096
e-mail: hrpc@hrpub.com
www.hrpub.com

If you are unable to order this book from your local
bookseller, you may order directly from the publisher.
Call 1-800-766-8009, toll-free.

Library of Congress Cataloging-in-Publication Data

George, Laura, 1955-
  Excuse me, your job is waiting : attract the work you want / Laura George.
    p. cm.
  Summary: "Applies the 'Law of Attraction' to the life experiences of losing or
getting a job. Helps you identify the qualities you want in a job and shows you
how to stay focused and upbeat to draw that perfect job to you. George offers
information on résumés, cover letters, internet job boards, interview strategies,
and more"--Provided by publisher.
  Includes index.
  ISBN 978-1-57174-529-3 (alk. paper)
  1. Job hunting--United States. I. Title.
  HF5382.75.U6G46 2007
  650.14--dc22

                              2006038248

ISBN 978-1-57174-529-3
10 9 8 7 6 5 4 3 2 1
Printed on acid-free paper in Canada

To Ted, Helen, Ken, and Magdalen

*The significant
problems we face
cannot be solved
at the same
level of thinking
we were at when
we created them.*

—Albert Einstein

Table of Contents

Foreword

What we attract as a job, and how we do the work, is simply a metaphor for life. Inspired by Lynn Grabhorn's bestseller *Excuse Me, Your Life Is Waiting*, *Excuse Me, Your Job Is Waiting* is chock-full of tips, strategies, exercises, and great advice on how to develop a bright outlook, empowering beliefs, and positive energy so that you can attract the work of your dreams. Work that is fulfilling, meaningful, provides opportunity, meets your financial goals, and, best of all, makes you feel great.

Our work deeply affects how we feel about ourselves, and ultimately our personal and financial freedom. Think about it. Do you feel stuck, frustrated, undervalued, resentful, or dragged down when you think about your job? If any of these words ring true, your beliefs about work are affecting more of your life than you realize.

Choosing empowering beliefs creates a better life, spawns success, and opens us to a universe of enormous possibility. But changing limiting beliefs is, for many of us, no more than a lofty ideal. How easy is it to have a feel-good outlook, staying calm, focused, and centered when your job is unfulfilling, a daily grind tethered to a much-needed paycheck—or, worse yet, you have no job at all? *That* is where the rubber meets the road. Meeting yourself where you are, taking an inventory of the way you approach work, and following the steps presented in this simple and sometimes sassy book will radically change the way you experience work *and* have a big impact on every other area of your life.

What we believe about ourselves and the world around us creates the filter through which we experience life. We don't see things as they are, we see things as we *believe* they are. The decisions we make and the actions we take, altered by the program of what we believe, draw to us people and situations that match the life-vibration we put out. This is certainly true with how we deal with work.

Author Laura George goes right to the heart of the matter, and each step she presents has the potential to make a big change in the way you approach the working world. For example: If we take action based on what we *don't want* to happen—such as keeping a job we dislike because we don't want to miss a car payment—that puts out a needy *"This is the way it is, I don't have the power to change it"* energy. Identifying what you really want, connecting with how good that feels, and investing your time, energy, and faith there will bring you the life (and job) you dream of.

Excuse Me, Your Job Is Waiting weighs in heavily on the intelligence of feelings. If you close your eyes for just a moment, you'll notice that you are feeling something *all the time*. Every moment, every thought pattern you have, every story you tell about how things are has emotion attached to it. Those emotions are full of good information. They answer important questions immediately: Is this good for me? Is this propelling me forward or holding me back? Is this fear or is this love?

As Laura points out, choosing to see the job hunt as a temporary process filled with possibility rather than a perpetual problem *feels* a lot better. Choosing strategies and a point of view that feels good can make a huge difference in the way you look for work and the work situations you attract.

Another powerful idea in *Excuse Me, Your Job Is Waiting* is the concept of personal responsibility. I'm not talking about blame or taking your lumps for making a mistake. That's a fear-based perspective. Taking complete responsibility is an *Act of Power.*

If you find yourself in a chronic situation full of negatives, with an outlook that isn't getting you where you want to go, there is good news. The good news is that whatever you believe is a point of view *you* agreed to. You have (and have always had) all the power you need to change it. Once you realize that, it opens a world of immense possibility. What we put out is often what we get back. Taking full responsibility and deliberately choosing and practicing what feels good will fuel your desire, creating an amazing shift in every part of life including your work.

How can you bring all these lofty ideas about attraction, belief, and feelings to your everyday life and something so pivotal as work?

Start with *Excuse Me, Your Job Is Waiting.* Follow all the tips, exercises, and practices. You will begin to notice right away that you *do* have the power to change your beliefs, your thought patterns, and the energy you radiate out to the world. And that's only the beginning. . . .

> With Many Blessings,
> Ray Dodd
> Author, *BeliefWorks* and *The Power of Belief*
> Boulder, Colorado
> December 2006

PART I

Energy

Chapter 1

Energy: The Basics

Master your energy, stir in a large dose of enthusiasm, entrench yourself in the process, and you will find your job search becomes empowered. You only need to employ both energy and economics to expand your opportunities.

In chapter 8, I will begin to address what I call "economic tools" because they deal with the business aspects of job searching: skill-sets, résumés, connections, etc. I will even touch on a few traditional economic concepts, such as demand for labor and maximizing utility. But, first and foremost, we are going to have a little fun with the energy side of job searching. The energy side involves thoughts, beliefs, and, most importantly, feelings. *How you feel about yourself, the economy, money, your occupation, and prospective employers has an immense impact on the outcome of your job search. Your energy has the potential to turn your job search into a smorgasbord of opportunities.*

This powerful energy is your *emotional* energy, not your stamina. Stamina is great, and very necessary, but it isn't the stuff that will bring your world into balance. Stamina is the stuff that keeps a puppy chasing its tail—necessary for physical movement, but not all that productive if applied without inspiration. You can have plenty of stamina and still be digging your grave with your low emotional energy. On the flip side, you can be very physically tired and have fantastic emotional energy. Great emotional energy can be compared with a runner's high: emotionally high as a kite while physically wiped out.

The concept of energy is easy to understand. In fact, its pure simplicity may be why some people discard it as kooky or nonsense, instead of looking at it as a powerful tool. The principle of energy, in a nutshell, goes like this: As humans, we are made of matter. As matter, we are made of energy, therefore we are energy beings. As energy beings, we are forever sending out energy and receiving in energy in the form of vibrations. You may have felt good or bad "vibes" coming from somebody at some point in your life—the strength and the frequency of the incoming vibrations were so powerful that you consciously felt the energy resonate! Most often, though, we are not conscious of the vibrations we pick up. We pick them up unknowingly.

Give Me the Keys, Please

The type of energy we send out attracts like energy. This simple concept unlocks the path to good experiences and favorable outcomes. It's the key to success. And shortly, you'll be taking it for a spin in your quest for a job. It's commonly known as the Law of Attraction.

Everything in your world, or not in your world, is a function of your vibrations. The vibrations you put out connect with like vibrations and, zappo, you've got more of the same. You are just a body full of vibes. Actually, it works much like a tuning fork. Think of a room of tuning forks set at a variety of vibrations. Ding one. What happens to the rest of the tuning forks? The ones on the same frequency start to vibrate. The others just sit there and do nothing. They don't connect.

The Law of Attraction

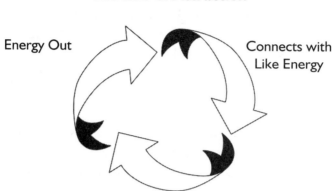

Energy Out

Connects with Like Energy

Brings More of the Same Energy Back to You

Like a tuning fork, you put out your own vibrations. Your vibrations hook up with energies vibrating at the same frequencies. These hook-ups work like magnets, bringing in experiences and things vibrating on your wavelength. Your vibrations cannot possibly pull in something vibrating at a higher or lower frequency. You can only connect with like energy. So, if you are putting out all sorts of bad vibes, you will get all kinds of lousy stuff back, maybe even a lousy job, but you can't get anything back that's different from your wavelength.

Unlike a tuning fork, you are not pre-set. You can change your vibrations from frequency to frequency by your thoughts. Most of us shift frequencies all the time. We may be sending vibrations way up on the scale, then a thought or two later, we might be sending out something pretty darned ugly. That's what keeps most of us in lives that are much the same—a little good, a little bad, but mostly just trudge, trudge, trudge.

Our vibrations are determined by our feelings. If we are feeling good, we send out high-frequency vibrations that connect us to even more high-frequency vibrations. If we are feeling less than good, we send out vibrations that are going to bring in something less than good.

Think about it. When you smile at other people, they smile back. When you give people an obscene gesture, what do you generally get in return? It only takes a little bit of positive or negative energy to get the process moving.

Vibes and Jobs

So, what does all of this have to do with landing a job? Well, just about everything. People who send out I-am-successful-and-I-am-a-great-employee-and-I-am-the-perfect-person-for-this-job energy get the job. People whose energy connects with the interviewers get the job. People whose energy connects with the corporate culture get the job. Many times, they get the jobs with less-than-stellar résumés. They get the job when everybody around them says it's impossible. This all happens because the energy they send out connects with what they want to bring in, and it all begins with their feelings.

How we feel at any given time impacts the energy we send out, which in turn impacts the energy we draw in. Therefore, it's our feelings, our emotions, that we need to master in order to bring good jobs into our lives. Lynn Grabhorn states this principle so wonderfully in her book, *Excuse Me, Your Life Is Waiting:*

> *We create by feeling, not by thought!*
> That's right, we get what we get by the way we feel, not by trying to slug things into place or control our minds. Every car accident, job promotion, great or lousy lover, full or empty bank account comes to us by the most elemental law of physics: like attracts like.

At this point you might be thinking: *Wait a minute here. This stuff is too off-the-wall for me.* You're not alone. We were not raised to think like this. Most of us were brought up to beat back our feelings. When you were having a bad day, what advice was dumped on you? If you're like most people, you heard, "Stop feeling sorry for yourself." "Stop whining." "Get over it!" "Don't wallow in self-pity." I think of it all as pull-yourself-up-by-your-bootstraps mentality. This mentality proved we were strong. We could get over our feelings. It was the only way we could do something about whatever situation was causing us pain.

We are a society of "doers," and when "doing" doesn't work, we "do" some more. Now, "doing" isn't bad—in fact, it is downright necessary—but problems arise when we get sucked into uninspired doing, or worse yet, doing simply for the sake of doing. I was once in that trap, sending out résumé after résumé, thinking that enough résumés would land me a job, as if landing a job were nothing more than a numbers game. Sadly, a lot of people seek employment from a throw-mud-at-a-wall perspective. If they throw enough mud, some is bound to stick. If they send out enough résumés, one will turn into a job offer. This process sends energy out all helter-skelter, and the job that comes back rarely has the potential to lead to a beneficial employment relationship.

Hindsight Is 20/20

If you are skeptical of the relationship between energy and employment, think back to your last interview. Whether the experience was good or bad, you felt something from the moment you walked into the interview and you sent off "vibes."

As a human resource manager, I was the gatekeeper for the flow of candidates. I had the responsibility to forward candidates to the hiring managers. When I started my career in human resources, I was not familiar with the principles of energy, but I constantly got a gut feeling about one candidate over another. I could seldom pinpoint what I felt or why I was an advocate for one candidate over another. I often had to tell the hiring managers that it was instinct, or gut, that made me want to give a less than stellar applicant a second interview. On the contrary, there were times when I told a hiring manager I just didn't feel "good" about a candidate whose credentials appeared to be nearly flawless.

As a job seeker, I have plenty of experience with the end results of my own energy. Here's a personal example of the kind of job I pulled in when I went job hunting with low vibrations. At the time, I had an upper-management position at a slow-paced company. The product was mature, the management team was lethargic, and the community was a picture-perfect country postcard. Unfortunately, that little postcard didn't have a place for me, a single woman. My days were spent in my solitary office, and my nights were spent in my solitary home. The only activity available to me was walking alone. During my employment at that company, I lost 18 pounds and resented my own companionship. This resentment was to play a key factor in my next professional position.

It was obvious that I needed a job in a metropolitan environment, so I began to submit résumés based primarily on geography. I got several responses and interviews. My first interview was for the position of Director of Human Resources for the United States Senate. I must admit I was pretty pumped up about the interview. Unfortunately, I wasn't pumped up about myself. Deep down, I felt I didn't deserve such a position. But I flew to D.C., hired a limo, and stepped into the interview with the necessary background and a crisp navy blue suit. My outward appearance was appropriate, but inside I was saddled with self-resenting energy. Ignoring my inner feelings, I went face to face with Senator Dole's Chief of Staff. The interview did not go well. Not only did I not get the job, but I also got the impression I was wasting her time. I walked out of the inter-

view on legs made of Jell-O. In retrospect, I had the skill-set—
I never would have gotten the interview without it—but I
didn't have the appropriate energy to stand on my own on
Capitol Hill.

After a much-needed vacation, I continued seeking employment in metropolitan areas. Each interview was in a great location, but each interview was a disaster. My self-resentment
fermented into self-loathing. A few interviews later, I gave up
actively seeking new employment and resigned myself to staying on at a slow but good job in a bad location. I figured I didn't
need, or deserve, anything better.

Back then, I didn't know the first thing about energy. I
didn't know then that what I put out is what I would get back.
I learned the hard way that my "I don't deserve any better"
energy was tacked onto résumés that had not landed into perpetual filing cabinets. One of those tainted résumés landed on
a desk that led to the worst professional job of my life. The day
I started the job, I realized I had hit some sort of professional
bottom with a painful crash. At first, I was pretty shocked, but
within weeks I began saying, "I am better than this." I said
those words when I drove to work. I said those words at work.
I said those words when I thought about the job and my life.
Within months, I was out of that place.

I would love to say that I learned my lesson about energy at
that point in time, but such is not the case. It took a few more
energetic explosions before I gave the concept of energy a peek,
but even then I did so with a great deal of skepticism. I wanted
to believe, I felt a connection, but I had reservations. I had to
look at my life in retrospect to confirm the idea before I applied
it to my future. My 20/20 hindsight gave me the confirmation
I needed to start working my energy.

I now realize that energy plays an enormous role in landing
a good job. People who work their energy get elevated to places
in the world of work that the rest of the population only

dreams about. They understand that they can "have it all." They take control of their energy and they take responsibility. Yes, *responsibility*. Unfortunately, I've seen too many people think that visualizing a job will bring it magically to them. Well, if they visualize a lot, and have the right feelings attached, it *might* happen, but generally speaking, people who succeed are far more proactive. They visualize, they feel good, and they move on a gut instinct when they are feeling good. If their good feelings lead them to believe they should be calling an old co-worker, or sending out a résumé to XYZ Company, they make the call or send off the résumé. They go with their hunches. They know their energy will open doors for them, but it's their responsibility to notice the doors and walk through them. Noticing such doors isn't easy. It takes practice to notice the doors, but all of this energy work takes practice.

Working energy becomes a way of life. It is a way of thinking. It is a way of being conscious. Our energy is at our command, but we must be willing to put feet on our thoughts and do the legwork necessary to succeed, as you will see throughout this book.

Personal Inventory

So what can energy do for you? Everything. There is nothing in your life that your energy has not brought to you so far. Your entire life has been orchestrated by your conscious, or, more likely, unconscious, use of your energy. If you have any doubt, look at your life through the clarity of hindsight. Remember a time when you were "on a roll" and everything went your way. For a while, you had the Midas touch. Then you started wondering when it would end. Perhaps a little voice in the back of your head kept telling you your good fortune wouldn't last, and your winning streak came to a crashing halt. Then there were other times when everything went wrong.

Nothing went your way. That same little voice started nagging about having your "luck" change, and it did. That little voice prompted a shift in your energy, and your life changed because your energy went forth and connected with other energy on the same wavelength.

Since the key here is to have your energy hook up with the energy you desire, you need to determine where you are and where you want to be. Take an inventory of your professional life. Think about it for a few minutes. Where you are today is a direct result of the thoughts and energy you created in the past. If you aren't fond of your current life, don't worry. Worrying will keep you trapped in negativity. Just look at your professional life honestly and accept that where you are is as good a starting place as any.

If you find that this personal inventory stuff isn't easy, you are not alone. In many cases, looking at one's life is downright painful. As humans, we don't care much for pain. When pain pops up in the personal-assessment process, it's quite natural to look for a scapegoat rather than to address the issue. It's far easier to blame a bad economy, a stupid boss, or a lousy company for a bad employment situation than it is to accept that your own energy is creating the havoc. Ahhh, we love to put out those bad vibes. But just because it's easy, or maybe even "normal," to place blame, it is not self-serving. A major component of working your energy is abandoning ideas, beliefs, and practices that no longer serve you. Therefore, if you happen to be one of those people who would rather blame someone or something else than accept responsibility, stop the blaming game now. Blaming creates a ton of bad energy. If you are blaming somebody else for your situation, then you are trying to deny that it's your problem. That doesn't work. You still have the problem, plus you have all of the negativity that goes along with the problem. By denying that you have a problem, you avoid resolving the issue. Instead, you sit and stew, whine and moan, and play the victim role well enough to win an Oscar, generating more negative energy in the process. That energy goes out into the world and joins forces with more negative energy. So, what do you get? More garbage, more stuff to whine and moan about, more negativity. In the case of job searching, it can very well bring you another lousy job or a longer duration of unemployment. So abandon blame and accept responsibility for your situation. Accepting responsibility is simply admitting to yourself that you put out energy that wasn't serving you well. It's nothing to feel bad about because you will soon be choosing to refrain from repeating that pattern.

Once you figure out where you are, it is time to figure out where you are going. You have to identify a job you want. This topic will be addressed in detail in the following chapters because knowing what you want is extremely important in getting it. As a human resource manager, I've interviewed dozens, maybe hundreds, of people who had no idea what they wanted. They would blankly look at me and say they wanted a job. From an energy perspective, they were putting out vibes saying, "I'm not worth much." In return, I put many of those people in dead-end jobs. I didn't do it to be mean; I simply did it because those positions needed to be filled, and filling them with people without direction was the easiest way to fill them.

I recently looked over a résumé from a young man who is a fresh graduate from a good college. It was thin and flat. He had no goals, no game plan, no idea of what he was going to do with his degree. He also waited until the last minute, two months after graduation, to do much about job searching. Currently, he is floundering, and until he gets focused, he will continue to flounder. I was privy to his résumé because he was passing it on to anybody who might know anybody who might be able to help him. People can only help people who know what they want. Knowing what you want is the first step to getting it, and this applies without fail to employment opportunities.

In some cases, people searching for work are not searching for work at all; they are simply searching for a way to pay their bills. They are not focusing their energy on positive things like a great future or a job they love. Instead, they are focusing on something they don't want: debt. This kind of thinking empowers negative energy. They are focusing on what they *don't* want, instead of focusing on a good job, and they are giving additional energy to that pile of bills they are trying to dodge.

Another important reason for knowing what job you want is that you can only begin to feel yourself in that position, the next step, after you define your perfect job. Feelings are like little energy connectors, sending energy out to like energy, connecting with it, and bringing it back to you, which is why feeling yourself in your new job is so important. How you feel is what you get. And you want to feel yourself in your perfect job. You want your energy to go out like a really big lure and tug that job back to you.

M.Y.O.B.

Mind Your Own Business. There's another important component to this equation: *Keep your feelings, and your thoughts, to yourself.* This was, without a doubt, the hardest part for me to master. I love to blab. I would start to feel myself in any given job, and I'd be telling anybody who crossed my path about the job I was getting. But my constant talking exposed my energy to the whims of others. No surprise, my big mouth was causing my troubles. I was putting out my energy, and it was getting muddled with the energy of all kinds of people who had their own agendas, adding extra weeks that turned into extra months to my job search.

A dear friend was once telling somebody about a great job she had on the line. Imagine her surprise when she got a rejection letter, and he got the job! He thought it was a great job and went for it before her deal had been clinched. She had put out all sorts of good energy to unearth that position, but he stepped in and put good energy around that specific job once he had wind of the opportunity.

In my case, I never knew how much I was hurting myself until I began to listen to the most successful people I knew. It took time, but I realized they played their cards close to their vests. The never talked about deals until their deals were done and the ink was dry. They never exposed their dreams, deals, and ideas to the murky energy of others. They kept their good energy on their most precious goals. And when negativity got in their way, they focused on their goals and flipped their energy back to the positive side of the playing field of life. They learned to master their energy and their world.

Chapter 2

What's a Want?

The Law of Attraction states that if we feel something, we attract it. If we want something, we simply have to feel it coming our way, and it plops into our laps. So why aren't we all just tripping over all sorts of goodies? Because we've been trained to *not* want, which pretty much explains why we have such a hard time creating good in our lives.

Why do we have it all so backward? It started eons ago when a few people decided they wanted all the goodies for themselves—the good food, the good cave with a spring-fed stream, the hottest babes . . . some things never change. So they started making rules that allowed them to have the best food, the best caves, and the hottest babes. Time passed, and this was all working out so well for a select few that they began to use God in their endeavors. Instead of passing on the truth that God is loving and benevolent, they turned him into an ogre that wanted humans to suffer on earth. Enough suffering, enough lack, enough toil, would eventually be rewarded with a glorious afterlife. So those without stopped creating via their vibrations and waited for their afterlives. The creation process slowed to a trickle. People lost their power. And, over hundreds and hundreds of years, even those that did not believe in God were convinced that life was one tough undertaking not something that offered a lot of goodies to the average Joe. Instead of creating people began waiting.

Now, waiting for an afterlife can be pretty damned frustrating. After all, getting a few parcels of goodies on Earth isn't all that bad. And if earthly goodies are such bad things, then why were those folks in the castles not abandoning them left and right? Some of those holding out for the afterlife began to look at life from a different perspective. They began to develop wants, but they were sending out such low-frequency energy that their wants remained unfulfilled. The unfulfilled wants generated more negative energy, and over time the wanters not only gave up wanting, but they told their kids not to want, and their kids not to want, and so it went. Pretty soon, most people forgot how to create with good vibrations. Feeling lousy became the norm and has pretty much stayed that way ever since. And just in case somebody didn't want to feel lousy, the human race developed a whole bunch more laws, rules, norms, and morals that made feeling downright lousy all the time the best thing in the world to get to that glorious afterlife!

Conversely, a few folks decided not to buy into the misery thing. They were willing to risk the castle in the sky with wall-to-wall plush cloud carpeting and a sound system that would blow you away for some joy right here on Earth. The nerve of them! They started looking around and decided that they deserved and expected more things. Oh, they worked, but they did so with joy in their hearts and anticipation of all the good things they could feel coming their way right here on planet Earth. They started getting the big houses, the good food, and the hottest babes. And what did they find? More joy!

I Waaaaaaant!

Most of us have issues with wants. We wanted candy as youngsters and found ourselves being dragged out of stores by our embarrassed moms as we cried louder in vain. We wanted a new Barbie doll, only to watch a sibling open the box with the doll at Christmas. We (okay, I) wanted to be cool in high school. Oh, God, that's too painful to remember. Bottom line, we found wanting to be disappointing and painful, so we stopped wanting a long time ago.

Instead of waiting for things we believed would make us happy, we settled for sure things. We wanted merely a roof over our heads, food, and a car, and, sure enough, we got a small home, lots of taco chips, and a Honda Civic. Life got safe. Our feelings flat-lined. No more getting excited about a want only to get that sinking feeling. We certainly weren't going to buy another ticket for a ride on that roller coaster.

Playing it safe sounded safe, but it was very costly. Those safe feelings lacked powerful, high-frequency energy, and we stopped the creative process. We forgot what it was like to get pumped up about something and the anticipation of feeling it come to us. Basically, we rolled over and played dead.

Oh, it gets worse. The wanting we could muster became wanting of things we saw in others' possession. Wanting went from desire to envy. Instead of anticipating the prospect of getting surf and turf at the latest hot spot, we started to get jealous of the folks who frequented such places. When that sweet little sports car passed us, we cringed with envy. If we were really in an energy sinkhole, we found a reason to dislike the driver, too. And when it came to beautiful homes, we simply stopped driving in such neighborhoods. The negative energy machine went into working overtime, and we found it hard to even keep that small house, those taco chips, and that Honda Civic.

All of this stuff happened because we forgot what it was like to want. We forgot what it was like to feel something we desired in our hearts and minds before we held it in our hands. We got stuck in the negative, and here's the kicker: We called it being *grown-up*.

Kids get more stuff not because people are willing to buy it for them, but because they can feel it. When they get it, they get really over-the-top happy. If you ask a kid who has just had a great day what kind of day he had, he will say "great" or "super cool" or "sweeeeeet" or any of a dozen other words that are over the top on the high-frequency scale. Ask an adult about a good day, and what do you get? "Not bad." Instead of a positive energy word, you get two negatives.

No Is a Two-Letter Word

Have you ever heard anybody say, "I ain't got no . . . ?" I ain't got no money. I ain't got no time. Unfortunately, most of us have heard that phrase sometime, someplace, and with some degree of discomfort. It's generally used to describe how downright down 'n' out someone is. People who "ain't got no" are scraping bottom and worried about the bottom falling out. But if you get out your old grammar textbook, you'll learn that "ain't" and "no" cancel each other out. Therefore, the true meaning of that expression is that you've got *something*, even if you are trying to express your lack.

Energy doesn't cancel out double negatives—it doubles the negative impact. If you focus on anything, regardless if you want it or don't want it, your energy magnetizes it to you. Let's say the last time you had a flat tire was when you were driving a "beater" in college. It was late at night and snowing, and you didn't have roadside assistance or an extra dime to your name. You spent what seemed like the entire night on the side of the road trying to change a tire without a flashlight. A trunkload of your most personal belongings was scattered all around you in the snow. That horrible night has burned a strong desire to never have a flat tire again into your very core. You really, really, really don't want a flat tire. You spend a lot of time worrying about a flat, and you spend a lot of money buying new tires so you never get a flat. You have the super-duper-deluxe roadside assistance plan. Guess what you get? A flat. Even if you have a new set of tires on the SUV, you will get a flat tire. Somehow you will run over something sharp and tough enough to rip a hole in those new radials. You focused so much negative energy on those tires that you made it happen—a flat tire.

I watch a lot of PBS. I'm somewhat addicted to *This Old House* and *Ask This Old House*. One episode of *Ask This Old House* had a piece on insulating water pipes. The team showed how to, and how not to, insulate pipes. They illuminated the most common mistake when it comes to pipe insulating—failing to insulate the elbow of a pipe. They showed different types of insulation, and some insurance folks even gave them data on the estimated costs involved to repair pipes that have frozen. They pretty much covered frozen pipes from A to Z. But just when I thought I knew all a non-pro like myself would ever need to know about pipes, a little story at the end caught my attention. They were talking about some poor soul who was really concerned about freezing pipes. He went to great lengths to insulate his home to avoid the problem entirely. What did he get? Frozen pipes. The insulation was installed on the wrong side of the pipes, protecting them from the heated indoor air and exposing them exclusively to the cold exterior air. That guy focused so much on a "don't want" that he got it—frozen pipes.

One of the best ways to extend a job search is to focus on not wanting unemployment. When you focus on how long you are unemployed, the ramifications of not working, or the stress of unemployment, you are sending out truckloads of negative energy. Keep it up, and you may find yourself sitting on the sidelines of the working world for years. Focus on bills, and they multiply like rabbits. You go from having one pile of bills you can't pay to having a broken washing machine and an idiot light on your dashboard that leads you to a problem that's going to cost you thousands.

It's Mine, Damn It!

We get attached to our own problems from an energy perspective and from an emotional point of view. Love them, hate them, it doesn't matter—they are all ours, and anything that might solve them is pretty scary. I worked with a woman once who put this all so plainly. She said if we all stood in a town square and tossed our problems into a fountain, and if we could all reach in and pull out any set of problems in the world, we'd all grab for our own. There's a comfort level within our own world, no matter how much we complain, so we hang onto it.

Oh, you might be thinking you'd let go of your problems in a heartbeat and you know exactly what you want, but I'd beg to differ with you any day of the week. This isn't an exercise, just a wake-up call. Take out several cards with one blank side—they can be old business cards or 3" x 5" cards. Now get a box. The better the box, the better the experience. A decorative box is great because you are going to make believe this is a magic box. This magic box delivers your wants. All you have to do is write down what you want, toss it in the box, and it appears. The only catch is that what you write is what you get. So, what are you waiting for? Get writing.

If you're like most people, you are thinking this is a trick. You are looking for the loophole. You are downright searching for the negative. This magic box is making you feel anything but good. Get over it. Start writing. You want all of your bills paid in full? It's a fairly common want. There's only one really massive problem with this want: The focus is on a "don't want," not a want. The focus, or root, is on bills. Bills! Bills, my friends, are a downright energy zapper.

Since this book is about employment, a job should be a want, but that too gets tricky because you don't want just any job, so you refrain from putting that in the box. After a while, you may realize you've put nothing, zero, zip, into this box. You simply can't figure out what you want, and you get frustrated when it doesn't show up.

Don't Wants

As we embrace our problems, fail to feel good about even good things, and allow our envy to flare whenever we see something out of our range, we send out more and more junk energy, and we bring back more and more junk energy. We end up with a bunch of "don't wants." Yeah, things that we don't want we get, and we get lots of them. We don't want lousy bosses. We don't want pink slips. We don't want our jobs to get shipped overseas. We certainly don't want to cash in our 401k plans before retirement. We don't want to tell the kids there's no vacation this year. We don't want to tap into that line of credit on the house. We don't want to go to the family reunion and sit in the shadows. We don't want to eat pasta for dinner for the umpteenth night in a row. For the unemployed, there are plenty of don't wants, and all too many of them come home to roost. Of course, the more don't wants that we get, the more icky energy we send out, and the more don't wants come back to us.

The only good thing about don't wants is they are the best roadmap you have to a want. Most don't wants hold a want. Yes, somewhere inside every don't want is a want just itching to get out. You don't want a lousy boss, flip, you want a good boss, or a great boss, or a fantastic boss. You are probably thinking you'd settle for a boss who wasn't sired by Lucifer. That's just the kind of thinking and feeeeeeeling that got you the boss from hell in the first place. If you don't want a lousy boss, then you want a great boss, or a fantastic boss, and believe it or not, there are lots of great bosses.

You don't want a pink slip—flip—you want a secure job. You don't want your job to get shipped overseas—flip—you want a job close to home. You don't want to cash in your 401k plan—flip—you want a financially rewarding retirement.

These simple flips start to get your feelings away from the negative and into the flat-line arena, but you need to catch onto that high-frequency energy to get them to magnetize into your life. Let's look at the 401k issue. If you flip from not wanting to cash in your 401k to wanting a financially rewarding retirement, you are on the right path. But you need to expand the dream to expand the energy. You have to feel yourself retiring in good health and playing golf a couple times a week. Begin to feel yourself traveling to those places you've always wanted to see, perhaps Europe or a road trip across the United States. Visualize yourself and your significant other sipping wine and watching the sun set over the ocean. Go whole hog with this line of thinking. Let those good vibrations take hold. Feeeeeel yourself living that fun-filled, secure retirement. Those are the feelings that will guarantee you the 401k. Let them expand. Think of a big balloon expanding with all of the stuff you could jam into your golden years. Keep pumping it up.

Well, here I come with a pin! Now, think about your lack of retirement funds. Pop! You may have gone from way-up-there vibrations to down-in-the-dumps vibes that can only possibly connect with some financial disaster. It's all about feelings, and that's why flipping don't wants into wants is so extremely important.

How does this apply to your job? If you're like most unemployed people, you are putting a lot of energy into what you don't want and very little into what you do want. It's easy to spot don't wants. They are in your face. Only by flipping them can you start to unearth the job you are seeking.

Law of Attraction (Again)

The Law of Attraction says energy out connects with like energy and brings it back to us. So, if we are sending out don't wants, we can only get more don't wants. In order to remedy the situation, we have to send out wants. By using our don't wants to identify our wants, we can get this entire process moving with four simple (although not always easy) steps:

1. Figure out what you don't want.

2. Extract the want.

3. Get a whole bunch of really super duper fantastic energy spinning around it and the anticipation of its arrival.

4. Be grateful at its appearance.

Enter Fairy Godmother

Lucky you, a benevolent fairy godmother just fell into your world! You get all your wants. What are they? Of course, the standard stuff comes to mind: a bigger house, more taco chips with sauce, a better car. But there are a lot of stuffed-up wants inside you. Now is your time to release them.

With your fairy godmother standing by, start to think of all the things you really want. Your kids' education paid for, some goodies for your spouse, 24/7 at-home assistance for your aging parents all come to mind. Perhaps some are just for you—a summer overseas, a new sports car, a beach house.

Stretch your imagination. Go into want overload. Let every pent-up want you have loose—everything from a good haircut to world peace. Allow yourself to feel your wants materialize. Don't worry about where they are coming from or who's going to pay for them. The goal is to feel them. How they show up is not your concern at the moment. What's important is to get back into feeling good things come your way.

Spend an hour or so just getting to the root of your wants. Feel good about them. If you want a sweet new car, feel the keys in your hand. Better yet, go testdrive one. Feel how it handles. Feel the seats. Don't let the pesky salesperson ruin the experience. Just feel gooooood!

Once you have your big wants defined, identify some small wants. Feel them, too. You will be surprised how fast they appear. Once you get used to the little wants coming your way, it will be much easier for you to work your good energy around big wants.

I've wanted some pearls for quite some time now. I've admired them on others and have thought about the day I buy them for myself. Well, a couple of weeks ago I was on a roll, on a frequency that was mind-blowing. Ideas and concepts were coming to me so quickly that I was having a hard time scribbling them down as I was driving across town. I had my local NPR station on the radio out of habit. It was fund-drive time again. Each pledge drive I always give a little, but to be honest there's a component of gambling with my pledge. I submit my pledge when there's a drawing for something I desire. Since my energy was sky-high and the drawing was for a two-day stay at a lodge I thought my parents would enjoy, I raced home to try to get my pledge in just under the wire. Later that evening, when I didn't get a call from the station, I must admit I was slightly disappointed. After all, my energy was in the stratosphere.

The pledge drive ended, and I forgot the entire incident until yesterday when the radio station called. As it turned out, I did not get my pledge in within the time frame for the two-day excursion at the lodge, but instead it went into the next drawing for a substantial gift certificate at a jewelry store. My pearls are on their way.

Oh, I am not saying you will win your dream car, but I am saying things have a way of working out that's beyond our comprehension once we start being conscious of our energy. It's our job to keep positive energy flowing and wait for the results. Your job is to focus good energy, continue sending out your résumés, and expect a job to be delivered in an unexpected manner.

Jobs, Jobs, Jobs . . .

Since this book is about procuring employment, it's safe to say you want a job. Good start, but why do you want a job? The next answer is generally "because I need one."

"Need" is almost a guarantee for a longer duration of unemployment. Need brings out the negative energy. Just thinking about needing something puts you in a state of not having, which is a real downer. "Want," on the other hand, is desire. Desire is great energy. When we think of desiring something, we begin to anticipate its arrival. It feels good. Desire and anticipation walk hand in hand. It's an uplifting vibration. So, first, go from *needing* a job to *wanting* it. Just this simple change of wording will shift your energy from desperation to desire. It will get you feeling good about your job search.

Why do you want a job? Is it for money, or self-expression, or a way to fill your days? Most folks say money, but money is nothing more than coins, paper, or electronic blips. Okay, you don't need a job for money; you need a job to pay bills. You are back to bills. You're in a negativity loop.

Jump out of the loop. Get beyond the car, house, and college fund. If money were no object, what would you buy and why? If money were no object in my life, I'd take my parents on a world tour. I would do this to see their faces and to watch their delight. In other words, I would like a lot of money to make my parents happy. Are my parents unhappy without my riches? Heck, no. I would just want to make them happier. So my want is defined as "making my parents happy." Guess what,

I can do that without much money! I can do that by visiting them, cooking a meal for them now and then, and forgoing annual spats with my siblings. I can get to the feeling of their happiness without money. And in my case, it's that feeling that will attract jobs that will bring me money to get more of what I want—making my folks happy.

It's the same with you. Why do you want your house free and clear? To not make a mortgage payment? Probably not. Most people want their houses free and clear to feel ownership, to feel secure, to feel that their house can never be taken away from them. It's the feeling of security they desire, not the lack of a house payment. It all boils down to feelings.

So if you could break out of the loop and get anything in the world you would want, how would you feel? Ecstatic, elated, happy, secure, content, proud? Well, there are things that you can do without a job that can give you the same feelings. Look for them. Once you get the feeling, you will bring more and more of the feeling into your world. Hence, you will bring in a job. If you want to feel secure, perhaps looking at a photo of yourself from long ago when you felt secure makes you feel secure. If you want to feel happy, perhaps a picnic with a friend lifts your spirits. Getting into the feeling is key.

Top Dollar

Say you've gotten your don't-want—bills—flipped to wanting money. How much money do you want? A nice $85,000 annually would be just fine. Okay, so you are developing a want. You want a job with an $85,000 annual salary. Your don't want—that pile of bills—flipped into a want—a salary, a concrete number.

It's important to set a number for your compensation from an energy perspective. Too many people look at their potential worth in dollars in a way that works against energy principles.

They set a floor, the least amount of money they will consider from an employer, and they focus on it. Since it's a worst-case scenario, it's double-charged with negative energy. If your want is an $85,000-a-year job, but you are vibrating your worth at a mere $60,000, you will only receive a $60,000 position. When you turn down that offer, your energy will sink even lower, and nothing is going to happen on the old job front. That's the tale and trauma of so many job searches. If you want an $85,000-a-year job, you have to get your frequency up to a level that connects with $85,000-a-year jobs. Now that you know about the Law of Attraction, you have the option, and the responsibility, to vibrate at a level that sends your energy out to get the good stuff. Stop focusing on a don't want. Extract your wants from your don't wants. Start the creative process.

Chapter 3

The Bad and the Ugly

The one thing I've always found amazing about prescriptive books is that so many are written by people who are peeking at the problem they are trying to solve, not living through it. Economists, protected from personal economic woes by tenure and college walls, write cures for poverty. Funny, people with full tummies writing about the inequity of income. I liken the process of people peeking at a problem and trying to solve it to tea drinkers prescribing a remedy for a hangover. Until you've had a hangover, you don't know what a hangover feels like. Until you've struggled to find a job, you don't know what struggling to find a job feels like. Believe me, I've lived through job searching more times than I'd like to admit. I know how job searching can be one big negative ordeal at times. I also know that I only got a job when I believed I would get one. When I sent out "this economy sucks, and I won't get a job" energy, I sat and fretted over bills. When I changed my thoughts and energy, a job always came my way, regardless of the economy or the gaps on my résumé.

Even if you aren't buying into this energy stuff completely, it's pure common sense that you will be more desirable to employers with a positive disposition than an ugly one. Therefore, it's time to sort through your emotions, dump the garbage, and bring up your self-esteem and your feelings. Your energy will follow.

Let's look at the down-and-dirty side of job searching, the side that makes you spew out negative vibes like a cotton-candy machine out of control. By doing so, we will be able to come up with some remedies to get you onto the feeling-good-here-comes-the-great-job express. Let's see what's blocking the good jobs from coming your way.

The Economy

Most folks looking for work believe the economy plays a role in their job search. Therefore, their feelings about the economy impact their energy. How do you feel about the economy? What is "the economy" to you? Is it some big boogie-man? Is the economy some elusive creature like the Wizard in *The Wizard of Oz* who pulls the levers and makes things happen? Is the economy some non-tangible that is relayed to you by faceless economists in some think tank or government office? If so, then the economy can be a pretty scary thing. The economy can be something out of your control. It can be something not quite understandable. As children, we learned that things out of our control and not quite understandable have the potential to cause us harm. Hence, they are bad things that make us feel bad.

Maybe you possess a strong knowledge of economics, and the state of the economy is making you mad as hell. Perhaps the national debt keeps you awake. You worry the government will refrain from fiscal responsibility and turn the Treasury into a printing press, turning inflation loose on the land. Bottom line is you worry a lot. Worry is negative energy.

Oh, there might be some bright spots in the economy, but

for job seekers, in a "jobless recovery," those spots are few and far between. Just the words "jobless recovery" can create a state of unease for the job seeker. For those reading about the economy on a daily basis, the feelings generated by the news can be confusing at best. When you read a report that states the economy is getting better, you may process that news and come up with mixed emotions. You feel better because a new job may be on the horizon, but you feel worse because if the economy is getting better, then your lack of success in your job search is personal. When you turn on the nightly news and hear a story about a company closing or another corporate scandal costing thousands of jobs, you again experience mixed emotions. You feel bad because more lost jobs means fewer opportunities. But you may feel better because misery loves company. Oh, does misery love company! Misery is negativity. Negativity loves negativity.

No matter what the economic news, it evokes emotions and feelings from all of us. Most of those emotions aren't warm and fuzzy. Economics is sometimes referred to as the "Dismal Science." If you think that putting the economy out of your mind is the solution, it might be part of it, but there is far more of this emotional baggage to dig through before we begin to address the solutions. So let's get to it. Let's get personal.

Ticked Off

If you are like most people looking for work, you are experiencing all kinds of emotions. Many aspects of job searching can make anyone feel pretty darned lousy. Everything from the constant question, "Gotta job yet?" to the bill collectors can ruin a day. Perhaps your spouse isn't pleased with your non-productive job search. Or maybe it's your fellow members at the club who are making you feel like an outcast. If none of them yank your chain, perhaps you are just plain angry with your former, or present, employer. Stewing about your mistreatment by the hand that once fed (or is feeding) you can be negative emotional fodder for hours at a time. It's also good for several months of simmering-just-below-the-surface anger. Anybody with a driver's license knows that kind of anger—the kind that prompts the using of hand language in traffic.

When you aren't angry, you may be keeping company with your old reliable companion, worry. Worry is always there. Worry keeps you awake at night and wakes you up in the morning. Worry haunts you as you draft what appears to be the millionth copy of a résumé and tells you in a panicked voice, "This one has to work!" Worry has you checking your e-mail a dozen times a day and calling your own phone number to make sure your phone still works.

When you get tired of worrying about your present state, you turn on the tube to escape and hear about the economy again. Yes, there is always some commentator willing to remind you that jobs are going on a not-so-slow boat to China. Oh, God, where does it end? The truth is that it ends when you decide it ends. But first, you have to dig a little deeper into your emotional garbage pail.

Hey, Buddy, Like Your Line of Work?

How do you feel about work? This may at first sound like a silly question, but it's probably one of the most meaningful questions you will ever ask yourself. Considering you spend about a fourth of your adult life at work, this question, if addressed, has the potential to change your world. Unless somebody created a trust fund with your name on it, or a winning lottery ticket is burning a hole in your pocket, or you've found some benevolent source who wants to take care of your financial needs, you probably have to work in some capacity for money.

But we don't work entirely for money. Money is important—in fact, it's so important that chapter 6 addresses money in detail—but money is only one component of the work/energy issue. In our society, what we do is what we are. I've worked many jobs over my lifetime. Some were at the professional level; others were at other levels in the corporate food chain. They all paid the bills. But the way people responded to me once they learned what I did for a living varied greatly with each position. People pretty much summed me up upon learning my occupation even though they knew little else about me.

There's no denying that your occupation plays an enormous role in who you are in our society. It's one of the reasons why being out of work is so painful for many people; they lose their identity when they lose their jobs. If you are feeling the pain of losing your identity, making a list of everything you liked about your former position or job and focusing on the key points will help you reconnect with your energy and bring a similar job into your world more rapidly.

The most successful people in the workplace like what they do and love to talk about their work. They can't get enough of it. It's not just CEOs who feel great about their jobs. Many people find their niche in life. I know artists living hand-to-mouth who wouldn't change a thing in their worlds. I know college professors who love teaching. Some of the craftsmen I've known over the years have taken great pride in their occupations.

On the flip side, people who dislike their occupations tend to want to steer conversations away from anything work-related unless they are complaining. I know a lot of those folks, too. They complain about their employers, their co-workers, and their lives. Talking to them is one endless whine. The only thing that makes them tolerable is their interests in things that are not work-related. These folks work for the weekend, they work for retirement, and, unfortunately, they work very hard.

When somebody asks "What do you do?" do you answer

with pride or do you rapidly find a way to change the subject? How you feel about your occupation plays a role in the energy side of your job search. If you don't like your occupation, you won't be energizing it and attracting it to you. And, even if you do manage to build up a good puff of positive energy to bring the job into your world, you won't be able to sustain the energy or the job.

Job-Search Energy

If you were to make two lists of your feelings—one side positive, the other negative—you'd probably find, like most people searching for a job, that the negative column is winning by more than a nose. That's a lot of negativity. All of this negativity is undermining your job-search efforts. Well, more to the point, it's crushing them like a bug. Playing around in negative energy is like playing around in a mud puddle. There is a certain amount of fun in playing in the mud, but it's impossible to attract anything other than mud in a mud puddle, and it's impossible to attract anything other than negativity while playing with negative energy. Being aware of the negativity traps is a good way to stay clear of them while job searching.

Chapter 4

The Remedies

Surprisingly, you don't have to walk around in some sort of dream world all day long to reverse your negativity. *Just a few moments of strong, focused positive energy can undo the damage caused by flat-lined or negative energy.* Get in the habit of taking your energy pulse. Pay attention! When you are spinning the bad stuff, *stop!* Change direction. Change your thoughts and your feelings. Work on producing vibrations at a frequency that will make your life a smorgasbord of opportunities.

Flip

Feelings are funny little things. They hold a lot of power, and you've probably been at their mercy for years. Well, no longer. You have the power to reign over your feelings instead of letting them set the course. And here's how it can be done.

First, flip those don't wants into wants. You have the power, so use it! You can turn your don't wants into wants and start getting the big house, the best food, the sweet wheels . . . and the best job. We talked about it in chapter 2, but this simple step-by-step plan bears repeating:

1. Figure out what you don't want.

2. Extract the want.

3. Get a whole bunch of really super-duper-fantastic energy spinning around it and the anticipation of its arrival.

4. Be grateful at its appearance.

Once you start flipping your don't wants into wants and are conscious of your energy, the world will get the message, and the goodies will multiply rapidly.

Thoughts about Job Searching

To change your energy, you have to change your thoughts. Thoughts lead to feelings that lead to energy and actions. As we discovered in the previous chapter, job searching for many is a whirlwind of negative energy. The best way to move from negative thoughts is to bear in mind that job searching is temporary.

Yep, job searching doesn't last forever. Oh, it might feel like forever at times, but it only lasts for a very short period in the final analysis. And all of the frustrations, financial struggles, resentments, and fears that go along with job searching are temporary as well. If you accept that job searching is temporary, it becomes easier to step away from the negative stuff flowing through your head like a raging river. By turning job searching into a temporary condition, you make it powerless over your thoughts, feelings, and results. You turn it into a process instead of a lifestyle.

Indeed, job searching is a process, not a crisis, a problem, or even a challenge. (Climbing the rope in eighth-grade gym class was a challenge!) It is composed of taking steps toward the goal of gainful employment. Each step should give you more confidence and have you feeling better and better about the process. With each elevated feeling, you get closer and closer to the job of your desires.

By turning job searching into a temporary process, it becomes easy to turn it into something rewarding. You can begin to feel that job being offered to you. You become empowered.

I've seen some pretty powerless folks sit across from me at the human resource desk. A few people just fidgeted themselves right out of a job. They gave little 5'2" me power over their entire futures. Ironically, I had no power over them until they gave it to me. I was just a woman with a title sitting behind a desk. All I could do was suggest hiring or not hiring them. That is very meager power in the entire scheme of things. In fact, it's pretty close to nothing. If I didn't hire them, they wouldn't cease to exist. The worst that could happen is they would simply face another human resource manager at another company. But they sat across the desk shuffling their bums from one side of the chair to the other as if I were a great big monster who would pounce on them if they sat still for ten minutes.

If you are going to empower anybody, empower yourself. Once you, as a candidate, believe that you have the power to create a world of opportunities, you will be comfortable around any HR person or hiring manager. You will be inspired in your job search. You'll become creative in both your methods and your goals. To become empowered, you need to figure out where you are currently frittering away your energy and power.

Anger

> Anybody can get angry . . . that is easy, but to be angry with the right person, and to the right degree and at the right time, and for the right purpose . . . is not within everybody's power and is not easy.
>
> —Ar

When we look at energy and feelings, we must look at anger. Anger is very powerful energy. Ironically, anger is not good or bad. Just check with your gut. Sometimes anger hurts like heck; other times, its release feels good. How we as humans decide to use that powerful energy is what's good or bad.

Although most of us have learned to think that anger is bad, anger is our servant. Without anger, we more than likely would have perished thousands of years ago. Anger has been pivotal in keeping humans alive for eons. Without anger, we would have just sat there waiting for that tiger to become a pet. Instead, we saw the tiger eat the neighbor, got angry, and high-tailed it out of there when big kitty came calling again. Anger triggers physical responses that can get us moving. In many cases, we hear about the "last straw," an action or event that made somebody so angry that it forced her to do something she should have done hours, days, weeks, months, or years ago.

Anger's force empowers us to perform great tasks. Anger has empowered people to get out of jobs they hated and search for jobs they enjoyed. Anger has empowered people to get out of destructive marriages and seek healthy lives. Anger has empowered people to change their lives for the better. When we use the energy created by anger to create a positive change, that powerful energy works for us. It has the potential to bring in opportunities beyond our wildest dreams.

The key to making anger work for you instead of against you is using that powerful energy as a motivator instead of an equalizer. When you have a good puff of anger rolling, use the energy to search for opportunities, instead of wasting it on "get even" dreams and schemes. Oh, it's human nature to want to go back and tell the tyrant who just fired you "HA!" but it serves no purpose other than to feed negativity. By feeding negativity, you will just get more negativity. Instead, use that energy to push beyond the "HA" and start thinking about how great it vill be for you to have the corner office and the big paycheck.

Think of what you will do with the money, status, or whatever else you determine constitutes your dream job. Use the physical energy generated by anger to seek out jobs. Use it positively and productively. Anger is powerful energy, and once it's created it can never be destroyed; it can only be used for good or for bad. Choose to use it wisely.

The way to turn the energy created by anger into a positive force is to be conscious of the anger and the energy it generates. Too many people act first and think later when they are angered; such actions are generally a destructive use of what could be good energy. We've all seen the behavior, and it seldom serves the person acting out. The key to using the energy generated by anger as your servant is to think immediately about what you want that energy to do for you. When you get angry, take a few deep breaths. If you are really angry, do something physical, such as running or cycling. Do whatever is necessary for you to focus the energy into a productive direction. The energy created by the anger isn't going to go away if you take a run. Energy once created cannot be destroyed; it can only be directed. If you decide to take a run or cycle 30 miles, you might find that you can easily get yourself into the "zone"—that place where ideas simply come from within so rapidly that problems solve themselves. That's angry energy working as your servant.

The only time anger becomes problematic is when we choose to use that energy in a negative manner or decide to hold it in. Holding onto it is a waste of powerful energy in the short run and a health hazard in the long run. Let it out. Anger is like gas. We somehow have this twisted view that good people don't get angry and good people don't get gas. But good people get angry and good people have to fart just like the rest of the human race. Holding in a fart doesn't stop the problem. Held-in farts eventually sneak out, silent but deadly. Anger is pretty much the same. Hold it in, and it too will sneak out silently but deadly. Don't try to hold in anger. Used properly, anger becomes your servant. Used improperly, anger becomes your jailer, holding you in a cell of negative energy.

Learning how to use the energy created by anger takes practice. Don't expect to turn every iota of angry energy into a genie overnight. In fact, it's a good idea to look at anger in different degrees. The big things that happen in life create a lot of anger and a lot of energy. The big things are what you need to turn into motivators. But you need to let go of the everyday garden variety of anger that's caused by hundreds of little things that don't exactly go your way. The newspaper that was once again thrown into the bushes, or the red light that slowed you down, or the kid at the coffee shop who couldn't get your order right—these are simply part of life, and it's better to let them go. They aren't large enough or powerful enough to help you. If you hold onto each and every one of them, they will soon become a large posse of negative energy grabbers ready and waiting to jail you.

Letting go of little irritants becomes relatively easy once you learn to prioritize things that push your buttons. What's worth getting pissed off about, and what isn't? Is the person with 14 items in his cart in the grocery line clearly marked 12 items or less worth a hissy fit? Probably not. The anger you generate by getting mad at the person in line puts out more angry energy, and in a few minutes you have a good cloud of negative energy all around you (like Pigpen in Peanuts) just waiting to bring more negative stuff to you. You must decide right there and then to turn that anger around to serve you or let it go. Most of us aren't that quick with harnessing anger, so it's easier to let it go. If you choose to turn it into your servant, do it quickly. Don't give it time to call in its cronies. They like to join forces like a big army.

Here's an example of angry energy on overdrive. I know of a string of car dealerships where the sales staff confused, intimidated, and at times bullied customers into buying cars. Those negative techniques generated a lot of anger and resentment in many customers. The entire environment was a whirlwind of negative energy. Unfortunately, the goal was to sell cars, not to worry about the vibrations. One day an angry customer returned in search of the salesman who had persuaded him into what he perceived to be an undesirable deal. He returned with a gun and shot the salesman. Were all of those closed deals worth a bullet? I have to say no.

Okay, this is all beginning to make sense to you, but you are wondering how to really apply it in everyday life. Practice. Practice. Practice. Let's say you are on the freeway. The car on your left cuts you off to get onto the exit ramp on the right. Now here are your options:

1. You can give the son-of-a-bitch the finger and blow your horn. Make sure you get plenty of attention.

2. You can shake your head and think that jerk needs to learn how to drive.

3. You can think that poor guy nearly missed his exit. It was a good thing you both had good driving skills.

All three are the truth. It's your option to embrace any interpretation of the truth you so desire. If you know that negative energy attracts more negative energy and you aren't skilled yet at flipping negative energy into your personal servant, why in blue blazes would you embrace number one? Habit. Is a habit a good enough reason to send out negative energy? All the first scenario will get you is more negative energy. The second scenario isn't as bad, but it still isn't going to bring in the good stuff. Practice number three.

Part of learning to harness your anger is being careful with your words and thoughts. If you use angry words, you will attract angry words, angry people, angry situations. If you don't believe me, watch any argument escalate. It doesn't take long for a minor disagreement to become a shouting match. Nobody wins, but everybody shouts. Therefore, listen to yourself. If your spoken and unspoken words are playing havoc on your energy and feeding your anger, change your vocabulary. Your vocabulary has the power to jail you or liberate you. If you think angry, if you think small, if you think lack, you will become angry, you will become small, and you will experience lack. But if your vocabulary embraces love, allows you to be a big person, and knows this is an abundant world, you will experience love, you will become a big person, and you will reap the riches of an abundant world. You have the power to change your vocabulary, change your perspective, change your energy, and change your life. It's all up to you. You can feel good. And those good feelings are the keys to magnetizing the good things into your world.

Fall in Love

Hopefully, you are beginning to look at your feelings with the emphasis they deserve. You are beginning to understand that your feelings can turn your world around. You are beginning to see the connection between feeling great and getting a great job. If you want to bring a great job into your life, you need to feel great. This may sound foolish, but we spend so much time trudging through life that we forget what it is like to feel good, much less great. What does feeling great feel like? At its best, it feels like falling in love. Remember a time when you fell in love?

I had a friend do this exercise, and she went a little too far. She recalled the falling-in-love part and the hooking-up part— but then she remembered the divorce part. The hook here is to hang onto the falling-in-love part, those precious moments, not to fast-forward to the good, bad, or ugly that might have followed. Just remember the falling-in-love part, period.

You will recall when you were falling in love that the problems of the world seemed to dissipate. You didn't have time to be hung up on trivial things like traffic jams, a boss on a rampage, and bill collectors. Your energy was focused on the person you were falling for, and all of life's little, or not so little, problems had to solve themselves. And, thanks to your energy, most of them did. You failed to give your problems energy, and they melted away.

Love has such a universal way of making problems transparent that weddings are a staple for boosting ratings on sitcoms. This tried-and-true technique isn't used during sweeps week because weddings are necessarily funny; this technique is used because weddings bring out the most bizarre behavior in people close to the happy couples, and still the happy couples emerge victorious. Most women can tell a tale of some fiasco from their wedding experience. At my own wedding, one of my aunts, whom I love dearly, decided that the bridal table had to be set with her personal china—a plan that had "disaster" stamped clearly on it from the get-go. Then, at the all-important moment when we exchanged vows, a bridesmaid vomited. Had I not been floating on air, such behavior would have set me off screaming. But with the feeling of love all around me, the quirks of the day had quite the opposite impact. I was touched by my aunt's gesture and generosity. I was very concerned about my friend's health, not her bad timing. Love was all around me, and nothing had the power to bring down my energy.

Love

Love and falling in love are two different things. Falling in love is finding some romantic partner over whom to swoon. Love is getting in touch with your Higher Self—that part of you that is all-knowing and pure joy—and allowing it to connect with all of the other good energy. We are so preoccupied with romantic love that we often overlook true love, which adds a richness and fullness to our lives. Our parents, our siblings, our friends, our neighbors, our acquaintances all bring with them qualities and security. They make us feel good.

Even though friends make us feel good, too many of us have been socialized to look for the bad in people. By seeking the bad, we are never disappointed. We find bad in the folks who drive on the roads. We find bad in the clerks who wait on us. We find bad in co-workers. We find bad in customers. We find bad in just about anybody who crosses our path. It is downright easy to find bad in people. But by taking this route, we are messing with our own energy big time. It's hard for the good vibes to squeak out when the bad vibes are running the show.

Of course, since what we focus on is what we get, it's just as easy to find good in people when we deliberately seek it. It's all a matter of choice. But this is far more than thinking positively and looking for good people. This is getting our good energy connecting with lots and lots of other good energy. When we find good in others, we find good in ourselves. We find unconditional love. Oh, not that gushy I-have-to-have-that-hunk's-e-mail-address love. Just the basic life-is-good love has a way of generating lots of good vibes.

You can love anybody anytime by allowing yourself to do so. Get quiet, focus on somebody you love, and just let those feelings expand. Once you've mastered love in this manner, start to focus on people you don't really know. Over time, you will find the sensation of your own self-expanding so rewarding that you will be able to generate these same feelings without getting quiet. You'll be able to generate love for strangers. You will be able to generate love for the people who drive you nuts—the clerks, the bad drivers, the entire lot of them.

There's an extra bonus in this type of behavior. The people who once drove you nuts lose their power over you. Their ability to push your buttons is diminished or downright disappears. Also, people come into your world who are connected with the good stuff in life, and they see the good in you. This opens lots of doors because people who see the good in you are generally willing to help you procure employment when they have the opportunity to do so.

Forgive

Okay, you can see the merit of loving, but a few characters in your life have harmed you to such a degree that loving them is just plain out of the equation. You hate them, and you want to get even with them. Well, as discussed previously, anger is one heck of a motivator, but that's no reason to keep it as the carrot. Once you are motivated, let it go.

Forgive and don't dwell. Most of us can deal with the forgiving part, but the don't dwelling part is a whole heck of a lot harder. After all, the human brain is hard-wired to remember things that cause us harm. If we didn't recall that moving trains can run over cars, a lot more cars would be run over by trains. We learn about dangers from others and from past experiences. If Sam caused you harm and got the promotion while you got the pink slip, your long-term memory puts Sam into a DANGER file. Those danger files are hard to delete because they have saved us as a species for thousands and thousands of years. So forgetting about a hurt, especially a serious hurt, is pretty close to impossible. We are hard-wired to remember. The only realistic option is to not pull up the file. It can't be deleted, but it certainly doesn't have to be your screensaver. File it. Let it be. Let yourself move beyond it.

Lots of really bad things happen to really good people until those really good people catch onto the Law of Attraction and stop putting out the bad vibes. If some really bad stuff has happened to you, you aren't alone. Letting it go and releasing the negative energy that's attached to it is the only insurance against more bad stuff. Once you choose to stop putting out bad vibes and make an effort to put out good vibes, the bad stuff stops happening. Once the bad stuff stops happening, you don't really care if Sam got that silly little job.

There's an old story about two monks walking home. Now in this particular order of monks, touching a woman was a really big NO-NO! So these two monks were hoofing it and, lo and behold, before them was a raging river complete with a damsel in distress. This woman needed to get from side A to side B and was lacking the size and strength to do so on her own. There wasn't a bridge in sight. The first monk looked at the situation and wordlessly picked up our damsel and carried her through the raging waters. Once on the other side, he silently set her on her feet. Not a word was spoken. The monks continued on for many miles in silence. As they approached their destination, the second monk broke the silence. He asked his partner how in the heck could he just pick up a woman? How on Earth could he have committed such a sin? The first monk looked at his friend with gentle eyes and replied: "I left her on the riverbank. It's you who are still carrying her." By clinging to a grudge, you are still carrying the energy of the person who hurt you just like that second monk was still holding onto the woman.

Think of a sack of rocks for a moment. Holding a grudge is like holding that sack of rocks on your shoulders. The rocks are heavy. They are really of no use. They weigh you down. They cause you to hold your body at an unattractive angle. Get the picture? By forgiving, you get to stand up straight again. You get to connect with high-frequency energy again. You are freed. You set down the sack of rocks.

How you forgive is your choice. It's not necessary to contact the other party unless you choose to do so. Most of the time, the person with whom you are angry has moved on. If you called old Sam to tell him you are no longer pissed off because he got the promotion you worked your butt off for five years ago, he'd say, "Who are you?" He's moved on. You've picked up the sack of rocks.

Forgiving is nothing more than letting go of the sack of rocks. You can forgive by simply telling yourself you forgive. It can easily be a solitary, liberating act. It will lessen your load and increase and liberate your energy. Of course, you are thinking that sounds like a good idea, but, but, but . . . but what? Do you like your sack of rocks? Are those low vibes helping you in any way, shape, or form? But nothing . . . let them go.

Tune In

When you are stuck with a sack of rocks, or a damned fool in front of you on the freeway, or an interviewer who is interested in just about anything except your skill-set, change your thinking. Retrieve a memory that gets your vibrations into a higher frequency. Think of the best day of your life. Once you remember it, fill it in like a color-by-numbers painting. Remember everything about it—how the day started, what you saw, thought, smelled, touched, tasted. Drink in the entire experience again. Close your eyes and see it for all of its beauty.

The goal is to get your vibrations up and get those little energy connectors working for you. Once you get the feeling-great part mastered, fold the perfect job into your emotional mix. Take it a step further to visualize what your life will be like when you have the perfect job. That's the recipe for success.

When you open your eyes, be conscious of your feelings. Notice how your energy is turned up. This simple technique will be pivotal in your quest to land the job of your dreams.

Learn to do it well. Do it at least three times a day. When you are feeling great, feel yourself getting dressed for your next interview. Feel yourself breezing through that interview. Feel yourself shaking hands with the person who just offered you the job. Feel yourself telling your spouse, parents, and friends about your new job. Feel yourself performing a valuable service for substantial compensation. Feel yourself buying that new car (clothes, boat, house) you've been dreaming about with your big fat paycheck. Feel it!

The Rut

One of most fun ways to shift energy is to get out of your rut. We are all in some sort of rut or another. There are things we simply just do. We get out of bed. We brush our teeth. We shower. We eat our breakfasts. Ruts are simply habits, some learned when we were very young, some developed later in life to accommodate needs in the most efficient manner. Ruts aren't bad. They simply are a repeat of the same sort of energy over and over and over and over . . . again.

If you're like most folks, you eat your breakfast in your kitchen or in your car. What would happen if you popped out of bed and ate your breakfast in your PJs in your back yard? I don't mean just grab a breakfast bar and stand in your doorway. I mean fry up some bacon and eggs, squeeze some orange juice, and enjoy a full-fledged breakfast on a table in your back yard. Throw in a tablecloth, too. Forego the morning paper until the coffee is cold.

Would the neighbors call the funny farm and ask for transportation? Highly unlikely. What would happen is you'd take one baby step out of your rut. You'd probably feel a little silly at first, but then, if you allowed yourself to relax, you'd probably feel happy, content, fun-loving, and joyful. Joyful is what we are seeking here. And ruts tend to pretty much squeeze out joy unless we've actually allowed it to flourish regardless of our activities.

Honestly, how joyful are you when you get out of bed? Are you grateful that the sun came up? When you brush your teeth, are you making funny faces at yourself? Are you joyfully looking forward to tasks that lie ahead? Do you savor the flavor of your first cup of coffee like the guy in the coffee commercials? If you've answered "yes" to all of the above, then your rut is serving you well. Let it be. On the other hand, do you stick your head under your pillow, silently cussing at the sun? Do you brush your teeth on autopilot? Do you chug down your first cup of coffee hoping to get the caffeine buzz a minute quicker? Well, your rut is causing you some pretty nasty energy right off the bat.

On the upside, there's opportunity for joy even in a rut. But generally, unearthing that joy involves taking a step out of the rut, if only for a few moments. A step away allows you to experience something other than the same-old, same-old. It creates an avenue to develop a conscious awareness of your energy. It's a wake-up call for good energy and the good things that follow.

A major problem with ruts is we don't think we are living in them. No, most of us would declare that we are too free-spirited to be rut-bound. Other people are in ruts. Your parents were in a rut. But you? Never. Nice myth, but out of necessity or habit, we all have some sort of routine that is one big, deep rut. Now, folks with jobs have morning ruts out of necessity. They have workday ruts carved out by work schedules, and they have evening ruts dictated by a society that currently believes being busy is the route to nirvana. If you are one of these and seeking employment, you are going to have to let the joy in somewhere, somehow, sometime, and it would be best if it's really soon.

What's really amazing are the ruts folks get into when they have far too much time on their hands. They find ways of filling up their days that simply put them into some of the deepest ruts of all. Some sleep until noon. Others play solitaire—one of my all-time favorite addictions. With the advent of the Internet, some people spend entire days on the computer. Oh, it starts innocently enough. They start searching the job boards for employment. They start going to the Web sites of some of the companies they're considering as employment options. That takes up a few hours, then they start going to more interesting places. They start sending e-mails, then instant messages. Blogs become a comfortable escape for hours. In just a few short weeks, what started as a job-search tool has become a lifestyle. Their primary source of human contact is e-contact, and they barely miss real flesh-and-blood people.

Months start to slip away, and these folks are only marginally concerned. They believe that all of their time on a computer is time spent in job searching, and they can justify their days. Unfortunately, this routine they've developed is sucking the life-enhancing energy out of them with a giant straw. Okay, they might be missing a little of the downer energy of road rage, but they are also missing out on any of the pure joyful energy that humans possess if they are not in lockstep with a machine.

Just a simple break in any rut or routine can have a dramatic impact on energy. Think for a moment of a married couple in a rut. Both the husband and wife are busy. There's nothing really wrong with the marriage, but nothing feels good about it either. Then, for no apparent reason, the husband buys the wife a $3.99 bouquet of supermarket flowers on the way home from work. The wife is overjoyed. The entire energy shifts. Instead of rushing through the meal, she flirts. There's a spark. That same spark is felt by the entire family. The energy in the family goes from the basic up-and-down stuff that we accept as "just life" to a higher frequency. All of this because of a simple step out of a rut.

If you are in a rut, and sitting in your back yard in your PJs doesn't appeal to you, then think of something that does turn you on. If you live alone, walk to the nearest coffee shop and have that second cup of coffee with other people. Connecting with the energy of working people is a great way to get energy moving toward employment. If you are sleeping until noon and not seeking a job as a bartender or a rock star, then it's time to give mornings a spin.

Get Physical

Get your blood moving—exercise! I learned to ride a bike when I was around five years old. Until I had a driver's license, my bike and my feet were my primary sources of transportation. Parents didn't play taxi driver back then, and if I wanted to hang out without somebody other than my siblings, it had to be somebody in close proximity. Fortunately for me, there were a lot of kids on my street and lots of nearby back roads for bike riding. When I got my driver's license, the bike got rusty. Then, 26 years ago, I decided cycling was a great antidepressant as well as a weight-control tool. It didn't take long for me to move up from a bike from Sears to a better bike to a Trek 1400 aluminum racing bike. Oh, I was cool. I had the racing helmet. I had the cutting-edge Oakley glasses. During the eighties, I had no qualms about dropping hundreds of bucks on Madonna-inspired cycling togs made of spandex and lace. I had the pedal system with the toe clips so the bike and I became one. I was sooooo cooooool! I rode an average of 40 miles an evening as long as daylight would allow. I went on the double centuries, 200 miles, on weekends for fun. Oh, life was a bike!

Needless to say, when I was on that bike, I was on some high-frequency energy. It was easy to untangle the problems of the days. When I would get in the "zone," I was connected with pure creative energy. Of course, at that time I knew none of this Law of Attraction stuff. I didn't know that the "zone" was high–frequency, powerful, creative energy. I just knew I felt good, and feeling good beat the heck out of the rest of the feelings that were consuming me for large portions of the days. Had I had the tools to harness that energy, I would have been able to flip a job that was good one day and bad the next into a promotion that would have put my career into fast forward.

Knowing how good I felt on my bike, I was planning to continue cycling well into my golden years, but back surgery put a big change in that plan. After the surgery, I tried cycling again, but developed foot, leg, and back pain. After one season of suffering, I gave up. A few years later, I was back on the bike with several adjustments that I didn't see as refinements at the time. The pedal system was gone. I had to wear Birkenstocks to prevent pain. The Oakleys were replaced by bifocals. The cycling togs became cycling shorts with long, billowing T-shirts. One day, I realized that I'd morphed into the kind of person I used to laugh at when I was really cool. Arrgghhhh! But, life is funny, and I am still on the bike and getting into a completely different sort of "zone." After two-plus decades, I am seeing things I never saw as I sped by in the past. This year, the honeysuckle took over large expanses of the overgrowth and smelled so overpoweringly beautiful that I had to get off my bike and sit in the scent. After the honeysuckle came the wild roses and their multitudes of pink to enhance my ride. I've noticed a goat farm. Now, I am uncertain if this goat thing is new, or if I just never noticed it before. I'd hate to think that I really missed a herd of goats— they aren't the most quiet of creatures, but they are very amusing. I am getting into the same fantastic energy even though my speed has decreased by about eight miles per hour. And it's all because I am getting out of my home, out of my space, and into a space full of nature and beauty. That's not to say my home isn't beautiful. I think it is, but it's not in a state of flux. I have order in my home. In nature, there's change daily. Getting in touch with the subtle changes has a unique way of lifting frequency. It makes you feel good. And getting the good life is all about feelings. Feeeeelings!

Pay Attention

Check out your neighborhood. Take a walk around frequently and notice the subtle changes. I read a book written by a man who made a fortune by watching the shifts in his neighborhood. He started noticing when houses sold and when they were stuck on the market. He realized he had not only an interest in but also a knack for real estate. His walks led to getting his real-estate license, which led to a new career.

It's highly unlikely you will jump into a new career from a walk around the block, but you may well get a feeling of whom to contact for a job, or find a new business on the block, or see an opportunity that you would have missed sitting on your computer.

Mostly, if you move daily into a space that's unfamiliar to you, you will begin to pay attention. Once you start paying attention to your outer world, it becomes easy to pay attention to your inner world. All creation starts within your inner world of feelings. By paying attention, you can take control.

Dismiss the Drama Queen / King

Drama queens never seem to get ahead. It's one thing after another. It's exhausting. It takes huge amounts of negative energy to just keep a drama queen going in any old direction. And for those men out there who are laughing, there are plenty of drama kings, too, who seem to invite one catastrophe after another into their lives. Energies of this royal family appear at first to be really out in the stratosphere. They are always on the move; they are always running from one disaster to another.

The truth is they are little more than sad characters running around in circles on a gas tank of negative energy. They get so very little done that they make some of the worst, and I mean worst, employees in the world. They send out armies of bad energy.

Drama queens and kings are vibrating like the rest of us, but they magnetize the most bizarre bottom-of-the-barrel stuff that it's amazing they even get out of bed in the morning. As employees, some don't bother with mornings. They show up around ten with a note from their doctor, their shrink, their lawyer. Dramatic types have energy that's sporadic on a good day. If they can get out of bed, manage a morning without a fight with a significant other, a kid, or a neighbor, get on the road without a motor-vehicle incident (anything from lost car keys, to an empty gas tank, to a stolen car), avoid a traffic accident and road rage, and actually get someplace, they have a pretty good chance of holding onto some good energy for at least an hour or two. But for some reason, they just can't maintain an even flow. Within a few hours, they have something going with a co-worker, or a computer, or a thought in their heads that just brings their energy back down to the ground floor, and the nonsense starts again.

Drama folks are addicted to the attention. Yeah, life might suck, but "Damn, I'm in the spotlight" hooks them every time. A few days without a spotlight, and they start to shrivel up like a thirsty plant. There's little value to talking to a drama person about change. They won't change until life becomes too uncomfortable, and then they only do so long enough to get some money in the bank, find a new spouse, or get a new job, and then they take the energy elevator right back down to the sub-basement to search for a spotlight.

Drama folks need to re-script. The biggest change in their script has to be letting go of the victim role. Most learned this role so long ago that they think it's their birthright. They just deserve to be able to point a finger at somebody and say, "She did it to *me*. Look at *me!*" Somewhere along the line, they have to realize that they aren't victims. Once the Law of Attraction is understood, there are no victims. And they have to decide that the spotlight isn't all that great—not an easy task for a spotlight addict. They go outside for the light because going within scares the living daylights out of them. They are afraid they won't find anything. Or they won't like what they find. Or that it might be dark inside.

Only by going within will they find the light they are seeking in the quest for a spotlight. It's a hard concept to understand, but if you are some sort of drama person, you need to go within. Take the trip slowly and quietly, and find the light within. Your Higher Self has been waiting for your arrival. Your Higher Self has been trying to reach you for years with those gut-wrenching warnings. It's time to listen.

Okay, you know lots of drama folks, but you aren't one. Here's a little test to determine if there's a tad of a drama person running your show. You might be a drama person if everybody loves your stories, but nobody wants your life. You might be a drama person if you exhaust others. You might be a drama person if you're a victim at home, at work, at play. Ask a friend if she thinks you are a drama person. If she starts to laugh, tears roll from her eyes, and she bends over in pain from laughter, you are probably a drama person.

If you are a true blue drama person, getting in touch with your Higher Self will only work for short periods of time. You will feel really good, but then something will happen—some fool will cut you off on the freeway, your ex-spouse will call to wish you happy birthday, something will happen that will send you spinning back into victim mode—and you will forget all about the Law of Attraction and your Higher Self until things get too painful again. But it only takes a little bit of high-frequency energy to get you back onto the path of good vibes.

Don't give up. Don't get so sucked into your old lifestyle that you forsake the concept of energy and the power to change. Just do it on your own schedule. You might have to plaster the Law of Attraction on your bathroom mirror, on your dashboard, on your coffee mug, but in time, you will find that attracting the good stuff is far more rewarding than the spotlight. Hang in, spin the good stuff whenever you feel yourself falling prey, and hold on.

Shhhhhh!

Get quiet. Meditation is the best way to get in touch with your good energy. Somewhere inside you is pure joy, some of the highest-frequency energy humans can experience. If you want to jump-start your job search, get quiet. A 20-minute-a-day meditation will do more for your job search than two hours on Monster.com. On top of getting energy into the high-frequency range, meditation also reduces stress and worry, and fine-tunes your hunches. When moving into a meditative state, put an intention into your mind, such as: "Where should I send the next résumé?" Don't expect a direct answer to come from some thundering voice. It doesn't generally work that way. But do expect that you will be opening the business pages of the newspaper soon and read an article about just the right company, or a friend may call you about a job, or you might get a flat tire in front of a company you never noticed before. If it's the right company, you will feel it.

Victims Need Not Apply

Accept that you are not a victim. You are not a victim of a bad decision. You are not a victim of a sour economy. You are not a victim of anything whatsoever. Once you grasp the Law of Attraction, you can never be a victim of anything. You become empowered. Empowerment is freedom. It's liberating to be free of the shackles of victimhood. It's a mighty responsibility and a mighty power.

It's Your Thing

As stated earlier, falling in love is a prime example of great energy, but it's not the only great energy to be found. Everybody has a personal experience that makes her or him feel terrific. To some, it's a memory of a day with a parent or grandparent. To others, it's a special holiday, a day at a beach, a mountain hike, winning a game, a great marathon, or a vacation, to name a just a few. One guy I've worked with uses the image of a great flight he piloted.

When seeking ways to tune up your energy, look at your own life. Some things may tune up your energy without you even knowing it. I know one very successful man who has convinced himself that his dogs love him more than any human. His dogs turn up his energy. Whenever things get tough at the office, this man creates a "dog emergency" and heads home to walk the dogs for a half-hour or so before making a decision or getting cornered into some disaster. He doesn't buy into this energy stuff in black and white, but he practices it unknowingly.

Visit an old friend. Walk through a museum. Watch a sunrise. Watch a sunset. Listen to classical music. Crank up some rock 'n' roll. Skydive. Swim. Fish. Fall in love. Take a road trip. Whatever makes you feel on top of the world is right. The goal is to feel fantastic and send out those good vibes. That's all there is to it. Your energy does the rest.

Value

For you, the job seeker, the last of my remedies to lift your vibrations is to unearth the value you bring to this world. We all bring value to our families, our communities, our employers, our friends, and our society. But we seldom look at this value; we take it for granted. When you are seeking employment, it may be difficult for you to see your value. You may choose instead to go into the market in search of work. You go in search of what the market will give you. A more healthy, holistic, energy-driven perspective is looking at what value you bring to the workplace, the community, the society, the world. When you flip job searching from strictly searching for work to adding value, your energy shifts. You go from a sense of lack, i.e., jobs are scarce, to a sense of value. Every employer is seeking value.

If you think you offer no value, think again. Every living thing has value. Trees offer shade and protection. Flowers offer beauty. Vegetables offer nutrition. Domesticated animals offer human companionship. All flora and fauna provide an intricate role in the balance of the world. You are no different. You have a unique personality. You have a set of experiences and skills that is yours and yours alone. Nobody else can bring to the marketplace exactly the skills you offer. Oh, you might be thinking you've worked as a cog in a corporate machine for so many years that you are nothing other than a cog. Not true. Once you begin to tune in to your Higher Self, you will discover you are far more than a cog; you are a valuable human being.

It's your responsibility to unearth your talents, your skills, and your value, and bring them to the workplace. You may find you have several latent talents that have been dormant as you melted into the form of a corporate cog. Let them breathe. Give them life. Then look at the world around you and see what value you can bring. Determine how you are going to sell this value in the marketplace.

Throughout my career in human resources, I've worked at little companies with less than 20 employees, and at a company with several hundred thousand employees worldwide. Some of the tasks I've performed have been downright sterile, such as setting up self-service benefits information stations. But some of my work has changed lives. I once assisted an employee in transitioning from a life with an abusive spouse into an independent life of security. I also had the displeasure of escorting a troubled man who had built a bomb from a facility into mental healthcare. When I had to determine my value, it was apparent my strong talent is working one-on-one with employees. My natural niche was working with small companies that allow me lots of one-on-one time with employees. I've also hired many people and have at times struggled in the job-search process. It was only natural that I eventually write a book about job searching without struggle. My errors led me to information that could help so many in the workplace. This is the value I offer to the world.

Everybody can add value. Your value may be something small but necessary, such as assisting the aged with daily tasks, or something as grand as discovering the next multibillion-dollar industry. If you think that every good idea has been taken, think again.

Ideas, Inc.

Around the early 1900s, the director of the U.S. Patent Office suggested closing the office down for good. He had personally determined that everything that ever needed to be invented had been invented, and there was no need for any further patents. I suppose Bill Gates would disagree.

When you have a really good idea, you will know it. You will *feel* it. Others may pooh-pooh it, but it will survive if it's from the gut. Xerox came out with a prototype of a copier several decades ago. It was reviewed by a group of economists whose job was to determine if there was a market for this monster of a machine. They came to the conclusion that the large, costly machine was unnecessary. Secretaries could always use carbon paper and make several copies of any document at the time the document was typed. Obviously, the opinions of the outside world aren't always on the money. When you have a good idea, stick with your feelings.

Go within, seek your value, then spin your good energy out into the world. You will be amazed at the number of opportunities that come your way.

Words of Caution

When you start to see the results of positive vibrations, you may become a tad lazy on your energy checks. After all, when things are going smoothly, there's no real reason to check one's energy. It's obviously spinning at some high frequency. True, but without a check now and then, it might start on a downhill trek without notice. It's all too easy to become complacent when things are going well. Don't get lazy and stop working your energy or abandon consciousness of your vibrations. We don't perpetually walk around day after day sending out good vibrations without putting effort into doing so. If we did, there wouldn't be any bad jobs, homicides, or wars. The folks on the six o'clock news would be working at Ben and Jerry's.

The funny, or not so funny, thing about working energy is that once you learn and master the techniques, you can't turn back. If you turn your back on your energy once you learn to work it, you will be inviting in all kinds of negativity, and you won't have anybody to blame but yourself.

When I started writing this manuscript, I was going after a contract that I knew was bad for me. I tried telling myself that I was going after it for the money, but the root incentive was revenge. Revenge is a large, really large, negative. It's the kind of negative that starts wars. And guess what happened to me? You name it. My car went from needing a few repairs to needing to be replaced. My hours got cut at my great job. The IRS needed to be paid. And I knew better! I just decided that the rules didn't apply to me because my life was going so well. Needless to say, once I realized what I was doing, I flipped it quickly.

Once again, I learned the hard way that I can't afford to play in one of those negative-energy mud puddles. You can't afford to play in one either. If you are serious about getting the job of your dreams, it's time to stop complaining, blaming, worrying, and whining. It's time to take the first step and become aware of your energy. Once aware, you need to practice the tools in this chapter to tune up your energy so it can begin to bring a good job to you. It's time to get your head and your gut on the same page and start putting your feelings and energy behind your desired goal. You have the power!

Feeeeeel!

At least 3 times a day, feel yourself getting that great opportunity. Feel yourself breezing through that interview. Feel yourself shaking hands with the person who just offered you the job. Feel yourself telling your spouse, parents, and friends about your new job. Feel yourself performing a valuable service for substantial compensation. Feel yourself buying that new car (clothes, boat, house) you've been dreaming about with your big, fat paycheck. Feel it!

Chapter 5

Set-of-Expectations

What we focus on shows up in our lives. If we expect something with enough oomph behind it, with feeling, we get it. If we go in search of something, we find it. Just by focusing on something, our radar goes into overdrive until it's ours.

The Color Game

Think of a color, any color. Hold your focus on it for a moment or two. Now, look for that color in your environment. Since the color is the object of your focus, it will appear. I play this color game whenever the cynic in me is on a roll or when I feel this energy stuff is too kooky to be real, which is usually after I've really screwed up and I want to blame somebody other than me for the state of my life. In other words, when I've pushed out a ton of nasty energy, got a ton of garbage back, and want to think, nah, it's not energy.

The other day, I was leaving a client I disliked for the last time. Needless to say, I had put out a pretty hefty amount of negative vibes to connect with a negative client. Even knowing I would not be returning, I was feeling as icky as ever. Actually,

I was feeling downright nasty as I pulled out of the parking lot. So, I decided to play this little color game and see if I could pin this entire experience on something other than my own energy. I was driving on a curvy, hilly, two-lane road, and I started tossing out colors to see if they would appear. I said purple, and as I rounded a curve, some purple flowers came into view. I said pink, and as I glanced in my rearview mirror, I saw a pink toy that was sitting in my car. I said orange and saw an orange barrel. (In Ohio in spring, that's a no-brainer.) Then I said yellow. I continued my drive with no yellow in sight. There wasn't even a random buttercup. My energy was not connecting with my want for yellow. I had a smug sort of satisfaction, the kind that only comes when the inner cynic is winning. I was beginning to second-guess a lot of what I hold to be true. I was wondering if any of this stuff has any merit. Oh yes, even knowing this stuff works doesn't prevent me from testing it every now and then when I'd rather be a victim than a creator. So if yellow didn't appear, what else wouldn't appear? Perhaps I'd lose a client. Or maybe I'd lose this book deal. Oh, I was well on my way to total scarcity and somewhat into it when I went to pass the car ahead of me. All I needed was a break in that double yellow line, and I would be flying. What color double line? Yellow. I had been driving along a double yellow line the entire time and never noticed it. I was so determined not to see it that I certainly did not see it. My inner cynic was crushed, and I actually laughed at myself out loud.

Focus

What we focus our energy on expands in our lives. This focusing is what causes some people to move seamlessly from one job to another and causes other people to hang out for months or years seeking employment. Some folks focus on lack. In the case of job searching, they focus on their lack of a job.

Too many people don't focus on getting a job when they are job seeking. Hard to believe, but they focus on all sorts of other things while their energy pings around waiting for some focus.

What do they focus on? Since I have a couple of extraordinarily large gaps on my résumé prior to learning this Law of Attraction stuff, I'll start from my own experience. Things I've focused on instead of employment: starting my own business (without enough dedication and filled with fear), a boyfriend (an all-time time killer), anger at a former employer (good enough for several months of unemployment), lack of opportunities (something like the yellow line), and a hodgepodge of all of the above melted together. No wonder I had such long gaps—there wasn't enough room left for a job to squeeze into my world with a shoehorn! I was busy sending energy out to everything but a job.

A former colleague of mine, who was a pleasure to work with, had an outstanding skill-set and a fantastic work ethic, and could have had a job within 60 days of losing his had he focused his energy on procuring employment. I brought this fact to his attention several times. His logical mind got it big time, but he could not tame his emotions or focus his energy. He felt betrayed not only by his former employer, but by himself for buying into the corporate world that he felt had taken the best years of his life. He also felt bad about moving his wife from the United Kingdom to the United States for his job. His wife was okay with it, but he wasn't. After seven months of anger, he packed up everything and moved back to the United Kingdom.

From the time he got sacked until the time he said goodbye, he never could get his feelings aligned with landing another job on this side of the pond, although his logical mind told him time and again that he'd have a better shot at a good job stateside. Instead, he floundered in his energy mess for months. Even across the pond, he found things to occupy his time and keep his focus away from his job search. So a guy with a stellar résumé—progressive responsibilities, no gaps for 23 years, and lots of education—sits on the sidelines of the world of employment. Even folks with the best of corporate behaviors can fall victim to their energy during job searching.

If you think this focusing stuff is easy, think again. We seldom live in the present. Human minds are generally busy rehashing some event from the past or mulling over the possibilities of some event in the future. When you mull over the possibilities of the future, you are creating a set-of-expectations. A set-of-expectations can work for or against you. If you are seeking employment and you develop a set-of-expectations that job seeking is hard and it's going to take you months to get a job, don't be surprised when the months start slipping away and no job comes your way. On the other hand, if you think that job searching is going to bring with it new opportunities, you will get new opportunities. Lots of opportunities. A set-of-expectations has a way of becoming a self-fulfilling prophecy when it's folded in with strong feelings.

Bam!

The more energy you put into a set-of-expectations, the more likely it's going to become your future. Not too long ago, two parties—one for me and one for my niece—were scheduled two weeks apart. No problem. But as I drove home one night, I started thinking that there would be some change in the schedule. Guests would have to choose one party over the other. I got myself so worked up over it that I recall being angry at my parents, who would have to decide which party meant more to them. This imaginary dilemma got a hold of me and was not letting go. I mentally jumped in without a parachute. Five minutes on this train of thought, and I was driving like a crazy woman, yelling at the top of my lungs over an event that was all in my head. I pushed it to the point that the entire family was split. After about ten minutes, I realized how much I was energizing this absurd situation and stopped. A week later, everybody but me was surprised when my niece's party was moved to the same date as the party in my honor. I had energized it to such a degree, and with so much force, that it happened. I had taken an event with a low probability of ever happening and charged it with such a strong burst of energy that it came true.

Thinking vs. Feeling

I've been told I think too much. I was forever getting myself in hot water with the maintenance guys at work. If I thought they'd appreciate a cake on an anniversary date, I was wrong. If I thought they'd be able to fix some little glitch in the wiring in my office within a day, I was wrong. If I thought they'd be receptive to a change in their job descriptions, I was wrong. I was forever saying, "Well, I thought . . ." hoping to get myself out of hot water. The team leader finally told me pointblank that the problem with me was I think too much. He may have had a point. Had I tuned into my feelings a little more often, I would have realized I was setting myself up for more grief. I usually had a hunch that I was doing something that would not set well with that crowd, but I ignored it.

Our thoughts impact our feelings, but thinking and feeling are still two different things. If you *think* you are going to have a short duration of unemployment, but deep down you *feel* a long duration of unemployment, the latter will occur. Feelings trump thoughts any day in the energy game, and the energy game is the only game in town. So regardless of your words, if your feelings are saying "no job," you are in for one heck of a doozy of a job search.

Setting Your Cruise Control

A set-of-expectations is sort of like the cruise control on your car. You set your cruise control to regulate the speed of your car. Once it is set at any given speed, your car maintains that speed until you change it. Once you develop a set-of-expectations, you send out energy to meet that set-of-expectations until you decide to change it. So, let's look at the set-of-expectations you are setting for your job search. Your set-of-expectations may be that you will have a good job in short order. Great. Now *feel* it! Or it may be that job searching will be an ongoing process for several months. Not so good. You need to revisit some of the remedies. Or you may feel there's a high probability of not getting a job at all. If you don't think there's a high probability of getting a job, what do you think will be the outcome? Do you think you will end up in bankruptcy court? That might sound harsh, but you are the one setting your job search speed. You can't set the cruise control at 50 and expect to go 65. Therefore, know what you want and go for it. You, and only you, have the power to set your cruise control. It's a mighty power, and it's all yours!

If you think you have your set-of-expectations in line with your goals, then it's time to do some daily tweaking. Start each day with some quiet time and an intention. This intention doesn't have to be that you intend to have a job by the end of the day. Intentions are more peaceful. They aren't demands or wishes or even to-do lists. They are little thoughts that align your energy with your want.

An intention might be, "I intend to stay peaceful today." Or "I intend to send out résumés from a state of joy and anticipation." "I intend to see the good in others." "I intend to find one skill that I have allowed to become dormant." Intentions should be said out loud. Hear your own voice. Follow your own instructions.

After your intention is set, calmly move into doing the

real-world work involved in your job search for the morning. Making phone calls from a state of peace will be far more effective than harping into someone's voicemail. Sending out résumés in a state of joy and anticipation takes the process from a down-and-dirty task of drudgery to a higher level of energy, a higher frequency. Remember, it's not what you say or how you say it; in the game of energy, it's how you *feel* about it. Uplifting intentions bring up frequencies.

Once you start setting intentions for the day, your set-of-expectations will subtly shift from a position stuck in fear to a position of expectation, which is exactly what a set-of-expectations is anyway.

Rocky Road

Many times, I've wondered why my career life took so many ups and downs before I learned the Law of Attraction. It all boils down to a set-of-expectations I hammered into my energy decades ago.

When I was engaged, my fiancé and I spent several hours a night discussing our wedding plans at an ice-cream place that was located near his office and my home. It was convenient, inexpensive, and as we rapidly learned, ice cream was one thing we really had in common. On slow nights, the owner would join in on our conversations. As the wedding day drew closer, she asked that we bring the entire wedding party to the shop, and she'd give us all a treat on the house. The only hitch was that nobody could order Rocky Road ice cream. She thought it might be bad luck. She didn't want us to start with Rocky Road and end up on one.

Well, I did end up on a few rocky roads in the workplace. They all started because of another event that happened that very same year. I had a good job with one of the top employers in the city. When I had started with that company a couple of years earlier, I was unaware that they were one of the top employers, and honestly I didn't care. I had left a job at a little company with no growth and had been hired at this big company where the human resource people read me a long list of perks, walked me to a very nice office, introduced me to my fellow office workers, and life got good. I didn't care that they went to great lengths to be one of the top employers; I didn't care that they had a long list of perks; I didn't care that there were rumors of the company moving. Oops, did somebody say the company was moving? Well, as I said, I didn't care. I was young, marketable, and far more concerned with becoming a wife.

By the time my wedding party had lapped down the ice cream, it was apparent that my job was anything but stable. I had breezed through the first few rounds of layoffs simply because my department was necessary until the bitter end. But by round three it was apparent that the good times were over for good. The last few months were the hardest on those of us who were to remain until it was time to turn out the lights for the last time. In fact, it was so hard that even young, uncaring me took notice. In my mind, I knew that I had a new husband who could pay the bills for a few months, so I was more concerned about the men in the office who I thought were just plain old. Yeah, there were a lot of those old toads around back then, most of them firmly planted in middle management. They came to work every day. The majority of them had been coming to work for the same company and sitting behind the same desks for two or three decades. On the last day of operations, some of them cried. That was the final straw for me. As I watched grown men cry, I vowed that would never be my fate. I'd never become so attached to any employer that I would some day sit and cry because some powers-that-be wanted to move to a location with better weather. No sirree, I was going to keep moving one step ahead of the corporate grim reaper.

I must admit, move I did. I never bought into waiting around for the gold watch. I did things the way many members of the generations that are following me are doing things. Generation Xers have witnessed very little company loyalty, therefore they aren't giving any loyalty to companies. They connect, and they disconnect. In order to be successful in their constant movement, they will have to feel themselves able to move with ease. They will have to know how to make their energy work for them in the workplace.

The workplace will always be fluid. Change is all it knows. As the world shrinks and technology expands, jobs will come and go at a much faster rate than they have in the past. Workers will find themselves having to be just as fluid. Those who realize life is all about energy will send out the greatest frequencies and move easily through the changes. They will feel exhilarated by the new experiences the workplace offers them. Their set-of-expectations will be of control. They will control their futures and not be victims to an economy, a company, or an occupation.

Chapter 6

Money Madness

As you may have started to see in a previous chapter, your feelings about money play a gigantic role in how you feel about your job search. Feelings act as our gatekeepers by establishing the frequencies at which we vibrate. They generate energy, and they only allow vibrations with like energy into our lives. Lots of things impact our feelings—our thoughts, our circumstances, even the weather—but very few things evoke more feelings from us than money. Lack of money can put our very existence in jeopardy. Lots of money can make us very happy. Oh, I know there's a contingent of people who like to buy into and promote the concept of pitiful rich people, but it takes only a look around the real world to see that rich folks have it easier. Sure, they worry about who's trying to get into their pockets. They may have concerns about the upkeep on several homes. They are generally so busy working at something they love that they may not have time to spend a hot afternoon on hard bleachers watching their kid strike out. But here's a news flash: The working poor don't have time to sit in the hot sun watching their kids strike out either. Bottom line, rich folks don't have to worry about the price of groceries, gas, or rent. They have the resources to fix what's wrong in their lives. When they get sick, they can fly to wherever the best specialist might be and get the medical attention they need. If their car is broken down, they don't worry about finding a buddy to install a rebuilt part on a Saturday afternoon. They take it to the dealership and get it repaired or trade it in for a new model. People who say money can't buy happiness are generally people who haven't experienced much financial prosperity.

Oops, Money Feels . . .

If you're like most people, you probably have a pretty rough relationship with Benjamin Franklin and his friends. We simply don't feel good about money. Oh, we might say we'd love a ton of money, but money is so cloaked in mystery and history for so many of us that it creates an entire emotional undercurrent that we rarely address.

Money is a very explosive topic. People would rather talk about their sex lives than their true financial situation. People who don't have money don't want to talk about it; people who have a lot of money don't want to talk about it. Just about the only people who talk about it in much detail are people who want you to think they have money—we all know a few of them. For the most part, people keep their finances to themselves.

People are secretive about money because we live in a society that puts more value on money than it truly deserves. Money—just plain banknotes—holds no value whatsoever. If you take a tour of a Federal Reserve Bank, you can get a bag of shredded money as a souvenir. Money is just a tool to transfer value from one entity to another. Its only value is a function of belief; money is only as good as the belief system supporting it. When a government collapses, the currency of the country becomes worthless. It's not that the people are necessarily any less productive or that the needs of the people diminish, it's just that the belief system fails.

With that cut-and-dried description of money—or M1, as economists call it—it's hard to attach emotions to the almighty dollar. But we do attach strong feelings to money. We also attach a great deal of emotion to people who have more or less of it than we do. In the United States, we claim to be a classless society, but we aren't. We indeed have a stratum system, which for the most part is a function of money.

So let's look at how our energy gets tossed around because of money. As a population, we love and hate rich people—oh, those filthy rich! Ironically, we love and hate them because of their money. If they are rich and get away with stuff you and I couldn't get away with in a zillion years, we hate them. If they are corporate crooks who are walking around their country clubs after wiping out our retirement funds, we really hate them. But, at the same time, we tend to cozy up to the rich people we know personally. This hating people as a group and loving them as individuals is not uncommon with any group we find threatening in some way, shape, or form. When it comes to the rich, they are perceived as taking cash from a very finite supply, hence leaving the rest of the population with very little. They rattle open our negative feelings.

It's easy to become jealous of people we perceive as having too many fingers in the cookie jar. I worked as a human resource manager at a mid-sized company where most of the managers earned around $50,000–$80,000. The general manager earned $120,000. At the time of this writing, his salary was approximately three times the average wage earner's in the United States. He had a comfortable life, but he was far from rich. He and his wife drove average cars, had an above-average home, but certainly not a showplace. He was always thrilled to get an invitation to golf at a private club, something out of his price range. He was hoping his kids would get some scholarships to help with college costs.

Being the human resource manager, I checked the bulletin board in the lunchroom often. A small contingent of unhappy campers weren't unhappy enough to seek employment elsewhere but just unhappy enough to express their opinions of management via the bulletin board. I arrived one morning to find an article on the board about the extravagances of executive compensation, with the general manager's name scribbled on it. These guys were so jealous of the general manager that they perceived him to be in the ranks of the multimillionaires whose salaries were making headlines. They disliked him for a lot of reasons, but their perception was that he was taking more than his fair share from the till. Of course, with the Law of Attraction, this angry group remained trapped in the same jobs by their own negative energy for decades, building up more and more resentment, hating rich folks more and more, and falling further and further behind the financial eight ball year after year.

So those living in lack continue to envy and dislike those who are living in prosperity, and by doing so they are generating more and more negative energy, sending out more and more bad vibes, getting more and more bad stuff. The process keeps this group trapped in negative energy. They create a cycle that feeds upon itself.

Why Them?

Most people who are self-made millionaires deserve to be millionaires. Although the early 2000s have given us headlines of corporate crooks, for the most part, the run-of-the-mill millionaires are pretty average folks who have just added more economic value to society than other pretty average folks. They aren't taking away; they aren't putting their mitts into the cookie jar and taking out extra cookies; they are creating value and being rewarded for doing so.

It's a given they are compensated well. Many of them are self-employed. They risk everything they own right down to their underwear to make their companies profitable. They work long hours. They forgo vacations. By the time they are millionaires, they are so accustomed to working that working is a way of life. They continue to put in the long hours. They are compensated well, not for their time but for providing a product or service that adds value to society. And, drum roll please, they are committed to being rich. They hold onto their "rich" energy regardless of what's going on in the world around them.

But, for some reason, we don't see the run-of-the-mill millionaires who work hard for their money. We tend to see a different variety that spends a lot of time in the limelight. We see the Hollywood sweetheart who is snorting cocaine and can't seem to recall what jean company is paying her several hundred thousands of dollars to wear their jeans. We see the corporate crooks. We see the sports stars. Most of these folks don't appear to be working all that hard and for all that long, and that evokes negativity from others.

I was at a friend's house earlier today. She's not a sports fan. The local basketball team had just signed its star player for a several-million-dollar contract, and my friend was livid. She was enraged about this guy's rise to sports stardom from a scholarship. She was ranting and raving about the publicity this kid was getting. She was on a total tangent over his outrageous price tag. She was so mad she wanted to contact the local paper and tell them to stop giving this character free publicity. This wasn't the first time I'd heard this, but today it was sucking the energy right out of me, reducing my frequencies to a place that could only cause me harm, so I wanted it to stop. I asked her why it mattered to her. She couldn't give me an answer except it was far too much money for one guy to be making to do something that wasn't even a job. I tried to explain that if the team didn't pay this guy, they'd be paying some other guy. As long as the fans are willing to shell out the hefty prices for the tickets, sports stars will be compensated royally. I reminded her it wasn't like this guy was taking food from her table. He certainly didn't get a job that any of her family members could have performed. Had she not been in such a state, I would have gone on to mention that his $20-million-a-year contract would put approximately $8 million back to society in taxes. A winning team would generate several hundreds of thousands of dollars in business revenues for the city. His endorsements for charity work would bring additional monies in corporate sponsorships for local charities. The price for all of this would be borne by people who wanted to see him perform. But she was not in the mood to hear it, and my energy was already so screwed up that all I could do was walk away from the conversation.

It's Show Time

Part of the reason why rich people are resented is because some of them flaunt their wealth. If you don't think the rich do certain things for show, think again. We have complete industries that function simply because people are willing to spend a lot of money for products that are expensive, but actually offer no value greater than a much lesser priced comparable item. Women's purses are a good example of just such a product. A purse has one function: to carry stuff. The most basic function of a purse can be done by a brown paper bag. But brown paper bags tear, stuff falls out, and they aren't very good in the long haul. So most women prefer purses made of a durable material such as leather. Leather bags sell for a wide range of prices. A woman can purchase a mid-sized leather bag for 85 dollars. At a designer boutique, a leather bag can go for several thousand dollars. Does a $12,000 purse carry stuff more effectively than an 85-dollar purse? Absolutely not. If a woman purchases a purse for the purest reason—to carry stuff—both bags will do just fine. So, why is there a market for $12,000 bags? Expensive bags display wealth. Some of the women who wear them do so to feel wealthy. They do so to keep their vibes up. Wealthy women who buy expensive bags to feel wealthy cause themselves no harm. They are feeling, and vibrating, at a frequency that's good for them.

Some women who carry expensive bags do so to evoke emotions out of other people—emotions of respect, or envy, or inferiority. This creates an entire set of energies that can mess up their worlds—and yours, too, if you buy into it. If they carry such bags only to evoke negative vibes from others, they are more than likely dealing with some money-related energy garbage from their own pasts. Energetically, they can cause the same garbage to reappear if they continue sending out negative vibrations.

If the bag is purchased on credit and the feelings attached to it reflect this debt, the owner will only attract more debt and feel downright miserable when the piper needs to be paid. If she can't really afford the purse, she may feel fraudulent. So she is going for the feelings of wealth, but getting negative feelings and energy instead. If you buy into this show by getting envious, you are also getting bad vibes. That designer bag is bringing bags of garbage to all sorts of folks. But you have choices. You can be envious, you can be neutral, or you can feel yourself in possession of a like goodie sometime in the near future. If somebody else's goodie is one of your wants, put out good energy to start magnetizing its equivalent to you.

These Shoes Are Made for Walking

Say you are looking for work because you've been downsized from a mid-managerial position. When you held your last job, you were far from rich, but you had enough disposable income to be comfortable. You had the money to get a weekly manicure and drop $398 on a pair of shoes now and then. Now things are tight. Your severance package has been exhausted, and you are living on your reserves.

That $398 pair of shoes can now induce all kinds of mixed feelings. Recall for a moment how you felt when you purchased that last $398 pair of shoes. Pretty good, I suppose. Wearing them to the office made you feel like part of the team. Those shoes were part of your uniform, your way of showing the world who you were. You felt pride, confidence, and maybe even a little superiority when you clicked by the administrative assistants. Now those same shoes are sitting in a box on the top shelf of your closet just above eye level in their little cloth bags. You don't have much use for them. If money is getting really tight, you might be thinking of them as an extravagance you should have bypassed, so you are glad to keep them out of sight, out of mind. When you even think of them, you feel a tad guilty for spending the now much-needed money.

Our stroll in these shoes isn't over yet. A former colleague calls, so you meet her for a cup of coffee. While exiting the coffee shop, she sees a pair of shoes she just has to have to complete an ensemble she bought last week. She tells you the purchase will only take a minute, so you step into the shoe store with her. She carelessly purchases a $398 pair of shoes as you look around the store wishing you were someplace else. As she tosses the shoes into the back of her car, you try to fight back envy, despair, and disgust. Two $398 pairs of shoes so far have evoked pride, confidence, superiority, guilt, envy, despair, and disgust. That's a lot of vibrations. Don't for a moment kid yourself that those emotions are a function of shoes. Those feelings are a function of the *money* spent on shoes. It's all about the money.

Too Little . . .

Possessions aren't the only things that bring forth feelings in us. People who have less than the average working stiff also evoke feelings. The next time you are in line at the grocery store behind a person using food stamps, check out the glances that poor soul is receiving from other patrons. Some scowl, some look away, some look at the purchase to see how the government assistance dollars are being spent. Why are these folks subjected to such glances? It's the pecking order in process. Somebody is a fraction lower on the economic food chain. The person who is charging groceries for the third time this month can feel superior to the person using food stamps—or possibly fearful that she's closer to that rung on the social economic ladder than she'd like.

Feelings

If you never notice a designer bag, or a luxury car, or the person on the side of the road holding a sign that reads "Will Work for Food," then you are head and shoulders above the rest of us on the energy scale. For most of us, those subtle, and not so subtle, reminders of money evoke all sorts of feelings, and each of these seemingly harmless feelings sets off vibrations that cause havoc in our worlds. They bring our frequencies up and down in roller-coaster fashion, connecting us with good stuff, bad stuff, and pretty much doing what unfocused energy does best: making life messy.

If you only work for money—and you don't have a healthy relationship with money—you are working for a negative feeling. Many people who only work for money don't work long. They get easily bored with a job and move on to some other job. Sometimes they get fired. Sometimes they simply walk away from their jobs. People who work for money attract flawed jobs—jobs that they want to leave as soon as their coffers are filled. So if your energy about money is all over the place, it's no wonder that a job hasn't fallen into your world. To make matters worse, there are even deeper reasons we have a tough time feeling good about money.

Money Rules

We believe money has rules. In general, we don't care much for rules. Rules are restrictive. Lots of rules appear to favor others. Rules impede upon our individuality. Yeah, we don't care much for rules at all. So it comes as no surprise that we can *really* hate the rules we've created about money. How does "money is hard to come by" make you feel? "Money doesn't grow on trees" makes it hard to harvest. "Too rich for my blood" is something we've all said from time to time. And who hasn't heard that "money is the root of all evil"? We call money evil, then we try to love it. So if you think you love money, think again. How does money really make you feel? Think of money with your eyes closed and feel your gut. If you're like a lot of people, you are getting a lot of negativity. If you wonder where all of these emotions come from, take a trip down memory lane.

Money Memories

Was money free-flowing or scarce in your childhood? Was money used to control you? Did you get money when you were "good"? Was money withheld if you were "bad"? Were you allowed to spend your own money, or did you always have to save your money for a rainy day? Were you forever dependent on your parents' money, with no spending cash of your own, making you a slave to their whims? These are all experiences that form your attitudes toward money.

For the most part, I thought little of money as a child. We lived in a modest house, but my brother and I were never denied anything we truly wanted, and all of our basic needs were met. Food was plentiful. Necessary clothes were provided and maintained. When we were small, we had a swing set and a sandbox, tricycles, bicycles, and assorted toys. Dad built a playhouse for me that even had a sink with running water as long as Mom was willing to run across the yard to refill the reservoir attached to the back of the house. We lived on a street teaming with other children who were playmates throughout our childhoods. The street was small with a lake at one end that provided us with hours of swimming in the summer and ice-skating in the winter. We didn't appear to have more or less than the other kids on the street.

But, like other people, I had a couple of experiences with money that simply helped pattern my thinking, and feeling, about money. Everybody has a few that stick out in their minds, whether they be the day they got something or the day they were denied something. I vividly recall two experiences that taught me money was hard to come by and very slippery to hold onto. When I was five years old, I wanted a Chatty Cathy doll. At the time she was very amazing because she talked when a string was pulled from the back of her neck. I wanted her so badly that I took another doll, put a rubber band around her neck, and pretended my lips weren't moving when I pulled the rubber band and talked for my poor, strangled doll. My mother took in ironing to buy me a Chatty Cathy for Christmas. My mother ironed other people's clothes so I could have the doll of my dreams. By the time Chatty Cathy appeared under the Christmas tree, Mom and I both knew well that money was hard to come by.

My second memorable experience was two years later. I had 32 dollars in savings. In February, I looked at my pass-book to see that the balance had been 32 dollars in November, went down to zero in December, then back up to 32 dollars in late January. Well, it doesn't take a CPA to realize that somebody drained my account. That somebody was Mom, the only person who could sign for my money. I was ticked. She spent a week telling me she was sorry, all to no avail. *Don't mess with my money*, I pouted. I also learned that money had a way of getting away from me. Sadly, I once embraced this belief, and money slipped away from me for years.

If you have hang-ups about money from your childhood—and, believe me, we all do—it's time to leave them in the past. Once they are identified, you can shift your energy around money. It's just a matter of feeling better about it.

Saving for a Sunny Day

There's another hang-up we have about money. We are always saving for a rainy day—for some unforeseen negative expenditure. Needless to say, those rainy-day funds are always being gobbled up by emergencies. Everything from a speeding ticket to a broken washing machine seems to crop up, and it always seems to be just about the same amount of money that's been tossed into the rainy-day fund. It's not irony; it's energy. Save for it, focus on it, and, bingo, it's yours. So if you are always tossing money into a rainy-day fund, you can pretty much expect to get rainy days.

It's far more fun and productive to save for a *sunny* day. One day, I will get out of bed, it will be sunny, and I will decide that's the end of my working days. Other people call it saving for retirement, but retirement to me holds a vision of being old and gray and worrying about pills. When I hold that perspective in my mind, retirement is not very inviting, and my retirement fund does anything but grow. In fact, it shrinks. After all, why save money to be old and gray and worried about pills? It's hard to think of putting money away for a life that's rather unappealing. It's much easier to save for that sunny day when I just decide it's time to do something else, something without a demanding schedule. It's the same money going into the same account, but one has a boatload of negative feelings and energy, and the other holds lofty visions and much higher vibrations. Even saving for retirement is all about feelings toward money. And feelings, my friend, are the key to putting a life in order.

Rich Person, Poor Person

When I was in college, I had just enough money for the bare necessities. My food money was spent on rice and caffeine—tea, soda, chocolate. When my tummy started rumbling for a real meal, a classmate and I would pool our meager resources and cook a feast of pot roast and potatoes that we would eat for days. Even with constant monitoring of expenditures, there were necessities that stretched my budget to the breaking point. One was toilet paper. I used it as sparingly as possible. I knew the sheet count on all of the brands. It was pathetic. I actually worried about it. As if exams and an overloaded schedule weren't enough to cause sleepless nights, I would actually lie in bed and worry about where my next roll of TP was coming from. Buying it took a chunk out of my food money. Well, that was all a long time ago. I now purchase packs of 24 when they are on sale. This works out pretty well except when I reach for the last roll. All of the TP feelings come back. I begin to feel poor, really *poor.* When I first discovered this little hang-up about TP, I thought I was a tad nuts. But then I realized it was all of those scarcity fears trying to generate their own brand of vibes, and if I didn't nip them in the bud, they'd go out and call in all of their overeager buddies to assist in some financial disaster. Whenever I'd get into a TP crisis mode, I'd get notices from the IRS, an extra car expense, you name it. Stashing a few extra rolls of TP in my home solves this TP-induced scarcity feeling and all of the bad energy that comes along with it.

If my TP thing makes me feel like a pauper, other things make me feel like a million bucks. I have a pair of earrings that put me into prosperity mode just by wearing them. They aren't the most expensive earrings I own, but to me they are priceless. I bought them at a turning point in my life. When I tried them on and looked into the mirror at the jewelry store, I knew I was seeing the inner me. I bought them without a second thought. I've had them for quite some time, and every time I put them on I feel energized. I feel rich. Ironically, nobody, and I mean nobody, has ever complimented me on those earrings. Only I know the power they possess.

Think of things that make you feel poor and make you feel rich. Those that make you feel poor may be as stupid as my TP thing. I didn't say they had to be good reasons, reasonable reasons, or logical reasons. A lot of energy stuff is pure emotions. If you can eliminate the things that make you feel poor, do so. If driving with the gas gauge bouncing near E makes you feel destitute, fill the tank when you see the needle at half a tank. You are going to buy gas sometime anyway. You might as well buy it before your vibrations bottom out. If wearing a certain item of clothing or carrying an expensive wallet makes you feel rich, do it. A wallet that costs $120 will last several years and make you feel wealthy every time you make a financial transaction. That's *good* vibrating!

Millionaires, Millionaires, Millionaires . . .

Becoming wealthy isn't merely a byproduct of hard work. There are plenty of jobs at the bottom of the corporate food chain that require hard work, but don't reward it with a high wage. While in grad school I waited tables. I was making ten dollars an hour on a good night and working my little body into the ground. It was hard work. I can attest firsthand that making money and hard work do not always go hand-in-hand. In the fast-food industry, it is stressful to have one time-crunched customer after another ordering in your ear as you're counting out change. It's boring to stand around during down times waiting for the lunch rush. It's tough to get everybody's order signed, sealed, and delivered in 60 seconds. In the manufacturing world, pulling the same little widget a million times a week is downright exhausting. These people are working hard, so why aren't they wealthy?

So, if hard work doesn't equate to wealth, what does? And why can't we all be rich? It's simple. We can't all be rich because we don't *feel* rich. Feeling rich is very foreign to us. When we get those rare fleeting moments of feeling rich, we can't make a commitment to keep that feeling regardless of appearances. Our life experiences have been limited to a given set-of-expectations and occupations. We look at the world around us and find a niche that meets our basic needs and accept that as our lot in life.

The truth is we could all be rich, but it would involve letting go of so much we hold to be true. Most of us would rather be right than rich! We also don't want to do what it takes to be rich, which is finding something to do that adds value to society, making a commitment to being rich, and feeling rich regardless of the world around us. Feelings, once again, are key. It's amazing how fast the good ideas flow once we begin to feel valuable and rich.

Good ideas come from looking at the world around us and going inside for guidance from our gut. Most of us aren't rich because we've been trained to do what we know instead of going within to discover what we can be. Oh, you might be saying you know lots of folks who go within daily, but are still eking out an existence. Well, I know them, too. They don't look very hard at the world around them, and they go inside with a flashlight looking for something that will pay the bills. They are seeking some way to do something they love, but they lack the commitment to become wealthy. They set their financial cruise control for $30,000 and stay there. To be rich, you have to *feel* it! Start thinking about how you will become rich. Start feeling yourself adding so much value to society that you are richly rewarded. And by feeling rich, I don't mean go on a shopping binge with credit cards. That will only make you feel rich for a day, week, or until the piper needs to be paid. Feel rich by thinking of the value you will be adding to society.

If the idea that everybody could be rich is outlandish to you, it's time to think of where your financial cruise control is set. Remember the concept of cruise control, or set-of-expectations, that we discussed in chapter 5? It's some number that's really the floor, the absolute bottom we are willing to earn. Somehow we get stuck at that number. Like cruise control, it's running the trip, only in this case it's your life. But it's possible to hit the gas and push your income above that number. It takes commitment, it takes desire, and it takes feeling it. It requires steps away from your comfort zone, which is really not all that damned comfortable. We all could do it. We all could go within with a search-light instead of a flashlight and seek out our value, then sell it to society. There's not one good reason in the world for anybody to be anything but rich. It's just re-setting the cruise control and taking command of our lives. It's all within your power. It's time to think of a world of prosperity instead of a world of scarcity. It's time to feel your way to a better world. It's time to put money back into perspective.

Is It Love?

Oh, you may still claim you love money, which is just fine and dandy, but is it conditional love? You love it as long as earning it doesn't put too many demands on you. You love it as long as it doesn't mess up your life. You love it as long as your relatives aren't checking your pulse to see if they will be getting into your pockets soon. Perhaps you don't love it at all. Perhaps deep down it scares you.

Your true feelings about money are more than likely all over the place. Therefore, it's time to tame them. If money terrifies you, read some books about it and take some courses that illuminate the issues. There's no reason to be held hostage to your fears. The best remedy for fear is knowledge. If you hate money because you perceive that it brings demands and responsibilities that you choose to avoid, then dissect the demands and the responsibilities from the idea of money. Just think of money as a tool to transfer value. Let your beliefs go, and let the money flow. It's not deserving of love, hate, envy, greed, or any feelings whatsoever. To generate good energy around money, have respect for it as a servant that will serve you well. Feel yourself in control over your finances. Feel yourself getting gut feelings about good employers, good jobs, good ideas. Feel the money in hand. Feel yourself pushing the gas on your job search, on your career path, on your highway to financial freedom!

Chapter 7

Synchronicity

As a kid, I loved to play Mouse Trap. When I turned the crank and watched all the pieces work together, I was delighted. Seeing the old boot kick the bucket and send the ball down the gutter just plain turned me on. Working your energy is sort of like a big game of Mouse Trap—when all of the energy is in place, things just sort of work seamlessly.

Energy delivers via synchronicity. People and things appear when needed. You happen to be having a casual conversation with a friend who has just heard of a company that's considering creating a position. Or you run into a former employer who tells you to give him a call since he might be able to throw some consulting work in your direction. Or you are standing in a line at the bank and the guy ahead of you is on the cell phone telling his human resource person he needs to fill that position pronto. Or a headhunter who's had your résumé on file for months calls out of the blue. All of these leads are little acts of synchronicity—and signs that you are putting out the right kind of vibes.

Here's an example of how synchronicity has worked for me. As a consultant, I go from job to job. I generate work via word-of-mouth, direct mailings, and radio advertising. Due to the nature of my work, I am always in the process of signing on new clients or resigning from clients who now have their HR systems in place. This process involves ongoing prospecting, something I find very time-consuming.

A few months ago, one of my clients needed the information that was to be presented at a luncheon, so I recommended she attend. She insisted I attend, too. I knew this luncheon would put a cramp in my schedule and cause me to be late to my next client. I tried to beg off, but she was insistent. Since she's my favorite client, I juggled my schedule and decided to attend, and to enjoy myself as well. Now, this client is an outgoing young woman who makes sure everybody at every table is introduced to one another. She introduced me not only by name, but as her human resource consultant. As the luncheon was breaking up, I was headed rather briskly for the door when a woman stopped me. I had never seen her before in my life. As it turned out, she was in charge of the continuing education program at a local vocational school, and she was looking for a human resource person to teach some courses on the subject to business owners. By the end of the week, she had contracted with me to teach the classes. Part of the deal included that I could take on any of the business owners attending my classes as my clients. So, just by attending a luncheon and sending out good vibrations, I was handed a fantastic marketing avenue.

Right around the same time, I got the great news that this book was going to be published. I knew I'd have to use the time I generally use for prospecting to finish the manuscript within the deadline. The book deal and the teaching gig fit together like pieces of some great cosmic puzzle. I couldn't have planned a better situation. That's how energy works. It delivers!

The Big Picture

But it doesn't deliver until all of the energy is on the same frequency. Streaming out good energy 24/7 is not our thing, so there will be times when things start to connect, then disconnect, then connect, and so it goes. And there are times when so much energy has to connect to make things work that it takes time for all of the pieces to fall together.

I started writing my first manuscript 17 years ago on a borrowed computer in my spare time around a job while in grad school. I must admit it was a horrible manuscript that fortunately was destroyed before I embarrassed myself. The good thing about it was I realized I could write. I kept writing until I came up with a manuscript that was marketable, and I started actively seeking a literary agent six or seven years ago for another manuscript that never sold. I never stopped writing. A year and a half ago, an agent at one of the top literary agencies took an interest in this manuscript. I was thrilled. She asked that I give her 90 days to review the materials. I gave her the requested time and then some. One hundred and ten days later, I shyly contacted her. She needed more time. We then moved to a monthly schedule of me contacting her and her needing additional time. Nine months later, I got an e-mail from her that she was leaving the agency to go solo. She was quite young. It didn't make much sense for her to be leaving a well-known powerful literary agency to strike out on her own. My heart sank.

But my energy was working on a delivery system in its own way. Two years ago, a small independent bookstore opened in an area where I cycle regularly. I found the store to be delightful and quickly joined its book club. I really hit it off with a woman who happened to be the owner of the store. She and her husband also own a publishing house, and we ended up talking about BookExpo America (BEA), the largest trade show in the publishing industry and a show closed to non-industry want-to-be writers. She invited me to BEA as a representative of the store and sent me on the lookout for books that I thought would sell. She also coached me as to how to get my materials in the hands of acquiring editors.

I enjoyed being with the crowd from the bookstore and being in New York City. I also enjoyed seeing the industry from the inside, but I was getting nowhere with editors. I came home with a handful of business cards and a pair of earrings from Tiffany's. I went back to waiting for a positive response from the agent who had been sitting on my manuscript for about five months at that time. When she pulled the rug out from under me four months later, I dug out the business cards from acquiring editors and decided to give my manuscript one last chance without representation. The worst they could do was say "no," and I doubted if it would take them nine months to do so. Within three months, a publisher expressed an interest. They had been discussing the acquisition of a book of this nature. Had I contacted them earlier, I could have gotten a very well-crafted rejection letter since this type of book was not what they had been seeking months earlier. A lot of energy had to be on the same wavelength to make this project successful.

Dedicated Line

Learning to tune into synchronicity and move on hunches takes some dedication. Decades ago, my friend, Kevin, then 28, was living in New York City earning a quarter of a million a year and perking with ideas of how to turn his well-paying job into a well-paying company. I, on the other hand, was struggling to hold onto a $25,000–a-year job and worrying about anything and everything. Long-distance phone rates were on a graduated scale with the off-peak time starting at 11:00 in the evening. Although Kevin was doing very well, he was one of the cheapest men I've ever known. When I flew to New York to visit him, he took me to an off-off-off-Broadway play and insisted we take the subway. It was hard to believe I was spending the evening with a guy who was earning in a year what I was earning in a decade as I descended into the foreign world of the New York subway late at night. Being cheap, he called infrequently, and his calls always came in after 11:01. One night sticks out in my mind because it was such a wake-up call. The phone rang at 11:01, and it was Kevin. When I answered the phone, he asked me what I needed. I was groggy and somewhat dazed, but I told him he had called me, not vice versa. Without hesitation, he told me that my phone number had been running through his head throughout the day, so it was obvious to him that I needed to talk to him. Now, if I wouldn't mind, he asked, would I please tell him what I needed so he could get some sleep! At first I was outraged, but then I recalled a problem I'd been having all day, a problem he could solve. And bingo, I stated my problem, and he had an answer. Before he hung up, he told me I should pay attention when somebody's name or number runs through my head so I'd stop missing opportunities.

Kevin learned early to move on hunches. When a phone number kept running through his head, he called it. When a name kept running through his head, he contacted that person or company. He was well aware that other people's energy impacted his life, and when their energy was connecting with his, he moved on his hunches.

Energy Schedule

When I was studying collective bargaining in graduate school, we had to study several negotiation models. Regardless of the model, the professor had the same input: Timing is everything. The same is true with energy. All of us have had something that we've desired, wished for, worked for, and visualized, but our energy failed to deliver it. We got so caught up in it "not appearing" that we pumped out bad energy after good. It would get close, and bingo, we'd push it away. And, as shown in the previous example, there are times when lots of energy has to connect for something big to happen.

If you think things are just plain off in the timing department, several things could be creating the traffic jam in the delivery process. Your energy might be so all over the place that your order simply is put on hold. Good energy, bad energy, up, down, it all cancels out. Nothing happens. So if a job is not appearing, get off the roller coaster. Get your energetic house in order. Go back to chapter 4 and find something that turns you on.

Also, things might be happening, but you might be missing the signals. Get in touch with your gut on a daily basis. Do a feeling assessment. When something feels right, when you get a hunch, when a phone number runs through your head, that's energy coming through. These little signals take practice to interpret. Being quiet is the best way to get in touch with your greater good. The good news is that if you are unemployed, you have time for a little quiet. Let that Higher Self communicate with you.

Leap

Okay, you're getting the messages. Yep, the communication is coming through loud and clear. It's time to move on your hunches. Oh, I don't mean if you hear three songs on the oldies station by Boston to pack your bags and get on the next plane heading east (although you might want to call the radio station to see if you won the T-shirt).

Since we learn by doing, start moving on little hunches. The other day, I had clients scheduled back-to-back. I was planning to grab a sandwich on the road when a colleague showed up unexpectedly at the first client's. I just got this hunch that we should have lunch together. I thought for a moment about my jammed schedule, but the pull to talk with her was so strong that I made a call to reschedule the second client. We went to lunch, which was pleasant, and she told me she wanted to talk to me about some ideas she had for my business. This was some good energy.

After lunch, I came home and parked my car in the garage and got busy on a project. Later in the early evening hours, I went to get my bicycle and noticed a large pool of something liquid under my car. My radiator was peeing green fluid. Had I not gone with the feeling to go to lunch, not only would I have missed out on the business ideas she had for me, but I would have blown the engine out of my car. The temperature was well into the nineties, and my car would have been toast before I would have known the radiator was defective.

Once you move on little hunches, you will develop a comfort level with moving on bigger ones. In time, following your hunches leads to a wonderful life.

PART II

Economics

Chapter 8

Psst, What Ya Sellin'?

I once had a friend whose career goals changed faster than fashion. She wanted to be a farmer, a preacher, a teacher—you name it, and it was her goal for a while. Needless to say, she never stuck with any desired goal long enough to get her energy wrapped around it or to earn the credentials that the position required. She floated from goal to goal like Peter Pan in Never Never Land. She never grew up and never got to enjoy the fruits of true labor.

A good job does bring pleasure to one's life in a variety of ways. A good job gives you a sense of accomplishment. It allows you to connect with other people in a stimulating environment. It provides validation of your value to society. It also supplies you with status and the financial means to allow you to enjoy a fulfilling personal life. Don't miss out on those pleasures!

What-I-Want-to-Be-When-I-Grow-Up

Figuring out what you want to do is not an easy task. Okay, being the CEO of an international company is probably a heck of a lot more fun than flipping burgers. CEOs get better pay, perks, and publicity. They don't have irrational customers witching about too much mayo, and they don't have to punch a time clock. They do, of course, have to meet some pretty outrageous expectations of Wall Street and make some very critical decisions every day, but for the most part the majority of them have it pretty darned good.

But they aren't the only folks who enjoy going to work day after day. I've worked in several industries. Some I've found very surprising because of the workers' loyalty and pride in their jobs, even if they don't enjoy high status in our society. I've learned a lot from these employees. Mostly, I've learned that it isn't the job but the mind-set of the person performing the job that determines if it is a good job or a bad job. I know tool-and-die makers who have more pride in their work than some college professors.

Jobs are public and personal. They are public because society defines who we are by what we do. What we can purchase in a materialistic society is a function of what we do. But there's a very personal side to employment. Each of us feels good doing some things and not good doing other things.

Only you can determine what will make you satisfied and put money in your pocket. Fortunately, you need not make this decision without guidance. Your Higher Self is standing by, ready to direct you to your most fulfilling life's work. You simply need to learn to tune into your Higher Self and get the message.

Most of us have had that feeling, that "I know what I want to be when I grow up" feeling. It's common to get such a feeling during the early morning hours just before dawn when the world seems clear and problems are easily solved. Many of us have not taken it seriously because it all seemed too good to be true or we simply didn't remember all of the details in the light of day.

If you are truly in a quandary as to what you want to do for a living, daily start tuning into that early morning message. It might mean putting both feet on the floor at a time of day when you'd rather put the pillow over your head. You may have to tip-toe outside for a quiet solitary reflection while the rest of the neighborhood is fast asleep. Whatever it involves, get into this habit and pay close attention to your feelings and thoughts. Keep a journal. You will notice a pattern develop in your thoughts and feelings that will lead you to your destiny. You may feel drawn to a certain line of work, or get good feelings when you think of jobs you'd like to perform. You may feel old rumblings of activities that brought you joy that can be incorporated into your job choices. You may unearth the feeling that you are valuable when you work with your hands, or numbers, or people. All of these feelings are keys to your destiny. You may or may not get a eureka moment—one of those grand moments when you know exactly what you want to do.

I recall my first eureka moment vividly. It was decades ago. In the wee hours of the morning I felt with every fiber of my being that photography was my calling. Oh, I got the message loud and clear and I did make some money off of photography, but it was by taking wedding photos, not doing what I thought of as serious photography. There's nothing wrong with wedding photography. I did a good job and I worked very hard at it, but it was not the photography that my Higher Self was trying to get me to do. *The Higher Self is a big thinker not a little mind.* It kept trying to push me in the right direction, kept putting the right people smack dab in the middle of my path, kept getting the right equipment in my hands, but I just didn't get it. I listened—I just interpreted the message in a mistaken manner. My talent was not photographing people; my talent was in my ability to capture light on film. I played with the camera for many years but never had the courage to move forward on a feeling.

Yet, the amazing thing is the Higher Self doesn't give up. It waits a while, then sends out another message that may or may not be heard. It goes after another goal since it thrives on change. All the while life goes on. More experiences are gathered. Another crisis forces another career change and again the Higher Self whispers. This process goes on and on until someday one finally realizes all of these crises aren't bad—they are just transitions. They are the spaces designed to connect with Higher Self. So eventually Higher Self gets through. Fortunately, by that time most folks have a pretty good understanding of how the real world works and why people are paid to do things in the first place. The whispers of the Higher Self and the requirements of the real world start to dance together.

Jobs exist because people pay other people to do things

1. they can't do themselves because they lack the skill-set,

2. they don't have time to do themselves,

3. they don't want to do themselves.

Whether your goal is to work for a company or to fly solo and work for your clients, you must determine what you can do that somebody else 1) can't do, 2) doesn't have time to do, or 3) won't do. You must see a need (a problem), and you must fulfill the need (the solution). By constantly looking for needs and providing the fulfillment of needs, you will be able to remain flexible and marketable in a shifting job market.

Maximizing Utility

Economists use the term "maximizing utility" to explain human behavior. Maximizing utility looks at why people make economic decisions using a broad range of criteria. When somebody maximizes their utility, they make a decision that is in their best interest in relation to their options and their desires.

When seeking employment, you want to maximize your utility. Maximizing utility requires looking at employment from a perspective greater than money. For some people, it's status-driven. Others want to work with their heads, or their hands, or their hearts. Some want to work for large companies; others desire the self-employment route. Here are some of the most common factors people look at when seeking employment:

• Money

• Healthcare benefits

• Stock options

• Retirement benefits

• Flexible working schedule

• Location

• Commute

• Social status

• Corporate structure

• Co-workers

• Good bosses

• Safety

• Working hours

Well, these are the more normal things one considers, but I've seen others. I know one guy who was made very happy when offered a corner office. Personally, I like commuting with the sun not glaring in my windshield. Yeah, I like driving west to work in the mornings and east from work at the end of the day. You may say that sounds absolutely insane, but I was once in a four-car pile-up on the way to work. I want to make my commute as agreeable as possible.

Money

All of this talk about variables isn't to minimize money. People work for money. People who say they work for something other than money would probably adjust that statement if their paycheck were to suddenly disappear. They would soon be scrambling for another paying job. Even those of us with an unhealthy relationship with Benjamin Franklin and his friends work with the carrot of getting a few dollars at the end of the week.

As stated in chapter 6, your relationship with money is probably not in the greatest of health. Well, now is the time to kiss and make up with money. The time to think about compensation packages is when you are searching for work, not six months after taking a job.

Ironically, a lot of people with good work ethics and skills have no idea how much they are worth. They go into the world of work taking any wage an employer offers. Some occupations, however, have really large pay variances from company to company. Case in point: HR managers make anywhere from $35,000 to $300,000 a year. Why such a large variance? Mostly the pay is a function of the size and structure of the company. When I was employed by a little 600-employee company, I worked really hard. My days were long, my phone at home rang at night with emergencies, and I had no clerical help. I left that family-owned company to move to a job at a company that was held by a holding company. My increase in salary was a whopping 70 percent. I had less work and a much shorter workweek. The policies and procedures were well-written and seldom needed amending. I had two clerks to handle the day-to-day paperwork that used to tack on hours to my workload at my former job.

Now you may be asking yourself why I did not seek employment at the second company and skip the first experience altogether. Honestly, I didn't know there was such a dif-

ference. Period. I did not have a roadmap to ste∕
low-paying companies, and I had no idea that c∕
ture played such a large role in compensation ⸗∕
out energy that I wanted a job, and that's what I got.

How can you avoid such a costly mistake? Know where to
look for the better-paying jobs. As you will see in chapter 9,
corporate structure plays an enormous role in compensation.
Location also plays a role. And, of course, supply and demand
of any specific type of labor is a factor.

There are several ways to determine how much the market
will pay for your labor. Some Internet sites, such as career
builder.com, provide salary and wage information. For those
seeking traditional jobs, a good starting point is the Department
of Labor (DOL). Although their data is dry, and it may take you
some time to find the exact data you are seeking, you should be
able to get a good sense of your worth from the DOL's data-
base. If searching the DOL isn't for you, ask people who work
in the field. If you decide to go this route, expect a little resistance when asking people about their income. Most people
shuffle their feet a little when asked pointblank about their
income. Also, expect the information you get to be a bit
tainted. Many people feel uncomfortable talking about their
earnings, so they state a figure that might be a little high.
Consider it a ballpark number. If you have a friend in the field
of human resources, see if you can get one of the several local
surveys that are created by corporate associations or chambers
of commerce. Small and mid-sized companies use these as tools
to determine their own wage scales. These surveys usually have
the low, medium, and high end of most job pay scales for a
given geographic area. If you are looking into work for the government, those numbers are available to the public.

One of the best ways to get a feel for the market is to look
closely at the job postings. Regardless of the source you use,
whether it is the Internet or the local newspaper, you will be

ble to find some classifieds with the salary range posted. Companies post the salary ranges to make sure they get candidates who fall into the range they are willing to pay or to attract the best candidates, depending on the number. Those who are the lowest payers often put the salary amount in the ad to scare away folks who want to earn more money. The high-end companies often put in the dollar amount because they want to attract the best employees possible.

Another source of regional compensation knowledge is counselors at community colleges. Since local employers use community colleges as a source of labor, their counselors are generally aware of what local employers are paying. If you are a student or are considering going to a community college, sit down with a counselor and find out how much you will really earn with your degree before you invest heavily in time and money for your education.

If you are just completing college, stop in the placement office. All college degrees are not worth the same amount of money in the job market. Some have little value, while others can demand some pretty hefty starting salaries. Your school's placement office is a great place to see what employers are offering for your degree from your school.

Keep in mind, some employers are willing to pay top dollar for the better schools, but not all employees see the value in a high-ticket education. Recently, I counseled a young man (I'll refer to him as my little buddy) who will soon be graduating from Case Western Reserve University. This is a well-respected school in northeast Ohio. I've known this kid since he was a little tike, and I know he went to Case because he felt it would lead to a high-paying job in the long run.

Thus, my little buddy initially approached his job interviews a little arrogantly. He assumed a Case Western Reserve University degree would be in demand at every company, so he didn't take his first few interviews very seriously. After all, it was months before graduation, and with everybody surely wanting him, what was the big deal? He soon found that a lot of local companies would not look at Case Western Reserve University graduates because they find them too costly. They aren't willing to pay for the higher-priced education. Therefore, even with a degree from a top school, this kid got the down and dirty truth. Everybody's skills, education, and experience have a given market. After he put out his "I don't care" attitude and lost three job opportunities, he began to listen to me. He realized he had to tap into his market or else he'd be in competition for jobs with employers who would pay him far less than he expected to earn. Now, keep in mind, this kid does not believe in energy stuff. In fact, he thinks I am pretty out on a limb by admitting I am into these energy principles, but he was willing to listen to me talk about marketing once he realized his primary market was limited.

Get the Money Upfront

As my little buddy found, it is very important that you know your worth to employers. The time to negotiate compensation is before you start a job, not six months later. If you take a job with the expectation of getting your salary adjusted upward after three months, six months, or a year, you may be setting yourself up for disappointment. The company has the upper hand once you are on board. Yes, you may be promised a review and a salary adjustment, but somehow those promises are pushed out further and further into the future once you are settled in. The company knows you don't want to look flighty by having a three- or six-month gig on your résumé. It also knows that job searching has costs attached, even if those costs are simply your time. Time is money. It knows you don't really want to start the job-search process again. And, in a tight job market, even if you do get fed up and go in search of another job in six months, it's easier for the company to replace you than it is for you to replace a job.

Once you start at a given salary, you can pretty much expect it to be a year before you see much of an increase. Regardless of the promises made to you, unless you have shined so brightly that you cannot be ignored, you will be waiting for your money, or asking for it. Also, if you are one of the lucky ones who gets your 90-day review and raise on time, your raise will probably not meet your expectations. It's best to get the money up-front.

Stepping Out

If you believe you know your true worth and can't find an employer who is willing to compensate you at market value, you may have an inflated perception of your worth, or you may be worth that amount on an hourly basis, but your skills may not be needed by an employer for a full 40 hours a week. In a fluctuating workplace, marketing yourself may involve looking at your skill-set and creating several small jobs. In other words, you might become self-employed. Self-employment isn't easy. It lacks the security of a company taking care of your medical, retirement, and other perks. Then again, in the last few years, so many companies have been killed with the cancer of corruption that thousands of people who were told they had these very things did not have them. And they had little to fall back on once their security blankets were pulled out from under them. Therefore, self-employment is an option not to be overlooked if you are planning on working for life because it gives you control over your life. If you apply energy principles to self-employment, you can turn it into your own personal gold mine.

World of Opportunity

As I said earlier in this chapter, people hire people for three reasons. But a "job" isn't what people get paid the most for in our society. What our society pays the big bucks for are really good ideas. Look around at the people who have made fortunes. They had ideas. The man who developed FedEx had an idea. He presented it in graduate school and didn't even get a very good grade for his idea, but he made a fortune when he presented it to the world. Bill Gates of Microsoft had a good idea, too!

You may say you have lots of ideas, but no money behind them. The amazing thing about energy is that it opens doors and brings in the necessary resources for ideas to flourish. With energy and persistence behind them, you can make your dreams a reality.

If you think there's no more room for new ideas, think again. I was listing to NPR a couple of years ago, and they had a short piece about a machine that tells people when to take their medications, dispenses the medications, and calls a family member if the medication is not taken. This isn't rocket science. It's a practical invention for an aging population. Look around, see a need and apply an idea.

In the eighties, I asked my grandmother, who was born around the turn of the century, what were the two best inventions of her lifetime. She had seen the automobile come of age, watched a man walk on the moon—a lot had happened during her long lifetime. She looked at me and told me that the two greatest inventions from her perspective were birth control and paper plates. I was pretty much floored. But, as she put it, no woman in her right mind would have had four children during the Depression if it had been avoidable. As for paper plates, she said they just made life easier, and with age she had little desire to drag out the fine china and silver for every holiday. As this demonstrates, people set their priorities, and their dollars, on things that make their lives easier. The things they buy don't have to be complicated, just effective.

Now, of course, lots of folks are looking for get-rich-quick schemes. Things don't work that way very often, although I do recall people plunking down cold, hard cash for pet rocks and beanie babies! But even pet rocks had value in the short run. Those little boxed rocks were whimsical enough and inexpensive enough to be a rather charming stocking stuffer for one season. But, in most cases, people only pay for products or services that have value in the long run. Your idea has to have some merit. Your idea has to be something that stirs your soul and your imagination. Your idea has to be something you can embrace and not let go of, no matter how many times failure smacks you in the face. You have to be passionate about your idea; you have to be enthusiastic about it long after the cheerleaders fall away. You have to have the ability to see its merits in the dark of night, and continue to hold it in good energy. Passion, energy, enthusiasm, and persistence make some people millionaires, while multitudes of others struggle on minimum wage.

Bottom Out

I am not an advocate of starting at the bottom of any organization unless it's strictly a short-term gig to learn the industry on somebody else's nickel. It's not that these bottom-end jobs aren't "real" jobs. I started in human resources in 1989, and I've never hired anybody for an "unreal" job. Oh, they are definitely real! Generally, they are really hard, or really boring, or really dead-end. But the major problem with most of the jobs at the bottom is they don't pay the bills.

So, the best place to start is anyplace other than the bottom. I've argued this case several times with a man I know who has several companies. He says people have to start at the bottom.

The bottom sucks. The bottom is full of negative energy. It's pretty damned close to impossible to live on minimum wage. Although most companies post jobs and have handbooks that say they promote within, in practice they fill the best jobs with talent from other sources. Even this friend of mine, who's an advocate of the work-yourself-up concept, couldn't give me one example of a person in his company who had started at the bottom and got above team leader. This man himself started in a rather lowly position, but he was the owner's son. That isn't really starting at the bottom.

Victor Gruen is probably not a name that is familiar to you, although you more than likely use his invention often. He invented the shopping mall in the 1950s. This Jewish man came to America from Austria during World War II. While crossing the Atlantic, with eight dollars in his pocket, he was told by another traveler to not become a dishwasher. Although this guy was clearly broke, he didn't feel broke or allow broke to define him and his energy. He look around, watched what drew people into stores and what kept them only window shopping. When he realized the role that architecture played in retail profits, he changed the architecture. Obviously, he did not become a dishwasher.

We do have plenty of dishwashers, and due to the laws of supply and demand, they make little money. It's easy to become a dishwasher. It's easy to replace a dishwasher. Therefore, they are compensated poorly. Conversely, not everybody has the skills, education, and composure to be a CEO. Therefore, the supply is low and the compensation is high. Most of us spend most of our lives somewhere in the middle. We strive to have our next job a rung or two above our last on the corporate ladder, and our goals are attainable because we have determined what skills are necessary and attracted the energy to put us in those positions.

The people who fare best in the workplace are those who

have goals. Oh, you might be saying they went to the best schools, had the best connections, or their parents paved the way. For many, this is true, but energy still played a great part. They "felt" that they were privileged, and that they were going to someday reap the rewards and responsibilities of those privileges. When you begin to truly feel deserving, the right position will come to you, too.

For the most part, people who come out on the bottom are those who have no idea what they want to be when they grow up. Over time, they stay stuck in jobs similar to jobs their parents held, regardless of their skill-set or desires.

Most people are exposed to the jobs their folks held and maybe a handful of other occupations. Therefore, they ultimately decide to follow the path of least resistance. The author of the book *Rivethead* looks at a factory job at GM as his birthright. When he tries to make ends meet painting houses, and fails, he goes to GM to collect his birthright—a job just like the one his old man had. My own occupation, human resource manager, didn't take me too far from my mother's occupation as an office manager.

Who Wins?

Over the years, I've noticed five patterns in the way people determine what they are going to do for a living:

1. The unhappiest people follow the path of least resistance. They choose a career path from a limited range of opportunities or they get a job because a friend knew somebody who knew somebody who could get them in a company or field.

2. Those with a little better energy (and a little more savvy) fall into jobs pretty much the same way, but they fall into companies or occupations they happen to find they enjoy a little.

3. Others study, toil, and eventually find work in a field they think will intrigue them.

4. Successful folks study, toil, and find work in a field that does intrigue them with the help of Higher Self.

5. The incredibly successful people among us look around, go within to Higher Self, and see a need they can fill with passion!

The major difference between number 5, the most successful, and number 1, the least successful, is that those at the high end know what they want to do. Yeah, simply knowing what you want to do can make all the difference in the world.

In order to decide on an interesting and challenging career it helps to be exposed to the wide range of occupations. There are several ways to gain such exposure; most involve research, physically taking a look at what folks do for a living, and talking to people in any given field of work. This research process can start with something as simple as looking at a long list of jobs. The Department of Labor (DOL) has 22 categories of jobs. Take a peek.

1. Architecture and engineering

2. Arts, design, entertainment, and media

3. Building/grounds maintenance

4. Business and financial operations

5. Community and social services

6. Computer and math

7. Construction

8. Education, training, and library

9. Farming, fishing, and forestry

10. Food and lodging

11. Healthcare

12. Installation and maintenance repair

13. Legal

14. Life, physical, and social services

15. Management

16. Nursing

17. Office and administrative support

18. Personal care

19. Production

20. Protective services

21. Sales

22. Transportation

Keep in mind these are just categories of jobs; there are several types of jobs within each category. Also, these are only the jobs that a governmental agency has boxes that fit. There are other jobs. A friend of mine travels the world teaching Tao. Some people are personal shoppers. A job can be anything you do well that you can find somebody else to pay you to do.

In this changing world, you must also change what you perceive to be a job. One of the best jobs I've ever had in my life did not fall into the parameters of what I considered to be valid employment, but it was just the job my energy was seeking. It was a tutoring job, something totally unrelated to my business experience. But it was fun, paid well, and gave me the time and resources to determine how I was going to work for the rest of my life. I am very grateful that my energy was stronger than my former narrow definition of employment.

I can't tell you what clicks your clock. I can't tell you what type of job will make you look forward to your daily toil. Only you can determine what makes you feel good in your gut and what makes your stomach turn. You have to look into opportunities and tune into your feelings.

Of course, you must be reasonable. If you have a high-school diploma and want to be a brain surgeon, all the vibrations in the world aren't going to get you hired at the Mayo Clinic. But what all those vibrations will do is open doors for you to procure the correct credentials, education, skill-set, and connections necessary to become a brain surgeon if you hold onto the vibration with passion and endurance.

Vibrations are powerful things. The road map you may have in your head as to how you are going to get from point A to point B might not be the same as the one your vibrations create for you. Energy, or vibrations, work quicker than rational thinking. Back in the eighties, I wanted to work in upper management, a pretty high goal for a female lacking a college degree and no financial means to make college an option. Day after day, I went to my clerical job and watched a bunch of men half as smart as me—some with just a high-school diploma—earn far more money, make a bunch of bad decisions, and boss me around as if I were some sort of dimwit. I felt like a crash test dummy that wanted to tell automakers how to make a frickin' safe car! That was my mental self-portrait.

A few months of those thoughts, and I became just that, more or less. It was a dreary January morning in the Midwest. I pulled into the parking lot at work and stepped into a mud puddle, breaking through the thin layer of ice and filling my shoe and stocking with cold mud. I spent the rest of the day trying to wash the mud from my stocking and shoe—kind of a Macbeth thing, out, damned mud, out! This behavior flustered my five male bosses, who couldn't seem to answer the phone with me locked in the ladies' room. By ten that night, I found myself heavily tranquilized in a not-so-comfy hospital bed. I had had a nervous breakdown.

After my crash, I went on to college, into management, and back to college for graduate school. Not only did I do it, but I did it in much less time than I thought possible. Of course, it all didn't go smoothly. There were IQ tests, and skill-set tests, and the Minnesota something or other test. There was breaking the news to my husband that it was college or he could expect breakdown after breakdown. There was financial aid. There was a string of part-time jobs. And there was, eventually, the divorce. But there was college with an environment in which I thrived. There was the knowledge I craved. I got that degree, that piece of paper that made me marketable. There was the management job I desired. And as I said above, it happened a lot quicker than any method I could have devised with my own means.

Although your energy will open doors you never imagined you still have to pound on a few doors yourself. Anything is possible, but putting the legwork—and the energy—into the process makes things far more probable. Knowing what you are selling and the market you are selling it to makes a world of difference in the long run.

Chapter 9

All Companies Are Not Created Equal

Now that you know what you are selling, it's time to check out the buyers. All companies are not created equal. Company size, corporate structure, and product all play enormous roles in how companies are managed, how employees are treated, and how career paths develop. Let's take a look at corporate structures to determine the kinds of cultures they have and the kinds of career opportunities they may offer.

Small Companies

I might be considered a glutton for punishment, but I loved working for these little operations when I was younger. They offer enormous growth potential for people with minimum education. Most of these companies are understaffed, and the employees are slightly underpaid to perform all kinds of tasks. Now this might not sound like a dream job, but I have always found the hardest part about nine to five, especially when I was only able to procure clerking jobs, was fighting the clock. With small companies, there is seldom time for boredom. Something always has to be done. Your skills are always being drawn out and used to their greatest capacities. If you tinker with computers in your spare time, you may rapidly find yourself in charge of the information systems department in a small company. So what if this department consists of only you? It can give you enormous freedom, status, and a strong argument for more money at raise time. It can also be a great résumé builder.

Because small companies need each employee to be as multi-tasked and useful as possible, they usually will do what they can to enhance your skills. These little companies may pay for some education, although you might have to ask them to do so. Since little is etched in stone or written in a handbook, "ask and ye shall receive" generally is the working mantra, as long as ye ask for something within reason. Education reimbursement generally falls into that category.

In 1977, I worked for a small company. Keep in mind, this was after the passage of Title VII, the Equal Opportunity Act, but women were still found mostly in clerical or light factory positions. I walked into the company and got a job as a clerk. It was soon noted by my boss, Joe, that I had plenty of talent, but none of it included typing and filing. He told me to file everything under "m" for misfiled because I was going to misfile it somewhere anyway. Joe was even less impressed with my typing skills. He even went so far as to inquire about purchasing Wite-Out in gallon pails with three-inch brushes.

I ignored Joe's remarks, and he continued to monitor my inability to perform clerical functions. Joe was looking for something other than my errors. Our energy had connected, and he felt I had potential if he could just unearth it. In time, he noticed I was able to handle vendors with ease, grace, and a few bullying tactics. He turned the purchasing work over to me and reduced my clerical workload. I think he even gave me a title at the time, Purchasing Manager or something of that nature, but titles at small companies can be quite meaningless. It is the work that counts, and I loved the work. Reading blueprints was a snap for me, bantering with salespeople was fun, and when a few salesmen refused to speak to me and wanted to see a "man," Joe would inform them that if they wanted to do business with us that I was "the man." A lot has changed since 1977, but small companies still allow employees to venture into new areas simply out of necessity. They can't afford to hire a full-time accountant, but they will have a part-time bookkeeper work closely with an outside accounting firm to glean enormous amounts of information.

Also, as these companies grow, which is the goal in most cases, employees who started "way back when we only had a few phone lines and some used office furniture" become the backbones of such organizations. They are the trusted ones who rise to the top like cream. They become the managers who are seldom questioned by the owner.

Let's say you are at one of these operations. What will your day look like? Most likely you will have to perform several tasks. If you are hired in for one duty, don't squawk when you find yourself being saddled with several duties that appear unrelated. After all, you are supposed to be the plant manager, so what in blue blazes are you doing on Excel creating an accounting system? You are doing your job. If you have the skills, they will be eked out of you and used repeatedly. Don't think of yourself as being abused; think of yourself as getting paid to go to the top of the market with this infant of a company, or at least getting one great résumé from the experience.

When employees "don't play well in the sandbox," it causes more havoc for small companies than missed shipments and unhappy customers. Therefore, if one person is continually throwing the first shovel of sand, no matter how productive he or she is, that person becomes a liability, not an asset. Small companies need all of their resources dedicated to making things work, not to sorting out petty politics. They cannot afford to play around with employees who aren't team players.

There are times when all must pull together to get that sand castle built, and somebody who is too busy building a fort alone will end up getting cut loose. Watching the energy of others, avoiding negativity, and keeping your own energy up are crucial to success in these operations.

Leaders can emerge in small companies regardless of their position. They know how to work their energy. Good leaders have ways of extracting information from the gatekeepers of such information. They are always looking around, seeing the writing on the wall, looking for clues. They watch inventory levels, shipments, and supply and demand. But most of all, they watch people and are aware of their energy, either consciously or unconsciously. They notice the unnoticeable—the ticks, the tricks, and the tempers. They know whom to listen to and whom to talk to when they want to get their message relayed. In many cases, they are the roots of the grapevine within a company. They have few reservations about walking into the owner's office. They like to get their information from the top. Although they may be the first to squawk about some unimportant nuance, they generally are dedicated and trusted, and, unofficially, they hold power.

As these operations grow, so do their needs. Jobs become more well-defined. The early hires usually are promoted, with or without education, to managerial positions. Their former tasks get farmed out to new hires with specific skill-sets and, in many cases, more education. This creates a dichotomy that is hard for well-trained and -educated new employees to understand. Many new hires are better trained, have stronger skills, and more knowledge than their bosses. They know how to get the work done effectively because they have been trained to do so, not because they picked up the skill on the job as their bosses did. The bosses want jobs done, but in many cases, they want them done in an ineffective manner—the way they always did them.

If you find yourself working for one of these bosses, it takes some savvy to get him or her to accept there is a better way. Also, there may be a tinge of resentment on the part of the boss. To make the situation stickier, many people who have worked their way up, without educational credentials, have done so over a period of years. Not only are they enjoying power, but they are enjoying the multiplier effect of those yearly increases. Their skills, in many cases, are company-specific and not easily transferable to another company. They are making good money and may not be marketable. Therefore, many are very territorial. Somebody coming into the company with a degree can be perceived as a threat. Bottom line, these folks can be downright negative, so don't pick up their vibrations.

Family-Owned and -Operated Companies

Family-owned and -operated companies have cultures established by the owners. Many are small and have the same pros and cons as other small companies.

Unless you are a member of the family or a very close friend, you will always be an outsider in a family-owned and -operated company. Regardless of how hard you work, or how small or large the company becomes, you will still be an outsider. Just look at Lee Iacocca and Ford. Lee Iacocca could dream, design, and develop the almighty Mustang, but he couldn't be a Ford. Despite his successes, he departed from the family-run Ford Motor Company, and went on to prove himself by turning around the dying Chrysler Corporation. He had to prove his leadership abilities elsewhere. Is blood thicker than water? You bet.

Families have alliances and, needless to say, fallings-out as well. The big difference between their family feuds and those in other families is that they can have an impact on your employment. Unfair? You bet.

At times these fights can be very nasty because, in many

cases, there is a large amount of money and ego involved. Money and ego are two components that can take any little irritation and turn it into a full-blown battle—a negative energy tornado. To make the situation worse, during a recession when resources are scarce, the methods of spending those scarce resources have the potential to determine the life or death of a company. When fights break out over spending, they can become very ugly. From the sidelines, it can be hard to tell what side is winning during such a battle. Waiting for the dust to settle plays havoc on the nerves. You must be calm, avoid picking sides, and wait. Watch your energy. Don't get sucked into a negative funnel cloud. Take a timeout and meditate for a minute or two. Feel things working out in the best interest for all involved.

Over any period of time, there may be changes and shifts involving family relationships. The owner may decide, after years of designing a succession plan, not to retire because he feels none of his offspring could efficiently run the business. On the other hand, the owner could die without a succession plan in place, leaving chaos. Or, the heirs could decide they want to make their own mark in the world and leave the business after years of service. A family feud may also become so irreconcilable that a family member, a key player in the organization, is banished.

There are too many variables to make a global statement about family operations. Therefore, you must be attuned to the players, the roles, the power structure, the market for the product produced, and the overall energy. All of these factors, along with your personal energy and behavior, will determine if a family-owned and -operated company is best for you.

Many folks who work for these companies have turned to the owners in times of personal need and have found the owners to be understanding and generous. The owners' understanding and generosity have been repaid with loyalty. These companies often have a good relationship with the community, which is an important part of the lives of employees.

Stockholder-Held Large Companies

Large corporations are held by stockholders and are managed by professionals who report to a board of directors. Working for one of these giants differs vastly from working for a privately held company.

After several years at small companies, I took a contract position in a Fortune 100 company and saw the differences firsthand. At small companies, employees are aware of the bottom line. Profits and losses are common knowledge, and each employee feels, to some degree, responsible for either. Each expenditure is monitored for value. I worked at one that was so tightfisted that employees had to take their used ink pens to the power-hungry office-supply keeper to get a new pen. At a Fortune 100 company, each expenditure is monitored, but an expenditure that would be considered a luxury at a small company, such as an expensive consultant, is considered a necessity at a Fortune 100 operation.

Even though there is a lot of talk about budgets at these companies, they have some of the best-compensated employees in the world. CEOs' compensation packages at many of these companies are so generous that they have been making headlines for years. And the good money doesn't stop at the executive suites. In the book *Rivethead: Tales from the Assembly Line,* Ben Hamper constantly reminds us of how much money he was making at General Motors as a member of the United Auto Workers (UAW), and he knows that his Thursday night paycheck was only part of his compensation package.

You may have to work in a culture within a culture. The mighty corporate giant has a culture, your department has a culture, and your cube may even have its own culture! In fact, many people who are in a given department for several years forget about anything in the next state, across the complex, or down the hallway. Those foreign lands are only revisited during talks of cutbacks or other bad stuff that comes down from some unknown face at corporate headquarters. Day to day, they focus on the culture and energy of their own department.

As stated before, compensation is generally above market value and benefits are rich at stockholder-held companies, but growth potential is also optimized for those who choose to acquire the skills and credentials to move up. These operations generally are very credential-oriented. They recruit at the best of schools and seek the best degrees, which are paid for dearly. Unlike small and family-owned and -operated companies, where the educated may be working side by side with an uneducated colleague, educational credentials are necessary to rise to the highest ranks in large companies.

Holding Companies

Holding companies hold the purse strings. They generally operate in one of two modes: "hands-off" or "hands-on."

If your company is held by a holding company, the holding company may maintain a "hands-on" approach in which the policies, practices, and benefits come from corporate. If the holding company is generous, the benefits will be generous. If the holding company is squeezing every penny, the overall compensation package will be a function of corporate beliefs and policies, regardless of the bottom line at your facility. For this reason, many of these companies feel like large companies regardless of their actual size. You may know everybody at the facility, you may have strong alliances and friendships with these people, but the operating decisions and money still come from corporate.

In a "hands-off" scenario, the operating unit manages the compensation, policies, practices, and benefits, giving it the feel of a small or mid-sized company. Corporate oversees the financial health of the operation, has a line of credit on hand, and makes the top management of the operations accountable.

The upside to working in one of these operations is that

you may have the best of all worlds, depending on the size and stability of the facility. If it is small, say less than a hundred employees, you may reap the rewards of a small company, by being busy, by keeping all of your talents in play, and by being flexible. At the same time, you are not as "under the gun" in the financial arena. If the company needs an injection of cash now and then to iron out the bumps in the economy, this cash generally is forthcoming from the holding company as long as the overall operations of the facility are good.

Franchises

People who work in food service or retail typically work for a franchise. How these franchises are bought, sold, and financed means little to most of you working at such establishments, but it means plenty in terms of your day-to-day life.

For most people, working in franchises is like working for a small company. There may be only a few employees (usually less than a hundred) at your store. You know everybody, and everybody knows you. Of course, there is that corporate shadow that dictates your uniform, your work rules and regulations, and your benefits, but corporate usually is somewhere else. Therefore, most people function within these companies as they would within a department of a large company, or within a family-owned and -operated company. These companies generally tailor their policies to make the employees feel like part of a family.

Government Jobs

The means for getting and keeping government jobs vary from job to job, so lumping them all into one category isn't possible. Some are political appointments. Some government jobs fall under the requirements of civil service, while others are unionized positions.

The energy at a government position is as varied as the types of positions. Some are high energy, such as campaign workers; others require a more nurturing energy, such as city workers who have to constantly keep their energy stable as angry residents complain about downed mailboxes during blizzards. Some of these jobs are boring; others are stimulating. Since the government hires everybody from clerks who look at the same documents day in and day out to forest rangers who patrol for poachers, it's not possible to put them all in one category. But, generally, the pay is at market value and the benefits are rich.

Dot-Com Companies

E-business went from boom to bust in a very short period of time, creating havoc with careers and energy. There was too much money, and then too little money. Many people who worked at these operations rose too fast and fell too hard. Take heart. In time, these businesses will stabilize and fall into the categories listed above, with the same traits.

Product

Company size and structure are only one piece of the corporate culture puzzle. The product also plays a role. If the product and the manufacturing process are mature, with stable markets, then the company has the potential to run smoothly and be a comfortable place to work, as long as the product is in demand.

For example, let's consider paper bag manufacturers. Remember when all groceries came home in a brown paper bag? What happened? The polymer people decided they wanted a part of a market with endless demand. In time, they came up with cost-effective plastic bags. In the process, they sacked job security at the brown paper bag companies.

Paper bag companies had to find new customers. They could no longer sit back and rest on their laurels because a huge chunk of market share was going to the polymer companies. This can happen to any mature industry if somebody comes up with a better, or cheaper, replacement product.

The market security of a product will play an important role in the security of your job within the industry and how you feel about the company. For that reason, you should look not only at the job, but also the product when you consider a position within a company. If the product is becoming outdated, and there is little research and development, the daily operations may go smoothly, but the company also may be nearing the end of its existence. This leads to a worrisome and negative work environment.

Products that are always changing offer challenges to employees at all levels, from design to sales to delivery. Some industries roll out a new and improved model every 6 to 12 months. If a new product is rolled out and it is well-received in the marketplace, these places can be cash-rich and fun. But the key to keeping such places operating is to roll out well-received products on a regular basis. Time offers no mercy in high-tech industries. In such environments, possessing the ability to work in a state of constant change is necessary. Constant change involves shifting priorities and regular energy checks. To feel good, you must learn to flow good energy, to think of it like a river of good water all around you, regardless of the state of the environment.

Who's in Charge?

Regardless of the company structure or size, or the product, the person at the top will impact your employment experience. I've always been amazed at the number of people who have no idea who the company president is. Some people feel they are just too far removed from the top person by hierarchy or location to care. But the top person's vision, energy, and agenda have an enormous force on any job. I worked for a fantastic company in the late seventies. It was the kind of company that employees stuck with until the gold watch was passed out. Unfortunately, I started just as the president was looking west. I suppose the ice and cold and union mentality of Ohio didn't click his clock. He had little concern for the upheaval he was causing in people's lives as he took the company from one of the top employers in the region to one of the former employers in the region.

Recently, we have also seen what the arrogance and negative energy of some of the top men have done to their companies. The top brass at Enron and Tyco caused incredible havoc in the lives of the employees of those once proud operations.

At the same time, some very large companies have benefited from strong leadership. I worked as a contractor at Alcoa on Paul O'Neil's watch. Mr. O'Neil believed in transparency and teamwork. He had so much faith in these concepts that he had the corporate headquarters designed with open spaces to encourage casual conversation and limit closed-door meetings. Although I did not work at the corporate headquarters, the principles nurtured at corporate were planted throughout the corporation. In other words, this leader's values permeated the entire operation worldwide.

At small companies, it's not uncommon to have daily contact with the person at the top. Depending on the leader, that daily communication can make the place heaven or hell. If the top person is great, the company will be a great place to work. If the top person is a kook, no matter how hard you try, you will find yourself working in a kooky environment.

For the past few years, I have worked for some great bosses. I am an independent contractor, but I still have to answer to the person who signs my contracts and the checks that go into my coffers. I got lucky because I was feeling good about myself when the jobs came my way. I was putting out good energy, and I connected with good folks.

Therefore, I know firsthand there are great bosses out in the world. Put out the energy and feel yourself working for the perfect boss. What energies would you have in common? Once you identify common energies, don't just think about them, feel them! Thinking is something the mind does to keep itself busy. Feelings are the vibrations that do the work.

Chapter 10

Hot on the Scent of a Job

Jobs are everywhere. Every financial transaction involves some sort of employee. If you think that an under-the-table cash transaction is free from somebody's labor, think again. Somebody had to print that cash. Oh yeah, some government employee plays a role in every cash transaction. The more complicated any business transaction, the more people have been employed to carry it off. So as long as we live in an environment in which we are not self-sufficient, there will be jobs.

Psssst, I Have the Goods on a Job . . .

First and foremost, there is no secret job market. Anybody who tries to sell you on that idea, or a Web page full of unpublished jobs, or any other sort of nonsense has latched onto your negative energy and is going to suck it right out of your wallet. Human resource people have to find the best candidate for any given position, so there is no reason to keep a job a secret. They are trying to find good candidates, not desperate ones. If you are connecting with any of this nonsense, it's time to go back to chapter 4 and shift your energy.

Some jobs are never posted anywhere. They aren't found on some secret Web page or list; networking unearths them. In order to network for a job, it's preferable to be around the types of people who have the ability to hire you or give you job leads. Stay connected with employed people. Employed people will see job openings where they work usually weeks before the public. If you let them know the type of job you are seeking, they can get your résumé into the right hands ahead of the rush.

Expand your networking beyond former business associates and current friends by joining new groups. Volunteer work is one way to get known in a community. Some people have done volunteer work for a particular organization, and when a paying job came around, they got it because managers like to hire people they know. Hiring a known person reduces risks. In many cases, volunteering in itself is rewarding, and therefore it has the potential to bring up your energy and bring a good job your way. Networking makes you aware that other people are in far worse shape than you. Such knowledge puts your situation in perspective and can get you out of your self-pitying mode. In other cases, just the interpersonal contact can be uplifting.

Checking the Classifieds

Networking is good for you on both the economic and energy side of the equation, but it is only one trail on the road to employment. Companies advertise for candidates. It may seem hard for a lot of computer users to accept, but a lot of employers still use newspapers as a primary source to recruit candidates. Many companies are only seeking local candidates. They don't want to draw from the whole world. They don't have the resources to sort through thousands of résumés. Therefore, they place ads in local papers and only seriously consider local candidates. Many local papers also post these ads on the paper's Web site, so check your local paper's Web site in addition to the larger employment sites.

Recently, I wanted to test the odds of getting an interview for a local job from a local paper versus getting an interview from one of the major Internet job boards. First, I went in search of a local employer on a large board. I found a job for which I was very qualified and spent several hours working every word from the posting into my résumé. I submitted my résumé and got a response within minutes. The automated response informed me that the company receives more than a million—yes, a million—résumés annually and that mine would be processed. Then I took a peek at the classifieds on the Web site of a local newspaper. I responded to an ad for which I had all of the qualifications, and within six hours I got a call from the employer requesting an interview. This is not to say that people don't get jobs from big boards and that everybody gets interviews from local papers, but it demonstrates the importance of looking at all options.

Internet sites range from large boards such as Monster.com, to specific job pages operated by business associations, to companies' own Web sites, to regional Web pages. If you are filling out an application on a company's Web site, the computer is sorting it and looking for specific qualifications, education, experience, etc. It will have a primary sort, then a secondary sort, and so it goes until it has a pile of candidates who look just about the same. In those cases, if you really want one of those jobs, you can't stick out in the crowd because the sorting system isn't designed to allow you to do so. Make sure you put all of the words in the job description in your work experience. The computer is looking for key words.

Some companies accept résumés electronically for higher-end positions since they don't want salaried folks to feel that they are being treated like hourly folks with an application. This is a nice little fantasy. Many of those companies have computer programs that seek out key words on résumés. Those programs are similar to the programs for applications. Some companies use a combination of data entry and computer programs to weed out résumés. They send the résumés to India or some other place where educated labor is cheap, and the résumés are keyboarded into an application format. So once again, a computer goes through a primary sort, then another, and so on until it has a pile of candidates who look just about the same. If certain key words are missing, the résumé is filed away, never to be looked at by a person with hiring ability. I'd love to say there are ways around this, but the truth is these programs are loved by hiring types. I worked for one company that had several lawsuits filed against it due to unfair hiring practices. In response, any paper résumés that came directly to the company were immediately shredded, unread. If they were read, they had to be recorded into an applicant-tracking program. Nobody wanted to take the responsibility for opening the company up to any greater liability.

Armed with this knowledge, the way to make it through screen after screen is to print off the job description for the job you are seeking. Read it, think about it, meditate on it, read it again, and make sure all words of any importance in the job description are on your résumé and the application.

Knock, Knock, Knock

Most people don't cold call. They assume that if a company isn't asking for help, it isn't hiring. Ironically, employment agencies cold call all the time because they know if a great candidate comes along that most human resource folks will take a peek. Don't wait for a third party to sell you. If you really want to work for a specific company in a specific field, cold call. Write a stellar cover letter, write a stunning résumé, and call the company until you get the name of the person who needs to see your outstanding abilities. I have created jobs and hired from cold calls—not often, but I've done it. I hired some great people who cold called. I know their energy woke me up to the fact that they had something to bring to the company.

When you cold call, you must know what you are selling. Fresh out of college, I tried this technique. I wrote several letters (sometimes it takes two or three to prove you really have an interest) to the CEO of a financial-planning company. Letter number three lassoed an interview. The CEO was incredibly receptive. She would have hired me on the spot if she'd had any idea of what I could have brought to the company. If I had shown her any concrete reason to hire me, I would have had a job at that company. Instead, I expected her to figure out where to put me. She did. She sent me packing. I learned the most valuable lesson of cold calling the hard way: If you expect somebody to hire you, you must know what you can bring to their operation, and you must be able to present your skills in an easy-to-understand manner. Know what you are selling and whom you are selling it to (see chapter 9). Make sure you have a strong argument defining exactly why the company needs your skill-set and why it needs you over somebody else who could perform the same function. Know your market worth. If the prospective employer has to be sold on hiring you, it will also need to be given a dollar amount for what your services are worth. A dream job without compensation is a dream volunteer opportunity.

One guy I know spent a summer backpacking through Alaska, letting ideas perk through his head prior to presenting himself for a job. The solitude, exercise, and self-sufficiency all cleared his head and his vision. When he returned to New York, he quickly turned his ideas into a $250,000 job. Keep in mind, the year was 1989 and this guy was around 27 years old. In fact, the company that hired him kept him hidden from customers who wouldn't have been comfortable dealing with a "kid."

Headhunters

Employment agencies are another option for finding employment. Personally, I am not an advocate of employment agencies. I am sure my publisher will get piles of letters for me on this one, but I've only had one good experience with them. Other times, they caused great havoc in my world. Of course, when I was desperate enough to use one for myself, my energy was so low that it attracted the bottom-of-the-barrel head-hunters. The job I got was the kind that anybody without a streak of desperation would have run away from fast. I can't say I care much for them from either side of the desk. As a human resource manager, they constantly hounded me with some mediocre candidate for jobs I did or didn't have on my plate. They had no concern for my precious time.

If you are seriously looking at employment agencies, get your energy up to bring a good one your way. When working with one, keep in mind that employment agencies are working for the client company, not for you. They are going to go a long way to sell you to the company to get the check, but they will take a much longer hike to sell the company to you, especially if it's a cruddy company that can't get good employees on its own.

The good experience I had with an employment agency was when my energy was up, and I was working a contract for a large company that I enjoyed. This company used a lot of con-tractors, and one was a one-man employment agency. His con-tract made him responsible for filling all non-exempt jobs in the facility. Due to years of nepotism, the company was in a lot of hot water with the regulatory folks. By outsourcing the hiring function and doing it off-site, the company was able to reduce its risks. Because that headhunter worked primarily for one great client, working with him was similar to working with the company directly. That is not the normal way employment agencies work.

Normally, employment agencies post one or two great jobs

and review a bunch of résumés. These résumés become their inventory. Once they have a stockpile of inventory, they start cold calling companies to sell the best of their inventory. You, being the inventory, may be sitting on that shelf for a long time. Unless you really want the one job they have posted and have great energy toward that job and that agency, your chances of getting a good job through an agency are not much better than getting one without an agency.

One of the first questions a headhunter will ask you is what companies you are already talking with about a job. They claim they need to know this information so they don't double their work by contacting the same companies you've already contacted. Think about it for a moment. They aren't working for you. They are working for the companies. They need to find positions just as badly as you need to find positions. If you start rattling off a bunch of companies that have you under consideration, don't be surprised when they call those companies offering one of the other items of inventory they have on their shelf. Be fair, tell them if you have something cooking, but remind them that you know they work for the company, not the candidate. Also remind them that you are sitting in front of them due to one classified they had posted. Don't be too surprised if they give you some song and dance about it being filled yesterday.

At very high levels in the employment hierarchy, employment agencies work as go-betweens, connecting talent from one company and quietly moving it to another before the stockholders get wind there will be a change at the top. In those cases, they are used to recruit and cloak a move. Folks in those categories have great employment energy and can easily move from company to company unless they become unbalanced and let their ego overtake their energy. When that happens, they become the fodder for the week in the *Wall Street Journal* as their demise is dissected.

How you decide to approach your job search is entirely up to you. While recently shopping for a new computer, I got on the topic of this manuscript with a fresh college grad who wants to go from his part-time job at the computer store into his first professional job. He's been submitting résumés for months via e-mail. When I told him to research a company and send out a paper résumé, he looked at me as if I were from another planet. The truth be known, I've helped a lot of people get jobs, and none of them found one on the Internet. They got them by putting some legwork into their job search and standing out above the crowds in some computer file. Of course, if a company only accepts e-applications, then that's the only way to go. But a lot of great companies will still look at a hard copy if it sees value in the candidate. As stated in chapter 9, the size and the structure of a company play a large role in the corporate culture; they also play a role in their recruiting tools. Keep all of your avenues open.

Chapter 11

Résumés and Other Paper Trails

No job is complete until the paperwork is done. No job search should be started until the paperwork is in order.

Résumés

An old saying goes something like this: Nobody ever gets hired from a résumé or without one. A good résumé is essential in procuring employment. The operative word in that last sentence is *good*.

What makes a good résumé? Ask 20 HR people, and you will get 20 different answers. Although my friends and colleagues believe I am an authority on the subject, the truth is I wing each and every one I write. Instead of using a form and having folks fill in the blanks, I take the time to conduct an in-depth interview with the person in need of a résumé. I pick up on their energy, unearth their skills, and only then can I begin to put their selling points on paper.

Skills aside, certain things make some résumés better than others. Neatness counts. If you write a sloppy résumé, you will be perceived as being a sloppy worker. Résumés are the first impression a company gets of you. You want to put your best foot forward, and you want to do it truthfully.

There are several types of résumés. The most common format is putting your job experience in chronological order, with the current or most recent job listed first. This format is great if you have gotten better and better jobs over the years and have no gaps. It also works well for people who have acquired new duties with each position. But they can be deadly if you have been out of work from time to time. Nobody should put a flaw such as an employment gap under a spotlight. If this is your situation, listing your skills first—putting your best foot forward—is a better choice of format. Whatever format you use should demonstrate the best of your assets and the least of your flaws. When you look at a draft of your résumé, your energy should be going up, not down. If your résumé brings you down, it won't bring in much of a job.

If possible, tailor your résumé to fit the desired occupation. Over the years, I have read thousands of résumés. Several stick out in my mind. One was from a woman who was just finishing her B.A. in art. I was the human resource manager at a company with an in-house art department. She sent her unsolicited, bright, bold, artsy résumé to me. In other words, she cold called. I was so taken aback by her creativity that I passed her résumé on to the vice president of sales, who created a job for her. Of course, such a résumé would not be appropriate for a job in banking or as a line foreman, but it fit her career like a glove. Her energy showed through on her résumé, and upon meeting her we knew such a talent would be an asset to the company.

A few other résumés have stuck out over the years, but not for the same reasons. One guy had a coat of arms on his résumé. His résumé screamed ego, not energy. Another had a photo of himself plastered center stage on the top of his résumé. Attaching photos will not help you procure employment in the current legislative environment.

Résumés are tools to transmit information. Give only the pertinent facts. Employers need to know what you can do, why you can do it, and where you've done it before you walked into their world. Mentioning a few hobbies is okay to break the ice during the interview, but other things aren't necessary. Information that indicates membership in a protected group (age, race, sex, national origin, and religion) is often covered with thick black ink by a clerk before a decision-maker ever sees the document. Photographs, too, will be covered with a big black marker. Facts of employment, not facts of life, are required.

Facts of Employment

Now what exactly is a fact? One would like to believe it is the truth, but this isn't a perfect world. Facts, like the truth, get stretched. Sadly, there are so many embellishments on so many résumés that many decision-makers expect some exaggerations—something like cheating on taxes.

What is a lie? Is leaving off a job that was a disaster a lie? Is adding a few months onto a job a lie? Is saying you quit a job when you were fired a lie? Is leaving information off a résumé a lie? There are jobs that were so brief and such a horrendous fit that leaving them off the résumé seems like the only sane solution. One bad decision along the way can make a gap in a résumé, but covering it up may make the difference between being employed and unemployed.

What you put on your résumé is really your choice. I can't tell you what is okay, or where the fine line between acceptable and unacceptable may be. What I can tell you is that over the past decade it has become easier and cheaper to perform background checks. As former employers become more and more reluctant to give references (good and bad), companies that specialize in reference checks have sprouted like weeds. Add a little computer technology, and reference checking is now a booming industry—so booming, in fact, that laws such as the Fair Credit Reporting Act have cropped up to protect the innocent. With a simple fax or e-mail, a company can, for starters, discover where you really were employed, your credit, your driving record, your arrest record, and your former addresses. Depending on the position for which you are being considered, a more in-depth check may be performed. Therefore, deviations from the truth can be unearthed quickly and cheaply.

Remember, energy attracts like energy. If you're putting out lies, you will get lies back. As stated in chapter 9, all companies have cultures, and some are pretty slimy. If you are putting out slimy energy, you will find yourself in some pretty slimy company.

Cover Letters

In most cases, when you submit a résumé, you do so with a cover letter. Cover letters are great sales tools. Write them to incorporate every little word that you find in the job posting. Cover letters are generally read prior to the résumé, therefore you want to pique the reader's interest before he has to sift through the facts on your résumé. Most importantly, keep them simple and to the point. Here's an example of an ad followed by the appropriate cover letter:

> HR MGR., 5 yrs exp., min BS, MBA preferred. The successful candidate will be a generalist responsible for recruiting, team training, benefits, safety, worker's compensation, employee relations at this ISO 9000 company with three locations. State salary requirements.

Name
Street Address
City, State Zip
Phone
E-mail

Date

Company Name
Street Address
City, State Zip

Re: Human Resources Management Position

To Whom It May Concern [if no contact name is given in ad]:

In response to your classified ad in the *Sun News,* I would like to be considered a candidate for the position of Human Resource Manager. I possess all of the education you are seeking and have experience in multi-site, multi-state operations.

As my enclosed résumé highlights, I have eight years of experience as a human resource manager in a generalist capacity. I was responsible for recruiting, team training, design and implementation of benefit plans, safety, worker's compensation, employee relations, and employment law compliance at a multi-site ISO 9000 certified company.

I possess an MBA from The University of Miami, as well as a Bachelor of Arts in Business from Ohio State University.

My salary requirements are flexible in the $90,000 range.

I want to thank you for your time and consideration in this matter. I look forward to hearing from you in the near future. If you need any additional information, I can be reached at the contact information provided above.

Sincerely,

Signature

Name
Enclosure (1)

Is a good cover letter a surefire way to land a job? No. I sent out hundreds of them, all with bad energy attached. I didn't want another human resource job and I didn't get one. But when I finally wanted one, when I had a gap that was large enough to drive a Mac truck through, one of these letters landed me a job. It's always a combination of the proper economic tools and energy techniques. I saw myself in that job, I felt myself in that job, and the economic tools worked. Never rely on one or the other; they work in tandem. By the same token, it's pretty hard to get a good job without a good cover letter. Most employment Web sites allow space for a cover letter. Companies that do not use filters generally look at résumés with cover letters with greater interest. I'd recommend reading a really good book on cover letters and tailoring your letter to transmit your information in the best light.

Follow-Up

Résumés and cover letters aren't the only documents you have to write to get a job. Follow-up letters are important and often overlooked. The young man I was recently coaching whined endlessly about follow-up letters. He whined about writing them. He whined about the "kissing up" component. He even whined about the cost of the paper. I told him I didn't care how much he whined as long as he wrote the letters.

Follow-up letters perform two major functions. For the candidate, they are an easy way to transmit information that may need additional emphasis or was overlooked during the stress of the interview. In other words, a follow-up letter is a sales tool. For that reason, I am always surprised by the number of people who fail to write them or dread the process. Personally, I find them far easier to write than cover letters or résumés, and composing them can become second nature once you master a simple format, which I will go into shortly.

From the employer's side of the desk, follow-up letters

show that the candidate carries through. Truthfully, I seld[om] notice the ones I receive, but I always remember when it comes down to decision time which candidates *failed* to follow through.

One of the best parts about writing these little letters is that you already have a sense of the recipient's personality and energy, so it's easy to compose one to connect with the reader. Even after interviews that involve several interviewers, it is fairly easy to personalize follow-up letters. First, be sure to get a business card from everyone who interviews you. If the interviewer fails to offer a card, ask for one. Immediately after the interview, in your car if necessary, jot down one trait each interviewer possessed on the back of the respective card—"all business," "a joker," "warm and fuzzy," "stuffed shirt," whatever trait stood out. Do this to make sure you draft a letter that will be well-received by the recipient. By putting these traits on the back of business cards, you will be able to keep several people sorted out in your mind when you write the letters. The last thing you want to do is send a "stuffed shirt" a humorous letter.

One batch of follow-up letters that landed me a management position had the following traits. To the General Manager who was moving to my old hometown, I put in a few anecdotes about the area, then moved on to my qualifications. To the Quality Control guy, who attended the same college, I mentioned how my education would be an asset to the company. To the Controller, a "class clown," I mentioned that I had worked in an environment that thrived on both humor and hard work. The second paragraph in each of these letters was the same: my sales pitch. The third, too, was a cut-and-paste product.

The best formula for follow-up letters is KIS: Keep It Simple. The first paragraph should thank the interviewer for his or her time and connect on whatever level possible. The second paragraph is for selling yourself and explaining why you

idate for the position. Paragraph three is a final
ı ramble on about yourself, your letter has a
tting read.

mple of a good follow-up letter:

Candidate's Name [as it appears on the résumé]
Street Address
City, State Zip
Phone Number
E-mail Address

Date

Name and Title
Company Name
Street Address
City, State Zip

Dear [Mr., Ms., or Mrs.—this is no time to use first names],

I want to thank you for the time you spent interviewing me earlier today.
As I could see by your desk, you are a busy person and your time is valuable, so I will keep this correspondence brief.

As I stated during our meeting, I believe I can bring several assets to XYZ
Company. [Write four or five sentences about what you can bring to the
environment: education, skill-set, experience, or whatever it may be. This
is also the place you'd add any information you left out of the interview
that might land you the job.]

In closing, I want to thank you again for your time and consideration. I
look forward to talking with you in the near future. If you need any additional information, feel free to contact me at the number(s) above.

Sincerely,

Signature

Name

If, by chance, you really screwed up during the interview—and, believe me, some folks do—it's even more important to get a follow-up letter out pronto. Sometimes the energy is great, but the message gets garbled. If this is the case, you still have a chance because the interviewer has a gut feeling you might be right for the job. A follow-up letter has the potential to be your best chance to get your foot in the door. Make sure you sell yourself well in paragraph two. Let the interviewer know her gut is right.

Follow-up letters must be printed on résumé-quality paper and posted with simple flag stamps. I have received follow-up letters on flowered notepaper, thank-you cards, and copy paper. The vibrations I got were anything but professional. Follow-up letters are part of a professional sales package, not a personal note of thanks. The message has to be professional, the medium has to be professional, and the energy has to be professional. Also, they must be timely. A follow-up letter two weeks after the position has been filled proves nothing more than you are a procrastinator.

My little buddy wanted to bypass the entire formal follow-up letter process by sending an e-mail to the interviewer. The interviewer had told him that he would be making a decision in five hours, but this is highly unlikely. Generally, interviewers make an offer on the spot or spend a day or two checking references, comparing notes with colleagues, then calling with an offer days later. In this case, the interviewer was seeing six candidates on a Friday and wanted to put the deal to bed before the weekend. I had a gut feeling that he would be putting it to bed by the following weekend. I was right.

If you've promised an interviewer additional information, an e-mail is a great way to transmit that information quickly. It shows immediate follow-up. But if you are thinking of using an e-mail as the only medium for a formal follow-up letter, consider the following:

- E-mails are age-sensitive. The younger the decision-maker, the more he or she will view e-mails in a favorable light. Unfortunately, you may not know who the true decision-maker is. In a family-owned and -operated company, it might be the owner, an older person you may have only encountered for a brief five minutes.

- Many managers get so many e-mails that they simply delete ones from addresses they don't recognize.

- Some systems delete e-mails from unknown addresses.

- E-mails are casual. Depending on the corporate culture, you may appear a little lazy, lame, or unprofessional. Therefore, the medium has the potential to be poorly received in a conservative environment.

- Finally, think of how your screen name sounds to prospective employers. If you are trying to get a management job and your e-mail address is something like *eatmeifUcan*, it will pretty much crush your chances.

No matter what medium you choose, keep in mind that a professional follow-up letter is a sales tool that works to the advantage of the candidate. Use it. The really great thing about follow-up letters is you can get yourself feeling good prior to creating them, and they will relay good energy.

Chapter 12

Dressing for the Job

Since feelings emit energy that bring back other like vibrations, dressing for the job serves several purposes. From an energy perspective, your clothes help align your thoughts and your energy with the position. Dressing for the position makes you begin to feel like you already have the job.

The truth of the matter is that experienced human resource professionals become very good at thin slicing. We take in the whole candidate in an incredibly short period of time, and we begin to determine if the candidate will fit into the environment. We look at posture, gait, carriage, eye contact, and attire, and we do it in seconds. I think of it as energy hitting or missing the mark. Although the right clothes are only a small part of the equation, the wrong clothes stick out like a red flag.

Tattoo You

Tattoos are age-sensitive. Yeah, I know that tattoo shops are prevalent around college campuses. Yeah, I know that this rock star and that Hollywood tart are tattooed. Yeah, I know it's young, it's *sweet* . . . it's whatever the word of the day might be. I also know that until a decade or so, tattoo shops weren't in marketplace U.S.A. They were in the same locations as cut-rate liquor stores, check-cashing stores, and anything-for-a-buck stores. They weren't in those locations for the cheap rent; they were there because their primary market happened to reside next door. Tattoos were a sign of low socio-economic status. Although that trend is shifting somewhat, the shift isn't getting up to the decision-makers and company owners.

Companies prefer to hire people who either appear success-ful or appear to desire success. They tend to shy away from folks who look like they are from the bottom of the socio-economic ladder. Oh, you can call me old-fashioned or a stuffed shirt, but you also have to call me one of the people who pass out the jobs, so I know what I'm talking about. Purple hair, tattooing, and piercing might set well for those under 30, might be hotter than Texas asphalt with your circle of friends, but unless your circle of friends is passing out jobs, you might want to hide or get rid of the hair dye, the tattoo, and the nose ring.

Of course, some large, progressive companies are scrambling like ants at a picnic to usher these new trends into their dress codes without offending customers and clients, but they aren't doing so because they are incredibly fond of the trend or because they think it's professional. They're doing so because they have positions that need to be filled, and every now and then some applicant shows up with some tattoo or piercing that falls under the protective umbrella of Title VII for religious reasons.

The rest of the companies are simply hiring out of really big stacks of résumés and aren't bending over backward to hire people who appear to have little regard for their own bodies or personal appearance. They certainly won't consider offering a job to somebody who grosses out the owner of the company. As stated previously, it's still the old toad who makes a lot of the final hiring decisions. And, here's the kicker: You might not even get two seconds to talk to the old toad. Old toads are busy old toads. They off-load the day-to-day interviewing on human resource folks and department heads. But they also poke around their companies a lot. You might not even know that the old toad who passed you in the hallway owns the place. He or she might have walked right by you without even as much as casual eye contact. But don't think for a moment that your purple hair, tattooed arm, or pierced tongue slid under the radar. Nope, that old toad picked it all up. That old toad made a mental note to pop into human resources and tell that frazzled interviewer to keep looking for a more suitable candidate. End of discussion. She goes onto a Web page and a stack of a few hundred résumés can appear on her desk with the click of a mouse. It won't be hard for her to find a more suitable candidate.

Oh, there are some jobs where the tattoos and purple hair are just fine. Hairdressers have always had hair that only hairdressers would wear in public. Behind-the-scenes computer programmers who have no desire to ever climb the corporate ladder do fairly well with tattoos. Art teachers at the local community college can get away with just about any outlandish costume. Some trendy boutiques hire young salespeople with spiked everything. Even some coffee shops will hire the more creative folks. So if your self-expression trumps your overall career objectives, then tattoo you. But if you think that maybe that's not the route you want to take, you might want to think about the message and the energy you are sending to the world.

Every generation has its signature look. The eighties had big hair and shoulder pads. The seventies had leisure suits and the introduction of pantsuits for working women. The sixties had love beads, tie-dyed shirts, prairie skirts, miniskirts, Afros, and bell-bottoms. The fifties had skinny ties and greased hair for men and poodle skirts for women. The forties had pencil-thin skirts for women who always wore white gloves on interviews, and any self-respecting man wore a hat. The thirties had poverty. The twenties had flappers. Each generation takes a step away from the previous decade to make its mark. Most generations make marks that are later considered fads. Life is fluid. This current trend of body art is unique in its permanence. It will be around for a while, but that doesn't mean it will take hold with the folks who pass out the jobs any time soon. Frankly, my dear, they don't give a damn about your social statement. They will pass you by and hire somebody who fits their mold. You don't appear unique; you appear in need of attention.

Interview Togs

One of the most important times to dress for the job is for the initial interview. HR folks want to make sure a candidate will fit in the environment, but they are legally prevented from asking a lot of personal questions. Therefore, they have to look for clues as to whether somebody will, or will not, fit in the work environment. Making yourself look like the perfect candidate gives you an edge over the competition. The rule of thumb is pretty simple: Dress for the job you are seeking. Dress like the rest of the folks in that particular occupation or organization.

So, what are the right clothes? It's a little hard to tell sometimes with casual days and relaxed work environments, but most companies still expect the first impression to be one of quality. For upper-management positions, the dark power suit is essential for both men and women on the initial interview. If you're not sure what this looks like, there are plenty of books written about dressing for these positions. Middle managers and recent college grads should also wear suits. Invest in a good suit. Good clothes are an investment because they pay a return on your outlay of capital by what they bring into your life. If you are just starting out and plunking over several hundred dollars for a suit is a bit steep, go to the best secondhand store you can find. I live in Ohio and have traveled to New York City to shop upscale consignment shops. The better shops are operated like private boutiques and carry the best in quality and labels. I save enough money on clothes to easily cover the cost of the airfare to the city.

If you are seeking a clerical position, you should dress conservatively, but not necessarily in a suit. Clean, tailored coordinates are fine. Factory workers have a lot of leeway, but again, dress responsibly and respectably. I've hired lots of factory personnel who have arrived for interviews in clean jeans and shirts lacking a social statement.

I've seen some pretty outlandish interviewing costumes over the years. Two come to mind. One was a young woman who was told to dress up for an interview at a bank. She did dress up—unfortunately, in her prom dress. This wasn't exactly the look the conservative institution was seeking. Another guy showed up for a factory job in a clean shirt, blue jeans, and a fresh shave. All would have gone well if he hadn't been wearing an AFL-CIO baseball cap at a non-union facility. Had he left his topper in his pickup, he probably would have picked up a job. Instead, I had a hard time calming down the general manager who wanted me to escort the guy from the building ASAP.

There are, of course, other little things that really blow interviews. Some people stink. Hygiene is important. It's sad that I even have to mention it, but poor hygiene has caused a lot of people to be shown the exit door. It isn't necessarily a lack of bathing—although there have been times when I wanted to send a candidate to the YMCA for a shower—it's usually the overuse of cologne. Both women and men have caused so much odor in my office that I learned long ago to keep a can of air freshener on hand. If you don't feel dressed without a little scent, that's understandable, but the operative word is "little."

Less is more. Keep it subtle. Nobody wants to wonder if you've bathed or just dipped in a vat of cologne. Also, keep in mind that many people have allergies. They will not even consider hiring a person who makes them sneeze.

Dress so you don't offend. Young women, especially, have a tendency to dress to annoy the hiring folks. Keep in mind that human resources is a field with lots and lots of women making the decisions. The vast majority of these women are middle-aged. They have moved into their positions by earning the right credentials and putting in a lot of hard work. They aren't incredibly receptive to some young woman strutting into an interview dressed like a high-maintenance super model. If you are young and beautiful, you may think these middle-aged bags are just jealous or mean-spirited, but the bottom line is that they are the decision-makers.

If you are fortunate to look like a super model, then go for a super model position. If you are going for an entry-level management position, dress for an entry-level management position. Wearing a short skirt with five-inch heels and having your makeup applied with a heavy touch will turn heads, but it won't land you the entry-level management position unless you have the credentials and are interviewed by a person with no concerns about sexual harassment. The overdone makeup might look great to you, but it will look like too many potty trips to the woman on the hiring side of the desk. As for the sexual harassment component, no human resource manager in her right mind hires with the prospects of a lawsuit on the horizon. Therefore, if you are blessed with great looks, use them to your advantage. Dress for the position, in a conservative manner, and let your inner beauty come out, too. Win over the human resource manager with your skills, common sense, and energy.

Women aren't the only ones who have to consider common sense when dressing for an interview. Casual Friday has added a strange twist for men. Their clothing choices used to be so simple, but those days are gone. After decades of dressing on autopilot, men now have to think about what to wear. One of the oddest questions I ever got on the company side of the desk was from a guy coming into our casual environment on a Friday for an interview. He was employed at a very conservative company and interviewing on his lunch break. He called to tell me he had to wear a suit or else his current employer would be onto his interviewing activity. I chuckled and told him I'd be looking for a suit on Friday.

A major issue with casual is it is hard to define. Casual varies from environment to environment. One thing is generally certain: Casual does not mean sloppy. T-shirts are not appropriate. Polos are a little too unstructured for a first interview. For men, casual can be a shirt, tie, and sports coat tucked on the back seat of the car just in case, but I'd never recommend casual for the first interview unless the person conducting the interview has specifically directed you to dress casual. If the job is high-level, regardless of the day of the week, the best option is a suit.

Women have always had to choose between a variety of images for the first impression. Women also have had to work harder at relaying their intended message because their roles in the workplace have changed over the decades, and their wardrobes contain more options. There was a time, when women were just entering the boardrooms, that women's clothing needed to make a power statement. Now clothing needs to make a dual, somewhat conflicting statement: power/position and approachability. And it's best to do it without making an issue of sexuality.

The message a woman relays with her clothing is a product of the way she feels in certain clothes and the stereotypes associated with certain clothes.

Each article of clothing, in the eyes of the beholder, has a role attached. In fact, anything you wear will evoke some sort of stereotype from a person who sees you. You will also feel certain ways in certain garments. Feelings play such an important role in dressing that on "bad" days you may have a hard time dressing up for a meeting. Your feelings will persuade you to dress in some sort of sack dress and hide behind a big wall. On up days, you may want to dress so powerfully that you can't help but get all of the powerful energy in a room pulled into you.

Now we'll look at the most common interpretations, or stereotypes, attached to certain clothes. Notice that most items have more than one message and some have quite conflicting messages. We are constantly putting out all sorts of mixed messages and vibrations with our clothing. Some work in our best interest; some cause us havoc. The goal is to feel good, put out good energy, and bring in a good working experience. How these pieces are put together in an ensemble will determine what they say and how you feel. Make sure they are saying what you feel about the job and how you feel you are perfect for the job.

Symbol Key: 𝖹Power, 🐾Approachability, ♥Sexy

𝖹	navy blue suit	𝖹🐾	white silk blouse
♥	black leather jacket	𝖹🐾	gold silk blouse
𝖹🐾	black knit dress	𝖹🐾	cashmere sweater
𝖹♥	very tight black knit dress	𝖹♥	tight cashmere sweater
♥𝖹	short black knit dress	𝖹🐾	cashmere sweater set
🐾	baggy black knit dress	🐾♥	tights
🐾	company polo shirt	𝖹	tailored suit
🐾	khakis	🐾	baggy jeans
♥	short shorts	♥	tight jeans
𝖹🐾	calf-length black skirt	🐾	well-fitting jeans
🐾	long flowered skirt	🐾	loose cable-knit sweater
𝖹🐾♥	red silk blouse	🐾	baggy sweatshirt
		🐾	white T-shirt
		𝖹🐾	tailor-cut T-shirt

sleeveless blouse

fitted jacket

freeform jacket

diamond earrings

dangling earrings

French manicure

two-inch fingernails

five-inch stiletto pumps

mules

penny loafers

pumps

clogs

beige fingernail polish

red fingernail polish

blue fingernail polish

red silk scarf

long flowered silk scarf

A-line skirt

fitted skirt

tight miniskirt

knit skirt, one inch above knee

lacy blouse

sheer blouse with lacy bra

low-cut sweater

bangle bracelets

charm bracelet

tennis bracelet

costume ring with large stone

costume necklace with large stone

ring on ring finger

rings on all fingers

pierced ears (one piercing)

pierced tongue

tattoo on shoulder

tattoo on leg

ankle bracelet

open-toed pump

slingback pump

Whether you're female or male, you must make sure your clothes are sending the message you want to relay to potential employers. Every industry and occupation has its "uniform." CEOs are expected to look like CEOs. Artists are expected to look like artists. We communicate through our appearance; be attuned to what your appearance says. Once you've defined your desired position, dress the part. Keep feeling yourself in the position. Know it's yours.

If you are truly in doubt about what to wear when you're called for the interview, ask the human resource person what's expected of you in regards to your garments. Several years ago, a major company from out of state sent a representative to my area to interview me over lunch at a country club. The dear soul had the decency to call me the night before and tell me to dress casually. Most human resource people will give you a straight answer if you ask them a straight question.

Chapter 13

Location, Location, Location

Companies interview candidates in all kinds of locations—the company's premises, job fairs, hotel lobbies, Starbucks, country clubs, corporate jets, you name it. Some spots such as coffee shops are incredibly casual. Others, such as a judge's chambers, are designed with the intent to intimidate. With any location comes energy.

If possible, interview at the facility where the job is located. This will enable you to determine if you connect with the energy in the working environment. As discussed in chapter 9, all employment environments are a little different. I have found that companies that won't show me my future office do so for a variety of reasons. The most common is they are hiring me to replace somebody who doesn't know they are being replaced. Others are afraid that their work environment might scare away the best candidates.

By seeing and feeling where you will be working, you can connect with the energy or, if need be, avoid such a connection. Unfortunately, on-site interviews aren't always possible. Some companies scatter recruiters across wide geographic areas to interview the best candidates. These recruiters can create a misleading image of the position and the company.

One time during an off-site interview, I connected so well with the interviewer that I was sure a job offer would be forthcoming. It was a beautiful summer day, the interview was at a country club, and it lasted for hours. When I got the airline tickets to make my appearance at corporate headquarters, I was looking forward to seeing the interviewer again. But from the time I got off the plane, things started to go badly. I missed a turn and got lost in a bad neighborhood with the clock ticking. When I finally got to corporate, the energy was chaotic. The interview schedule was a mess. Nobody knew for sure what job(s) I was interviewing for or whom I was supposed to be seeing. When I finally got a moment or two with the initial interviewer, she looked at me and shook her head. It felt like I had lost an old friend. Our energy connected wonderfully off-site, but on-site, she was a stressed-out mess, and I wasn't connecting. It wasn't until I got back to the airport with seconds to spare that my good energy connected to another soul. It connected with the woman at the car-rental place who personally got me to my flight on time.

In the previous example, even though I had a great experience with an off-site interview, that isn't always the case. Off-site interviews can play havoc with energy and presentation. One morning I was having coffee with a writers' circle. We were a pretty loud bunch with piles of papers and red pencils. In the same coffee shop, an interviewer was interviewing candidates for an entry-level management job. During our three hours, I saw six candidates come and go. All six had a hard time sitting comfortably in their suits in the casual environment. They felt uncomfortable, and it showed. All six had a hard time selling themselves over the writers' circle's little outbursts when one or another of us would come across something we had to discuss. The interviewer did toss us a few unflattering looks in the hope of getting us to quiet down, but the bottom line was that the interviewer had chosen a casual location to perform a not-so-casual function.

If an interviewer chooses a lousy spot, you have to work hard to keep your energy up. You have to feel yourself in the job, not in the coffee shop. On the upside, you can make the environment work for you. If it's close to your home, go to it a day or two before the interview and get a feel for the environment. Close your eyes and feel how you are going to make this environment work with you, not against you. Feel how you will be able to feel comfortable in a suit when all around you are in jeans. Imagine how you will feel at ease in the perhaps noisy environment.

Job Fairs

One of the all-time worst interview sites is a job fair. In all fairness, some of the organizers of these events have the savvy to have private interview rooms available, but most are large, noisy, and allow little or no privacy. The best way to make one of these circuses work for you is to keep your energy up. Feel yourself being offered jobs by half of the companies in the facility. When you are pulled aside for an interview, give the interviewer a crisp, professional copy of your résumé, a strong handshake, and just the essential facts. Tell the interviewer that you are checking out several companies at the fair. Ask for a business card and tell the interviewer you will be calling soon.

You absolutely must keep your energy up at these fairs. If necessary, run to the restroom and look at yourself in the eye for a few minutes. Remind yourself of your value. Remember, these fairs attract a large population of people who are sending out a lot of bad vibrations. They may have been looking for a job for a long time and are feeling very abysmal about it. Don't become a magnet for their garbage. Keep your energy up and keep the interviews short.

Don't Talk with Your Mouth Full

Interviews involving food are always tricky. My little buddy called to ask me if he could have a drink at a dinner interview. As a frat boy, he prided himself on his ability to consume alcohol. I doubted if the company would consider this to be an asset. I told him that if the company folks ordered a drink, he could have one if he really could handle it. If the company folks ordered a second round, it was time to switch to tonic water without gin. He didn't care much for this advice, but as I told him, the big difference between them and him was they had a job and he didn't. That part he understood.

Interviewers use dinner situations for interviewing for several reasons. Interviewers can use expense accounts to cover the cost of their food as well as yours. They want to see how you will fit in socially, especially if you will be representing the company in a capacity that interacts with the public, such as sales. They can extract more information out of you during a dinner than in a stuffy interview. The timing fits into their schedule. And if the company is out of town, it may be easier for them to put a couple of company representatives up in a hotel for a week than to fly several candidates into corporate.

Dinner interviews can be tough. It's hard to eat, think, and talk at the same time when under a microscope. To make matters worse, we have all heard of the extremists, such as the man who was famous for taking interviewees out for dinner to see if they salted their food prior to tasting it. If they did, he assumed they assumed too much and job offers were not forthcoming. Also, the more upscale the restaurant or club, the more nerve-wracking it may appear for fresh college grads who were not raised with a silver spoon. If you don't know what fork to use, get a book on etiquette and get the basics prior to the interview. If you're still perplexed as to which utensil to use, follow the leader. There is no reason to err from ignorance. And believe me, some people do. A colleague watched a man eat an entire meal with the fork from the shrimp cocktail. Did he get the job? No. The story only became cocktail fodder.

If you have to go to an eatery for an interview, if possible, check out the place prior to the interview. If the eatery is casual, check out the clothing of the patrons and plan to dress a notch above their attire if you are told to dress casually. Otherwise, it's suit time again. It's always better to be overdressed than underdressed. Remember how good you felt about yourself when you were dressed up for special occasions as a child? Well, those feelings are still a part of you. Most people feel better about themselves when they present themselves in a powerful manner. Dress up, feel up.

Regardless of where the initial interview may be, if at all possible, try to get an on-site interview prior to taking the job. You need to feel the energy of the location.

Detective

Several years ago, I got laid off. I was feeling damned angry about the entire situation, but had no idea of the connection between feelings and procuring employment. I sent out résumés and soon had an interview—a long-distance phone interview with a guy at corporate headquarters several states away for a job at a division near my home. I made the first cut and was scheduled for the first round of in-person interviews when the interviewer flew to town. The interviewer was nice enough. In fact, I thought I might like being his colleague. He told me they had just gone through a buy-out, but that it had gone smoothly, the compensation model was being reviewed, and the benefits had just been revamped to incorporate the best of what the employees had had prior to the buy-out. We discussed how the labor force had been a little restless after the buy-out, but things were calm now since a series of town-hall-style meetings had been implemented. It all sounded pretty good.

Due to time limitations, he had to cut my interview short, so he asked the woman who would be my secretary (if I were offered and accepted the job) to take me on a plant tour. She was a nice enough person, the kind of person I'd want living next door, not too nosy, but friendly. She promptly took me to the production area.

On the plant tour, the body language and energy of the employees spoke volumes. They refrained from eye contact with me, but when I passed them and looked over my shoulder, I noticed work had stopped so they could check me out. The work being performed was done in an extremely sloppy fashion, but my escort seemed to think little of the display. When we got back to what would be our offices, I asked about the buy-out. She said it had been a hard pill to swallow. I asked about the compensation model. There hadn't been raises in 15 months, and nobody knew if any were forthcoming. I was batting a hundred so I asked about benefits. She told me flatly that the workforce was up in arms about having to contribute toward benefits for the first time ever and for a package that seemed to be tailored for a big city, not their little community. She told me all of this with her smile intact, like a doll with plastic molded lips, unable to frown. Her smile couldn't hide the edginess in her voice or her bad energy. Red flags went up in my mind.

When I wrote my thank-you note for their time and consideration that night, I also requested that I no longer be considered for the position. The corporate culture was the mirror image of the one I had just left. I needed a job, but I didn't need to be looking for one again in a year or two. I may not have understood energy, but I understood unemployment.

Therefore, look for any clues about the company culture. Look at the employees. Are they "happy campers" emitting good energy, or do they resemble faces from a horror movie? Look at the furniture. It might be old, but is it cared for, or is it junked? Do employees do anything to make their cubes little homes away from home during the day? I knew one place where the telemarketers went to great lengths to fill their cubes with Happy Meal toys, photos, and other little mementos to bring joy to their environment. On the other hand, walking into a bank where such frivolous decorations are banned may feel like walking into a pit each day. Are the restrooms clean? Is the toilet paper cushy? I'm not kidding. Scratchy TP is just another way of being cheap with employees, of saying, "I don't care" about them. If you are looking around and see an environment that you find distasteful, it's a sign you didn't put out the best of energy to bring in a good job.

Chapter 14

Face to Face

Lo and behold, it's time for that interview. If there's ever a day to get your little energy connectors on board and working for you, today's the day. You want to connect with as much good energy as possible, and it all starts with you.

Start the day quietly. Oh, I know this isn't always easy, especially when interviews involve air travel, breakfast meetings, or a hurried schedule prior to the actual interview. I, too, have jumped through those hoops. But it's worth forsaking that extra 15 minutes of sleep to get some quiet time. You owe it to yourself to go within and get in touch with your good energy, regardless of your schedule.

When you first get quiet, you might find you have some negative stuff just below the surface. Let all of your nervousness, anxiety, and fear bubble up. Feel them for the moment and address them. If you are nervous, ask yourself why. Are you nervous because you think you are a weak candidate? If so, remember the company believes you have enough talent to look at you. Are you nervous because you are worried about the competition? Forget it. You have absolutely no control over the competition. Focus only on things you can control—your energy and your behavior. Address all of your pesky feelings. Keep poking holes in them until they surrender. If you can't unload all of them, flip them. Turn anxiety to anticipation.

If you are fearful, that's just an old tape running over and over again. It has no place in your new energy-driven world. Dismiss it. Know that you are the best candidate for the position. Don't let fear and insecurity be part of your energy equation.

Once you've addressed your fears and anxieties, you should become comfortable with yourself and the day facing you. In this space of comfort, you will be able to bring up the over-the-top good energy that will fuel your day by focusing on your value. Focus on your value as a person, your value as a member of society, your value as an employee. When you focus on your value, you expand your good energy. You allow the true you to come through. You move from a limited scope of being a candidate like a dozen other candidates with the same limited skill-set to a full person who brings not only a skill-set, but a personality, a set of experiences, and a sense of worth to the table. Continue focusing on your value until you feel a sense of lightness come to you. It is then that you have connected with the true you. This is also the energy that moves you smoothly through your day—hold onto it!

Before you move away from your quiet space, begin to visualize yourself getting dressed, getting in your car or on the train, arriving at the company, being greeted by the interviewer, explaining your talents and skill-sets with charisma and confidence, shaking the hand of the interviewer. Feel yourself knowing that if this is the best job for you, it will be yours. Hold those feelings. Once you have them established within you, begin to join the real world and perform the mechanical tasks at hand. You have your good energy working for you; let the synchronicity begin!

Physical Preparation

Your good energy is important, but following through on the physical level is necessary as well. Your energy will shine through, synchronicity will begin, but you still need to take action. Yesterday, a former client of mine had been talking to one of her business associates who just so happened to need a human resource consultant. She told him about the outstanding work I had done for her company. As the conversation developed, he thought of several people in his trade association who could use my expertise as well. She called me after their meeting to give me his contact information. This is all wonderful, but until I set up a meeting, put on a little blue suit, and pitch my services, it's all energy. I need to put the physical steps into motion to turn the energy into income. The same is true with interviewing. There are certain steps that are part of the process, so let's walk through them.

First of all, be prompt. Arrive at the interviewer's office four to six minutes prior to the interview time. Arriving 20 minutes early appears desperate. Arriving even one minute late is tardy. Tardy doesn't fly well in the real world. If the interviewer has asked you to come 15 to 20 minutes early to fill out an application, then he means the interview for you starts 20 minutes before you see him.

When planning your trip to the interview site, consider the traffic for the time of day, the location of the company, and the physical size of the company. Don't estimate your drive time during perfect driving conditions and leave out the time necessary to get from your vehicle to the interviewer's office. I had to go to a wedding recently. A friend was driving, and I told her to arrive a half-hour early. The church was two minutes from my home, but the real time from my home to the pew was much longer. My elevator can take up to three minutes, so I always allow myself three minutes to get an elevator. There's a half-minute trek through the lobby and parking lot to get to a car in the visitors' parking lot. The direct route from my parking lot to the church has two traffic lights that could add minutes to the drive. Then there's the time to find a parking place, walk into the church, and wait in the queue for an usher. Considering my friend was meeting me in my apartment, I figured we needed 12 minutes to make a two-minute journey, and we needed to include an additional seven minutes to be seated in a reasonable amount of time before the bride walked down the aisle. When figuring the time necessary to be prompt for your interview, consider all components of getting your body from your place to the office chair, not just the drive time. If you're not familiar with the company's location, make sure you build in extra time in case you get lost or make a wrong turn. If possible, make a practice run to the company a day or two before the interview so you'll know right where to go on the actual day. Once you get there, allow for time to find the right office. A guy once called me from out of state as he was walking around looking for the proper office. It was a downtown location, and the office he was seeking involved going through three buildings before he found the company. Every step takes time.

Once you enter the building, turn off your cell phone. Do not have it vibrate. Do not have it silenced. Do not have the little red light blinking to let you know you have a new voicemail. Have it off. Cell phones are like excuses—everybody has one, and nobody wants to hear yours. The goal here is to focus your attention and energy on your value, the company, the interview, and the interviewer, not an incoming call. People who have the potential to get really important calls turn off their cell phones during important meetings. They make other arrangements to have crises handled in their worlds for an hour or so. An interview is a really important meeting.

Why Do HR Folks Do THAT?

Depending on the position and company policy, you may have to fill out an application when you report for your interview. Some companies forgo the application until after the first interview. Some companies allow candidates to take applications home; others insist they be filled out on-site. No matter when it's filled out, if you are to become an employee, you will be filling out an application before you go onto payroll.

Companies that interview you from a résumé without an application are doing weeding interviews. They are weeding out the first round of candidates. They may be looking at a handful or a few dozen candidates. These interviews are important since they have the potential to lead to a second interview, but don't expect a job offer from a weeding interview.

Other companies insist that all candidates fill out an application before they even offer a candidate a cup of coffee. This gives the company a signature that allows them to check references. Applications also contain language that allows for termination if the information is inaccurate. It never ceases to amaze me how many candidates claim they went to colleges that have never heard of them. And, depending on the state, applications may have a clause that says all employment is at-will, meaning the employment relationship can be terminated at any time for any reason or no reason.

From a human resource perspective, applications make extracting necessary data easy. The forms are designed to make all candidates put their information in a specific format. The human resource person can easily determine how much relevant experience and education each candidate brings to the table without playing connect the dots from résumés. Therefore, some human resource folks just have them filled out to make candidate selection easier.

Along with an application, many companies request that a candidate fill out an additional form that asks for information on a candidate's ethnic background. These forms are used by companies that are either under an Equal Employment Opportunity (EEO) order to curtail discriminatory hiring practices or by companies that are collecting that information to make sure they are drawing a pool of candidates that reflects the demographics for the type of position they are filling. These forms do not become part of am employee's employment file. They are logged into an applicant tracking system that looks at the company workforce overall, not any one candidate specifically.

Some companies allow a candidate to participate in the first interview without completing an application, and if they're interested, they give the candidate an application to fill out and bring back for the second interview. I never do this. Since I interview candidates from all walks of life, having them fill out the application on-site gives me some much-needed information about their literacy, accuracy, and, in some cases, their honesty.

Prepare, Prepare, Prepare

Considering I am not the only stick-in-the-mud HR person who insists on applications being filled out on-site, it's advisable to have an extra copy of your résumé with you when you report to the interview. By doing so you will have all of the necessary information to fill out the application. Applications generally request information that's more specific than the information on a résumé. Applications request the names and phone numbers of your references. Have a list of references attached to the working copy of your résumé for your use. A completed application can speed along a hiring decision. One with gaps can get you placed at the bottom of the pile.

Know as much as you can about the company before you walk in the door. Even many small companies have Web sites you can read before the interview. Know the company's mission and vision. Know the product. Know who's in charge. By knowing these things before sitting across from the human resource person, you demonstrate that you are interested in not only employment, but the company as well. A few hours of research can make you appear to be an enlightened candidate, or at least save you a lot of grief. Say you start looking into a company and you find there's a lot of negative press on their treatment of employees, or they are under investigation by the Securities and Exchange Commission. Armed with such information, you may decide to hold out for an opportunity that better fits your values and ethics. It's best to know these things before you step in the door rather than afterward.

But let's say you've done your homework and you like the company. Since you've read pretty much everything you could find on the company, what do you do when the human resource person starts her spiel about the merits of the company? Listen. I've found that many candidates are so intent on selling themselves to me that they fail to listen to what I am trying to tell them. From the human resource desk, such behavior is frustrating and rude. Let the interviewer set the tone for the interview. That's her job.

If the company is small and there's no HR person, you might find yourself sitting across from the owner. She may load you down with company brochures. Don't leave them when you walk out the door. She's worked hard to get the company off the ground. She's very proud of those brochures. Accept them with pride. Let her know you'd be proud to be part of her team.

In addition to knowing all you can about the company, it's important to know thyself. Keep focused on your value. Know you have the skill-set required for the position, and you are a unique person who has the potential to do this specific job in such a manner that the company will be glad to have you on board. Feel comfortable with what you bring to the company and let your light shine.

Communication

The trick to interviewing is to say the right things, at the right time, in the right amount. I've had candidates who interrupted me. I've had candidates who wouldn't talk. I've had a few candidates who said some of the most outlandish things that I wondered if they were even aware they were interviewing for an employment opportunity. Keep in mind at all times that you are there to bring value to the company. This value is marketable in the form of your skill-set, your set-of-experiences, your education, your personality, and any other unique characteristics that make you the best candidate for the job. You are there to become part of a team. You are there to be an asset. Keep in touch with your good feelings and let yourself move smoothly through the process. Put yourself in the best possible light and say what needs to be said to show your skills, talents, and abilities.

Style

I've taught interviewing, and I've interviewed hundreds of people over the years, and I've seen several methods for interviewing. Personally, I like to get the candidate talking and sit back and take in as much as possible. Since that's my style of interviewing, I look for hobbies or activities on their résumés that will start the ball rolling. I've always found it easier to ask somebody about a hobby, get them relaxed and comfortable, then lead the conversation toward work-related issues rather than hit them with hardball questions from the get-go.

This method allows you as a candidate to put your skill-set on display. If given such an opportunity, have examples of your accomplishments that show the interviewer your skills. Show, don't tell! Case in point: I am good with employees. When I was seeking employment, I used the following example to demonstrate my strength in employee relations. I showed how

I went that extra mile to work with a good, but troubled employee. This woman had been a good employee for a few years when her supervisor came to me concerned that she was drinking. Her attendance had become very problematic, which is a key indicator of substance abuse. I looked at her attendance records, and unless she was drinking morning, noon, and night, her behavior wouldn't have had such a dramatic shift in such a short period of time. I decided to ask her directly what was going on in her life. Within a few minutes, I learned she was 37 years old and homeless. She had left an abusive spouse and was living in her car. After nearly two decades of marriage, she had no personal assets, no credit, and didn't even have a checking account. She was also very scared. It was hard for me to relate to a person who was lacking basic life skills, but that's exactly what I was facing. I had options. I could have told her to straighten out her life. I could have written her up for poor performance. Or I could help her and hope that she turned her life around and became productive. I opted for the latter. I helped her open a checking account. I helped her get a little apartment and get the utilities turned on without a credit record. I helped her get her life back on track. I was not running a social-services operation, but I was trying to retain an employee who had once been very productive. Within a few weeks, she was back to being a good employee, in fact, even better than before, because she was grateful for what I, as a company representative, had done for her. So when an interviewer asks me if I am good at employee relations, I have that example I give in detail. Instead of saying "I'm good at employee relations," I show it. No matter what line of work you may be in, if the interviewer is letting you talk, he wants you to start showing him what you've done. He wants concrete examples.

Because of my employee-relations experience, I am well aware that people's personal lives have a great impact on job performance. Therefore, when I am interviewing a candidate, I look for clues as to what's going on with this person overall. Laws prohibit me from asking many personal questions, but allowing candidates to talk generally reveals a great deal of personal information. Most human beings come with a certain amount of baggage and drama, but no human resource person goes out searching for a candidate who has *extra* baggage and drama. If your life is full of turmoil, the human resource person is not your shrink or social worker, so keep it to yourself. If you've honestly been working your energy, your baggage and drama should be lessening, but it's still not something you want to tell an interviewer. I am always amazed at the personal stories I hear.

Although I prefer allowing candidates an opportunity to talk, some interviewers ask specific questions and take lots of notes. They do this to make sure they extract the same type of data from each candidate. When faced with this type of interview, take a few seconds to really think about the question before answering it. Make sure your response answers the question and allows you to present yourself in the best possible light. Interviewers are looking for the best candidate for any position. You have good energy. Keep it flowing. Keep yourself connected to the good within you and allow it to come out in your answers.

Questions

There is a whole list of questions that are popular with interviewers. One is: What's your biggest weakness? Your weakness has to be a weakness for you, but one that works as an asset for the company. For example, you might say that you are the type of person who works long hours because you can't seem to rest until a job is well done.

Another question: Where do you expect to be in five years?

This question made more sense when companies hired for life. Now it's a bit trickier. The correct answer is along the lines that you want to be at the company as long as the company wants you. Putting that into a sentence that makes sense takes some finesse. It has to be tied to the position you are seeking. Say you are coming on as an engineer. Your five-year goal may be to lead the company into new markets by engineering and designing new product lines that work within a global economy.

Another question: What would you change about the company? This one is loaded. The correct answer is you would need to be a part of the team to determine what is currently working and not working, and then give examples of positive changes you implemented in your previous position, along with the costs they reduced or the profits they increased. Unless you are applying for the position of CEO, nobody really wants to hear of all of the changes you have in mind until you are an insider. Lots of the changes you may have running through your head have already been tried and abandoned. Your goal is to bring in positive change, not to reinvent the wheel.

Round Two—the Second Interview

I was sitting in the dentist's chair the other day, and the dental hygienist was having a one-way conversation with me since my mouth was full of tools and her fingers. She was going on and on about how her niece went on an interview for a job she had envisioned and got an offer on the first interview. Offers on first interviews seldom happen, not because the candidate isn't a perfect fit, but because any human resource person with an ounce of savvy is going to want to take the time necessary to run a reference check. Reference checks need an applicant's signature. That's why they aren't done prior to an interview. It's also one of the reasons few job offers are extended during the first interview.

Out-of-the-chute offers generally go to people in specific categories. For instance, they go to the young folks who haven't had enough time to screw up yet. They go to a friend of somebody in the hiring process who can vouch for the candidate's character. And they go to candidates for jobs at the lower rungs of the company strata.

So most candidates have to go through the interview process more than once to get a job. A lot of candidates expect the second interview to be a carbon copy of the first interview, or even easier than the first. The truth is, they are usually tougher. During the first interview, the interviewer is weeding down the field of candidates. During the second interview, the interviewer is looking more closely.

My past experience has been that the person on the top of my list for a second interview is the person I want to hire. The same has been true from the other side of the desk. I recall vividly the day I stood in front of the desk of a company president who told me not to panic when I saw the same ad in the next day's paper. He told me pointblank that he had pretty much made up his mind to hire me, but he just needed a night to sleep on it. The job offer came the next day.

So, on the upside, second interviews mean the company is really interested in you. Your energy connected with the initial interviewer, who has more than likely been selling you to somebody else within the organization. There are good vibes in the air. From an energy perspective, this is in your favor. You just have to keep those good vibes going out. That's where things get a little tricky.

Sometimes the second interviewer has heard so many good things about you that there is a set-of-expectations that you have to meet. Therefore, make sure you tell interviewer number two the same things you told interviewer number one. You don't want to leave out the one thing that might be the selling point. Keep up your energy just as you did on the first interview.

Them against Me!

Sometimes the second interview is conducted by a group of people. These types of interviews are held for several reasons. They take less time. Actually, they take less of your time, but they take the same amount of everybody else's time. But they are perceived as time-effective for the company because you will be answering questions in front of a group, therefore each member of the group doesn't have to ask you the same question time and again. Another reason for such interviews is to see how you fit into a group situation. This is great if you are going to work in a group situation, but my experience has been that some of the people put in these groups have nothing to do with the position you are seeking. Nevertheless, you must play along.

Answering questions about your education, skill-set, what you have done, where you have done it, and giving examples are all standard. Be prepared. Have the data. Groups can only process data; they can't process much else because there is too much energy floating around the room.

Here's my thought process during a one-on-one interview: I ask the question. I focus on the answer. I ask another question. I focus on the answer. Ditto. When this part is done, I ask the candidate if there is any additional information that might be helpful in my decision-making process. I listen for an answer. That pretty much sums it up.

Now, in a group interview, here's my thought process: Good question, Tom. I intently listen to the answer. Pause as the duck-duck-goose game of who's going to ask the next question is played. A question is tossed out. Oops, I missed part of it. The interviewee did give some pretty good information, something I hadn't caught during the first interview. I jot down a note. I ask a question. I intently listen to the answer. Again, duck-duck–goose. Oops, nobody has a question. I'm hungry. I wonder what flaw Sally is going to find with this candidate. It's amazing how the least competent manager in the operation can always find fault with every candidate.

See how the process has little to do with you personally and everything to do with you on an energy level? In group settings, interviewers are paying attention to just about anything but you on a personal level. The major difficulty for the candidate is getting the attention of any person in the room for more than a few seconds. Best bet is to answer any question to the group, but zero in on the person asking the question. Focus your energy on that person because that person is the one who is probably paying attention and is, for that brief moment in time, able to connect with you.

On an energy level, group interviews are tough because there is so much energy bouncing around, looking for like energy, ricocheting, bouncing, connecting, and on it goes. Therefore, you have to be putting out positive energy. That way, you'll only connect with the good stuff others are putting out, and deflect the stuff that causes you harm. The overall effect will be to bring up the energy overall and bring in the job.

Marathons

Other scenarios are also common for second interviews. Some are what I think of as candidate marathons. I used to schedule a lot of these when I was with a Fortune 100 company. They involve candidates seeing several company folks back to back to back. If scheduled properly, you'll have time to step into the restroom and catch your breath between interviews. If scheduled improperly, they can be exhausting. I once went through one of these marathons at General Electric—seven hours, and they forgot I needed lunch. At 2:00, I asked for a candy bar and figured they were more than inconsiderate.

If scheduled properly, marathon interviewing can be fun. Yeah, you read that right, fun. After all, you get to meet a whole bunch of people in one day who want to listen to your story. It doesn't happen often. Some will make your life easy by telling you their own story, which makes for a nice rest. Mostly, these folks want enough information from you to have some input at some meeting scheduled sometime when you aren't on the premises. From a business perspective you will have a chance to meet a lot of people you may be working with and determine if you feel good around them and want to work with them. You also get more insider information on the company, since each employee has a little different spin on what it's like to work for XYZ Company. Most interviewers will ask you at some point during the interview if you have any questions. Ask what a day in the interviewer's shoes is really like. You will learn more about a company by asking seven managers what their days are like than you will learn from hours of research. Marathon interviewing allows you to put your good energy out to interviewers one by one. This allows your good energy to connect with their good energy, leaving them with a "gut" feeling that you are the right candidate.

Tests

Some companies use second interviews to give you pencil-and-paper tests. (Actually, some companies will even give them at the first interview as another screening tool.) They generally say it's just a formality and that the test scores don't really count—don't buy it! Companies use them because they hold up well in court. Over the years, I've seen tests that ranged from personality profiles to basic math skills. One headhunter I know always tells his clients to answer the personality tests from the company's point of view. He says to think of what kind of person the company would want and act it out on paper. If you really want the job, this might work, but it certainly won't help you keep it. If your personality or energy isn't a fit, it won't stick.

Regardless of the method of interviewing, hold true to yourself. Continue to focus on your skill-set, your personality, your education, and the overall value you can bring to the company. Human resource people are paid to find the best candidate for the job, but at the same time they don't want to engage in long, protracted searches. They need to fill positions effectively and efficiently. Therefore, they work hard to bring candidates on board who they feel will be able to bring value to the company. Be that person.

Chapter 15

When to Call Back

When Lily Tomlin did her telephone-operator routine, she would count the rings: "One ring-a-dingy, two ring-a-dingy." Regardless if your phone makes a ringy-dingy sound, plays Pop-Goes-the-Weasel, or the National Anthem, when you are waiting for a call and it doesn't emit a sound, it's maddening.

We are not a patient society. We eat fast food no matter how unhealthy. We push thousands of pounds of steel inches toward an intersection if we think the red light is too long. We even want our pregnancy tests to be over and done in three minutes.

Most of the time, we are up and running in an "instant" society. But when it comes to searching for a job, we can get derailed by a human in human resources. As a veteran of both sides of the human resource desk, I know how slowly time crawls when seeking employment, and how fast it flies when the task at hand is to fill a position. Human resource people don't get their entertainment by making you wait for an answer. It truly takes them time to get an answer, and the process can get snagged by traveling decision-makers, slow reference checks, a backlogged human resource department, or any of a number of things that have absolutely nothing to do with you.

Time Warp

Usually, problems arise due to differences in time perception. As I said in the previous paragraph, time does not feel the same on both sides of the desk. As a human resource manager, it was not uncommon for me to interview somebody on Tuesday, tell him I'd get back to him by Friday, and be no closer to a decision on Friday than I was when he sat across from me. In truth, there were many times I was further from a decision. Many times I knew I wanted to make the offer when the candidate was in my office, but I couldn't because I lacked approval from other members of the organization. As time passed, some positions were deemed unnecessary, and others were put on hold. Some positions were still on the front burner, but waiting for someone along the line to have a few minutes to perform a second or third interview. The delays never ceased. And time flew. Tuesdays melted into Wednesdays, which faded into Thursdays, which blurred with Fridays.

As a candidate, time feels different. Tuesday seems to go pretty fast; on Wednesday the phone seems unrealistically quiet; Thursday is maddening; and Friday is a roller coaster of emotions. Time all but stops at 5:00 as another week goes by without a job offer.

This time issue puts stress on both sides of the desk. Here are a few suggestions to help you keep your energy up and reduce the negativity generated by waiting. One, when you are truly interested in a job, tell the human resource person you want the job. Some folks fail to express interest in a position. This might make the human resource person assume, rightly or wrongly, that the candidate is only seeking a paycheck, not a position.

Make sure you get the HR person's business card. Many interviewers will hand you one at the beginning or the end of the interview. Use the card wisely. Follow up the interview with a well-crafted follow-up letter. Your follow-up materials and methods will keep you on the top of the pile of stuff on her desk.

Take Control

The most effect step for gaining some control over the situation is to establish a timeline with the interviewer prior to the end of the interview. This is simple, but something few candidates do. When the interview is drawing to a close, first and foremost express your interest in the position. Say not only that you are interested, but also why you are interested. Then ask, pointblank, when you can expect a decision. Most human resource people won't give you an etched-in-stone answer to this question. Many don't have that information at their disposal. If it were up to them, it would be in two hours so they could get onto the next task at hand. But they should be able to give you some sort of ballpark answer, such as, "By the end of next week." Take that information and turn it into an open invitation for your follow-up phone call. Respond by saying, "Great, then if I don't hear from you by next Thursday, I'll give you a call on Friday." If the human resource person abhors calls from candidates, you may get the "don't call me, I'll call you" response, but usually the interviewer will be willing to accept your boldness.

Of course, if you need to make the follow-up call on the agreed-upon day, don't get your hopes up that you'll have a solid answer. You may still hear that the candidates are under consideration, but getting some news is better than nothing. It may also prompt the HR person to unclog whatever glitch she has at her end to try to fill the position.

If you don't give yourself permission to call the human resource person, your call may not be well received when you get frustrated enough to call. Also, timing the call too early makes you appear desperate. There's a fine line between showing interest and appearing needy or pushy.

In the Driver's Seat

The one time when it's okay to call the human resource person soon after the interview is when you really want the job and have another job offer pending. I've lost a few candidates over the years because they took other jobs before I could get an answer to them. If you have a solid offer in hand, but prefer the position with the company that has you on "hold," give the human resource person a call. Give it to them straight. Tell them you want the job, but you have another offer pending. If they have any interest in you, they will make something happen if at all possible. If not, you know it is time to move on. Keep in mind, a lot of folks use this technique when there is no other option on the horizon, but they want to move things along. Just remember, any time you give a prospective employer a take-it-or-leave-it option, they may choose to leave it.

If you have written the necessary follow-ups and are going mad waiting for a call, it may be time to fall back on your intuition. Meditate on the situation—and I don't mean meditate with the TV blaring, a little righteous anger brewing, and an attitude. I mean meditate. Get quiet, stay quiet, and seek guidance from within. Get your energy up. Feel yourself making the call, getting the call through to the right person, making the connection, being a professional. Feel yourself getting the answer you really want to hear. If you can't get yourself into the "feeling," don't make the call.

You will notice when you are ready to pick up the phone prior to meditating, you want to do it and do it now! After meditating, you will either be ready to make the call in a calm, professional manner or be ready to wait a while longer.

Technology has given you another easy option. Call after hours and leave a voicemail. This, too, is best after a meditation so that you can come across as cool and calm. Think about the message you are going to leave. It should be brief and just a reminder that you are interested in the position. If it rambles on and on, you will appear unprofessional and desperate. If it's brief, upbeat, and in a professional tone of voice, it should get your paperwork shuffled back up to the top of the pile.

Chapter 16

Rejection

Okay, if this plan is so foolproof, how can there possibly be rejection? After all, if the up energy is flowing, it has to connect. True, it has to connect, but it connects with other like energy. Your energy might be up and flowing, but it may not connect because somebody in the equation is putting out some pretty muddy energy. Usually, it doesn't connect because what you think you want isn't really what you want. Your energy is going to connect with what you really want. Rejection is your good energy protecting you from something that isn't in your best interest.

Think of a cruddy job you once had. Most people have had one somewhere along the line. When you went in search of that job, you had bad vibes, they attracted other bad vibes, you got a job, but it wasn't a good job for you in the long run. The goal here is to get a good job that you will enjoy. You don't want another job that sucks the life out of you. So if you're all pumped up, and you don't get the job you've been pumping up over, it isn't your energy—it's the energy at the company or it's your energy seeking something even greater for you.

Once, a company strung me along for five months. To this

day, I can't remember the name of that company, although I could drive to it pretty much by rote. During my initial interview, I really connected with Andy, the HR guy. We chatted a lot. After all, I'd be taking his old job as he moved somewhere else in the company. Andy and I were on the same wavelength. We had both worked in human resources long enough to have plenty of stories to share—employee gambling, employee sex, and union contracts. We had been in human resources so long that those three things in one sentence didn't even seem strange to us any longer.

Weeks passed. I had a lot of time to think about the interview and Andy. I played it in my head over and over again, and I couldn't see where I had erred. Furthermore, my daily check to the mailbox for a rejection letter came up dry day after day. Finally, I called Andy. He was still all gung-ho for me. A couple more weeks came and went, and I was finally sitting in his office again. This time we were both a little frustrated. Things seemed to be going slower than either of us wanted. We chatted briefly, and then he sent me on to another interviewer.

The second person was a woman. Again, we had war stories to share. Things were looking good. A month later, Andy called. He sounded exasperated. He wanted to get the position filled and asked me to come in for a third interview. Another person needed to see if I'd fit into the environment.

For the third time, I met with Andy. This time I sat in his office as he went in search of the person I believed would sign off on the fill-job order. It was a windowless office with all of the charm of a backyard shed without a view. I couldn't picture myself sitting there day after day. I was uncomfortable about having to meet with yet another interviewer. I was feeling pretty lousy. My energy dropped.

Andy returned and escorted me to yet another office. The interview was brief. This guy was all pumped up about his recent relocation and had little interest in me or what I could bring to the table. I sat, listened, and gave him a few pointers on navigating his new neighborhood. After the brief interview, Andy came in to walk me to the door. He looked disgusted.

A couple more weeks went by, and I called Andy again. He was chatty, but frazzled. He actually sounded tired since he was still pulling double duty. In fact, he was pretty much holding down two full-time jobs for half the money. He was a real bargain. I had been a real bargain once, and I can't say I liked it much. Andy told me for the umpteenth time I was the primary candidate and that he wanted to get things moving along.

A week or two later, Andy finally called to schedule a meeting with the top banana and me. The next day, I was firmly planted in a chair in front of another newbie to the company. Here was another guy with another pile of ideas that he was going to implement to get this place turned around. Turned around? I had heard earlier it was doing well. This was beginning to sound far too much like a job I had had in the past.

Again, Andy escorted me to the door without a job in hand. A few weeks later, you guessed it, another interview. By this time, the process was no longer even slightly amusing. Except for that carrot of a fatter paycheck than the one I was currently receiving, I felt this company had nothing to offer.

The last interview was the worst. The interviewer was late. He was too impressed with my address and not concerned much at all with my former performance. He had reservations as to why I wouldn't fit into this dirty environment. I wasn't concerned about the physical dirt; I was very concerned about the dirty tricks being played on Andy. If they were playing them on Andy, they would someday be playing them on me. But I smiled, answered the questions appropriately, and was told there would be an answer soon.

Andy called a week or so later and said they would not be offering me the job. I thought I'd feel bad at the news, but I felt nothing but relief. My good energy saved me from a bad job. In other words, rejection was protection, not the end of the world. I stayed with the job I loved until I opened my own consulting company.

Even if you cannot think of rejection as protection, never, and I mean never, take rejection personally! If you take it personally, you will be growing all sorts of negative stuff such as "I'm not good enough," or "Nobody will ever hire me," or "Now I will never be able to pay my bills." None of those thoughts are uplifting. None of those thoughts will get your energy up. Abandon them. Accept the fact that you and the company didn't fit. That's it. If you've been working your energy, the fit failed because you were too good for the company. Think closely about what you really want, not what you think you want. Your energy is around your real desires. Your energy will connect with what you deep down feel you deserve.

Live and Learn

From a business perspective, rejection is the best of teachers. Look over your documents. Do you see flaws in your résumé you failed to see earlier? If so, fix them. The great thing about the electronic age is that résumés can be cranked out, and out, and out. Tailor the next résumé you send out to fit the position to a T. Did your cover letter fail to sell you? Did your follow-up letter do its job?

Remember my little buddy, the soon-to-be college graduate? I wrote his résumé. After a couple of interviews without offers, he called me, whining and begging, for me to rewrite his résumé. I frankly told him that if he was getting interviews, then the paperwork was just fine. It was his interviewing that failed him.

So go over the interview in your head. Don't go over it until you can repeat the errors on automatic pilot. Go over it to examine what you think you did wrong, and more so, what you know you did right. The things you did wrong are over and done. You can't undo them; you can't call up the interviewer and ask for another chance; you can't do one thing about them. Forget them because they will nurture negative energy if fed. Forget them because if you focus your attention on them, you will do them again.

Ever notice that the things you focus your attention on happen even when they are exactly what you don't want to happen? It's kind of like calling out an old lover's name when passionate with a current lover. It's something you never want to do, but you're so paranoid that it might happen that it does! Well, focusing on all the errors in an interview is pretty much the same. If you focus on them enough, they will happen again.

I talk fast. I hate talking fast. My mother talked fast, and it's how I learned to talk. With people I know well, I can pace myself. In front of a crowd, I am just fine. In fact, in college my public speaking even took awards. But when I have to meet somebody influential in my life for the first time, I am a wreck over the speed of my speech. I worry that I won't be able to sound intelligent. Of course, without fail, I trip over my words and sound like an idiot.

One time, I was in conversation with a total stranger at a party, and I was talking well. Our energy had connected, and we were soon bouncing from topic to topic with great ease. As we chatted, I noticed out of the corner of my eye that a substantial crowd of people was waiting for this man's attention. Finally, I asked him who he was. He looked a little surprised. It was apparent from the look on his face that he thought I was kidding, but I wasn't. I really didn't know who he was. He smiled and told me his name, smiled a little more, and told me his title. He was a federal judge. In fact, he was one of the five most powerful people in the state. Not knowing who he was, or what he was, I had no trouble talking with him. But once I had a grip of the situation, my tongue went every which way, and I nearly choked. Fortunately, he found the entire situation amusing.

Yes, what we focus on appears and re-appears in our lives. There are entire industries based on this premise. The diet industry comes to mind. If you think you are fat, you are going to eat like a fat person. If you think you are thin, you are going to eat like a thin person. But the multimillion-dollar diet industry tells people they are fat, so they have to eat like fat people who want to be thin. It works for a little while. Some of these folks shed a few pounds. But they still feel "fat" because they aren't eating like normal people. They return to their old eating habits. In short order, they become fatter people. This works well to fatten the wallets of the diet industry. If you want to be thin, feel thin. If you feel thin, you simply won't want to eat like a fat person.

Let It Go

Let's get back to rejection here. Don't keep your thoughts and feelings attached to the bad parts of an interview. Acknowledge them and abandon them. Focus on what you did right. Even some of the toughest cases I had to interview did something right. They were punctual, or they wore the right clothes, or they had the necessary paperwork. They did something right.

Also, keep in mind, most people do something wrong. I once interviewed three minority candidates at a company that hired few minorities at the time. These three gentlemen did everything right. They were punctual. They had résumés that were well drafted and on appropriate paper. They filled out the application with perfect penmanship. They answered all of my questions and volunteered enough information to make me believe they were personable people. I hired them on the spot. My only reservation was that they interviewed too well.

Nobody interviews that well, much less three people back to back. I felt something was out of kilter.

Within days, I learned my feelings were right on the money. They had interviewed too well, and they had done it for a reason. The company had a reputation as having discriminatory hiring practices at the time. The truth was that few minorities ever applied, but that wasn't the perception from anybody walking through the operation. These three gentlemen had been coached, and coached well, by a group that was considering suing the company for unfair hiring practices. They believed that if these minority candidates couldn't get a job, no minority could get a job. They had no case because all three of these gentlemen had job offers.

The above demonstrates that interviewing is a skill. It's a skill that can be coached, self-taught, or learned in the school of hard knocks. Most people learn it in some mix of the three. Rejection is just part of the curriculum in the school of hard knocks. Learn the lesson well. Remember your strengths, what you did well, and rehearse it time and again. Rehearse in front of a mirror if that helps you get your presentation down to a smooth performance. While rehearsing it in front of a mirror, notice your performance getting better and better. See the energy you can get going when you do it well.

If you believe you have just botched an interview so badly that you want to crawl under a rock, it's time to call on a friend to do a little role-playing. Pick a friend with empathy, compassion, and some business savvy. Do a couple of mock interviews. If a friend in need isn't a friend indeed, then seek out a professional coach.

If you have been practicing the energy techniques throughout this book, it's highly unlikely you botched it badly. Your energy was probably your saving grace from a job that could have caused you months, maybe years, of frustration. Move on.

PART III

Equilibrium

Chapter 17

Getting to the Root

So you've been spinning good energy, following hunches and leads, following up every interview, using a smashing résumé, and still no job? You're not alone. I decided to use the principles of the Law of Attraction to get a job, and it failed. Well, that's my story, but upon closer examination the Law of Attraction worked perfectly; it was my application that had enough flaws that it's pretty much a miracle I ever got any work. Oh, I just love hindsight.

During the onset of a recession, my boss, Scott, called me into his office and told me that my job was to be eliminated in 90 days. At the time, he offered to have me work part-time on a contract. My ego went ballistic. Part-time? Contract? Absolutely NOT! I tore out of his office, raving about the law that prohibits turning employees into independent contractors. Why he didn't follow me and escort me out the door is somewhat of a mystery. Instead, he insisted that I show up and train an administrative assistant to handle the day-to-day functions of what was soon to be my former job and trusted that I would not sabotage the process.

Oh, believe me, I considered sabotage, but I happened to

like the poor soul who was getting the workload. She didn't want my job. She hadn't done one thing to cause this to happen. In fact, she was dreading my departure. Harming her would not make me happy. I also thought of walking out, but even in my somewhat unstable state, walking out had no benefit. Three months of paychecks and guaranteed unemployment benefits trumped no paychecks and a fight for unemployment compensation. So I decided I'd play along and not throw sand in the sandbox. By this time in my life, I had a pretty good understanding of the Law of Attraction—or so I thought. All I had to do was turn my attitude around, and I'd have a new job before my current one expired. I stomped my foot and demanded a job in 90 days.

I started my 90-day plan pretty gung-ho. I drummed up some positive energy and began looking at employment opportunities. Considering I was already "fired," I spent a couple of hours every day using my office computer and the Internet to search for jobs. I used my company-purchased membership to the Society for Human Resource Management to get me onto a Web page just dripping with HR management jobs. The first couple of weeks went pretty well. No job offers, but my résumés were getting some responses, and an interview or two materialized. I was pretty much on track and appeared quite chipper. Well, at least that's how I thought I appeared. But appearances can be deceiving.

My energy was actually in a downward spiral, and my version of the story in retrospect goes more like this. First and foremost, I was ticked, no pissed, no downright livid about the way my jerk of a boss handled the situation from day one. The whole saga had started a couple of years earlier when Scott had hired me to take human resources from a maintenance function into a partnership function with the rest of the management team of the company. To do this, he had to hire me away from a job I enjoyed and a company where I had colleagues who also happened to be friends. Scott also had to terminate a long-term employee who was great at clerical functions and quite well-liked within the company. But his goal was to take human resources to the next level, and I was just the person to do it. At the time, I took that move as a good sign. He was serious about turning human resources around and making a professional environment.

In fact, Scott had expressed his desire for professionalism so many times during our interviews that I had been pretty much chomping at the bit to get my professionalism and expertise into the environment. So I said ta ta to my former colleagues, and I walked in the door with years of management experience and the desire to really shine. I was reeling with anticipation to begin working with rest of the management team.

My first annual review was stellar. I was damned near close to walking on water. Things were sweet for me. I looked forward to year two. I had a barrel full of ideas that I wanted to implement over the coming year. I began mentioning them one by one when I could get Scott's ear. Unfortunately, within a few short months after my anniversary, Scott was spending more and more time away from the office. It was becoming difficult to get his attention. Things were changing, and I couldn't get my bearings as to which way the wind was blowing.

As Scott became more and more distant, it was apparent things were amiss. I continued on my path, but I noticed Scott was no longer on my side. He seemed to be on another path altogether. Each move I made toward professionalism was thwarted. Scott had one excuse or another as to why I couldn't take my department in the right direction. I was spinning. At night I would wonder what had changed. As the months dragged on, things got worse. Scott was trying to steer me away from the professional environment and into clerical work. I reminded him often that my clerical skills were weak on a good day, and my compensation was managerial, not clerical. My words fell on deaf ears. I decided that two could play that game. I started to ignore Scott's requests when he asked me to perform clerical functions for others, or answer the phones during lunch, or order food for other departments. I wasn't an administrative assistant, and I wasn't going to morph into one. It felt like we were both stuck on one of those Chinese finger games, both pulling, not able to get away from one another or able to get anything done as a team.

So I was stuck trying my hardest to be a professional in a less than professional environment, and Scott was dragging me down. Ironically, at the same time he was elevating a woman named Deloris. Scott hadn't been impressed with Deloris's management skills in the past, so this turnaround was puzzling. To make matters worse, I didn't like Deloris, and she certainly despised me. She thought little of my professional experience and the fact I had gone to graduate school. I was equally unimpressed with her lack of education.

The entire situation was maddening. Although I talked a good game about my 90-days-to-a-new-job plan via the Law of Attraction, it was easy to see anger all over me. I slammed doors. I walked out of meetings. I sulked. I am almost embarrassed to write this next sentence, but it shows, literally, how I felt. From the day I was given my 90-day notice until my last day, I wore the same black miniskirt and the same black jacket. Keep in mind, even with great legs, there's an age when miniskirts just aren't proper. I was beyond that age. Not only did I wear the same clothes, but I wore angry clothes. I wore clothes that screamed, "I am here, I am tough, I am up for a fight." No happy vibes flying around me. No sireeee. I was pissed, and I was drawing in all of the pissed-off energy my little energy connectors could find. Damn, it makes my blood boil just to think of it all again.

In all truthfulness, Scott cut me loose at the right time.

Since I wasn't allowed to shine professionally, I was bored out of my mind with that job. I was frustrated with the environment. I was trapped by the lack of professional growth opportunities. It was time for me to leave. What I had been thinking about for months was opening my own consulting operation. Nothing big, just a few small clients where I could do HR work a few hours a week and really be productive. I didn't want to keep my job; I wanted to be my own boss.

What had Scott offered me before I took a ride on the lowest frequency in town? Exactly that. He had offered to become my first client. My energy had sent me my exact request, bingo. And what did I do? I pushed it away with both hands. I shoved it as far away as possible. My pride, my ego, was bruised. I couldn't imagine going into that environment as a part-timer with Deloris gloating. I was also scared. Those bimonthly salary checks are tasty. They are addictive. They are secure. What if Scott were my only client? Oh, my God, I'd starve. So with fear running my life, with negativity running amuck, I took the negative route to anything but security. I must admit, I really blew it. Scott was well-connected locally, and had I continued to work with him, he probably could have assisted me in getting other small accounts. Instead, I did it the hard way.

So, what happened to me? I walked around in my full-blown victim role for several months. I even wrote a little song about Deloris whose name was remarkably easy to rhyme with words that aren't worthy of print. I let that little ditty run through my head when I really had an ax to grind with the world of work. Deloris was my sack of rocks, and I was holding onto that sack with both hands. I had lots of sleepless nights. I aged, and not in a fine-wine sort of way.

Over time, I started thinking about the self-employment concept again. I held tight to it and began spinning out as much positive energy as I could muster. Eventually, I was offered a contract in a different line of work. I enjoyed the work and starting sending out more and more good energy. The situation forced me into opening my own company. In due course, it led to where I am today, president of a business/human resources consulting firm.

To avoid all of that pain, emotional and financial, I should have taken a look at my "root want" as soon as Scott gave me my 90-day notice. A "root want" is something you *really* want. It's something you believe deep down you really deserve. A "root want" can be good or bad. The only thing it can't be is ignored. My "root want" was to be self-employed. I received my "root want" the day I got my 90-day notice before my energy took a nosedive. Had I had identified my "root want" at the time, I would have jumped at Scott's offer. I could have stepped into my own company the day I left my job. I could have avoided months of negative energy.

So, if your job hasn't arrived in a reasonable amount of time, take a look at what's really going on with your energy. Are you, like me, saying one thing and feeling something else? If so, you are playing havoc with your own world. You need to unearth your "root want."

Spotlight Please

In the process of unearthing your "root want," you must be completely honest with yourself and go in search of it with a spotlight that can get into all of the crevasses of your emotions. You must ask yourself if you really want to work. Now, don't go getting defensive on me. There are times in life when another job just simply isn't on the top of your priority list— it's not a "root want." You may have something on your internal radar that's driving your "root want." Some of these things are fairly easy to detect, such as time with family or time off to recharge from burnout. Perhaps you want to open a café or go to grad school. Maybe it's another geographic location that calls you. Other times, "root wants" are little more difficult to unearth. There may be a cross-country trip you never had time to take in college still waiting for an opportunity. Maybe that vintage car under the cover in your garage is haunting you.

Then there are "root wants" driven by emotions that are close to impossible to ferret out without deep soul-searching. Not only are they buried deep down, but they are also very powerful. Unfortunately, the emotions driving these wants do not need to be logical. In fact, some of the most powerful emotions lack logic, which is why they are so deeply buried. An example is the desire for a spouse's financial support as a show of love. I know at first this sounds like absolute nonsense. It's illogical. The logical side of you screams you wouldn't risk your family's financial foundation to prove you are loved. That's the logical side talking, but the illogical side might be running the show. It happens all the time. And the logical side goes to great lengths to prove it's not happening. So, before you slam this book shut because you are still struggling with your root want, it might be time to give yourself a deep-down energy check.

Think of yourself as a car for a moment. The tires might be fine, the body might be shiny, but if the check-engine light is on, good tires and a shiny body mean nothing. Somebody has to find out if the light is on because the gas cap is loose or because the crankcase is down a quart or two of oil or because the entire engine is on the verge of costly repairs. The same is true with you. If all outward appearances are saying "I'm ready for a job" but one isn't here, it's time to dig deeper.

Getting to the deep stuff doesn't necessarily mean a couple of years on a couch are necessary. It could be just looking at a key moment, or a key behavior, from your childhood that has set the script for your adult life.

All of our primary scripts are written when we are children. How we feel about ourselves, how we perceive ourselves, our strengths and our weaknesses, all come from childhood. As children we learned we are smart, or witty, or clever, or hard workers, or lazy, or dumb. We learned all of these things about ourselves during our childhoods. Most of the stuff we learned was reinforced. In my case, I was the smart kid. I didn't hear I was smart once; I heard it time and time again. It became part of my script.

Unfortunately, for some people, the scripts aren't positive. In fact, some people become successful to disprove the script. They may go on for years and years running from the script, but the script is still running inside them. When times get tough, that script has the potential to become the underlying energy behind the scenes. So if you are one of those souls who heard you'd never be a success, perhaps it's that old tape that's generating your core energy.

Perhaps your script went something like this: When your folks loved you, they lavished you with gifts. When they were displeased with you, they took things away. The script you learned was that love equals things, and no love means no things. So if your spouse loves you, your spouse will want to give you things, money, food, shelter, etc. Not working gives you the perfect opportunity to determine if your spouse really "loves" you or not. If you are saying this is childish, well for crying out loud, of course it's childish. The script was written when you were a child. It was developed as a piece of your core survival skills. Unemployment jeopardizes survival, so you will fall back on any and all survival skills that worked for you at any time in your life. Think of it like swimming. If you learned to swim as a child, and you are pushed into a pool as an adult, the first thing you are going to do is swim. If you learned that basic financial security was a function of being "loved," then you are going to prove you are loved to survive.

These scripts for the most part are good things. They stop us from eating rat poison, walking in front of buses, walking barefoot in the snow, and other such things that prove useful throughout life. There's no reason to dig them all up and analyze them one by one.

But if you aren't getting the job, if you aren't getting the good energy, you have to tackle the deep-down energy culprits. Try meditation. Get comfortable, get quiet, get alone, and focus on unearthing anything that's buried deep inside. Let it bubble up. It will. The good news is that you don't have to do anything about it. You don't have to call your mother and tell her that when you were six she said you could never be an engineer. Just acknowledge it, let the feelings flood you until they are exhausted, and move on.

Meditation will bring out the little buried scripts that were written as a child. It will dislodge some defining moment that stuck. It's generating energy, and it's causing havoc.

So what can you do once you unearth these little buggers? Deal with them. If you are angry, get angry—but get angry in the right amount for the right reason. Feel it, acknowledge it, and let it go. Say you dig up some comment made by an angry parent that left you with a script that you'd be a failure. You've spent the last two decades working your tail off, and bingo, your job gets shipped off to China. You are angry, and you are scared, and you feel like a failure. That failure feeling lingers and lingers, and you realize that you were told 40 years ago you'd be a failure. Your energy has connected. It's here to stay unless you decide to flip it into something that works for you, instead of against you. Remember, how you feel is important. In fact, sometimes saying one thing and feeling another only causes you to stuff the bad stuff deeper inside, making it harder to detect, harder to process, and harder to eliminate. So, if you are pushing a nagging worry deeper inside, it's time to face it, square off with it, and bid it farewell.

Then write a new script. Let it start with a daydream. Let your mind take you to where you want to be—employed. Spin the web, fall into it, feel it. Once you have it running in your head, start writing it. I mean, seriously start writing it. This isn't Fairy Tale 101; this is serious writing with the research behind it. Write a business plan for your job search. Write how you will work, where you will work, and what you will do to make the job come your way. Get creative. Put in details, such as how much you will earn, how you will live, the kinds of people you will call friends. Most of us earn within 20 percent of what our friends earn. Think about it: If you are hanging around with a bunch of people, all struggling, it might be time to broaden your circle of friends. Don't worry, really successful people don't bite. So write about the kinds of people you will be calling friends. Write how you will help others with your resources. Once you get it fine-tuned, read it aloud. Read it to yourself in a mirror.

How does your new script make you feel? Can you easily step into it, or does it feel clunky? Massage it until it's you. New scripts are like seedlings—they need attention, they need to be nurtured, and in time they take root. So, if this is the script you truly desire, it's time to replace your dysfunctional "root desire" with this new root. There are a few ways to do this. One of the best is to enlist the assistance of a good hypnotist. Have the hypnotist hypnotize you and incorporate your new script word for word as part of your subconscious thinking. The process is the same as using a script to stop smoking or to lose weight, but the message you are feeding to your subconscious is one you've written yourself and have consciously decided to adopt.

If the idea of hypnosis seems a little too over the ledge for you, you can perform the same function solo. Just write the script and read it to yourself aloud when you get out of bed, sometime during the day, and just before bedtime. Make a tape of it and play it as you doze off in the evening. In time, it will take root. (Actually, a good hypnotist will make a CD for you of your session or your script since hypnosis needs to be reinforced every 72 hours.)

The bottom line is that if the job isn't coming your way, it's time to check your energy. Be honest. Don't say you are spinning good energy and dragging in gunk. It doesn't work that way. And don't say this stuff doesn't work because it's woo woo. The problem isn't that it's woo woo; the problem is that we are all far more negative than we would like to admit. And even when we think we are staying out of the negative zone, it's easy in retrospect to see how much of that negative stuff we are still generating.

Ironically, when we think we are spinning the best of energy may be when we are spinning the worst. A few weeks ago, I got some good news. My mood skyrocketed. Then things got delayed, and I started worrying. Then I started expressing my worry to a few close friends. That was getting me lots of attention, so I started expressing it to anyone who would listen. So what had I done? I had taken some really good news, turned it into worry, and spread it around like mud. What happened? I got the worst client ever. My invoices weren't paid. My tummy hurt. I floundered with a client I should have cut loose, and I came close to losing my favorite client. My hair and skin got dry. My nails flaked away. Stress does those things to a body.

Fortunately, the bad stuff was so in-my-face that I had to do something. I spoke with a friend who has a way of pulling me out of some of the energy holes I dig for myself. Once I was freed, my manicurist gave me a free pedicure, the credit-card company resolved an old issue, and the nightmare of a client dismissed me but cut the check. Sometimes even good things can generate bad energy if we let our minds run rampant on them.

Reflections

Since energy out connects with like energy and returns, what is going on in our lives is a reflection of our energy. If things are good all over, then it's a sure thing you are sending out all sorts of good energy. If things are pretty good, you are sending out more good than bad stuff. A little tweaking could make things better. It only takes a few moments of sending out over-the-top good energy to stop the connective forces of the bad stuff. If things are just not moving, or getting worse, it's time to take action.

Working energy is something like dieting—the proof is in the results. I have been fighting six pounds for quite some time. I like to think of them as hangers-on due to my midlife metabolism, but I have to admit the candy bar after the bowl of Special K in the morning probably has just as much to do with the unwanted weight as my age.

If you're still holding onto old fears and patterns, you are still sending out the old bottom-of-the-barrel energy that goes with them. If your job search is trudging along at a snail's pace and you can't seem to connect with any worthwhile employer, it's time to go back to chapter 4 and take a couple of the tips out for a spin. This stuff works. The proof is in the results.

So make sure the energy you are sending out is the good stuff. And dig deep for your "root desire." If it no longer serves you, let it go. No fanfare necessary. Just a simple "thanks but no thanks" will do. And write a new script, one that will bring in the best job of your life.

Once your new script is written, step seamlessly into a good life. Feel yourself getting that great opportunity. Feel yourself breezing through that interview. Feel yourself shaking hands with the person who just offered you the job. Feel yourself telling your spouse, parents, friends, about your new job. Feel yourself performing a valuable service for substantial compensation. Feel yourself buying that new car (clothes, boat, house) you've been dreaming about with your big fat paycheck. Feel it!

Chapter 18

Immoral, Illegal, and Fattening

Charlie the Tuna is forever trying to do things to prove he has good taste. Over the years, he has read the classics and performed other such antics in pursuit of a pedigree as a tuna with taste. Regardless of his efforts, the result is always the same: He's told, "Sorry, Charlie, StarFish only wants what tastes good, not tuna with good taste."

Our energy has a way of saying "Sorry, Charlie" to us as well. It doesn't give a damn if you are good or bad by society's standards. Its only concern is that whatever you are doing makes you feel good or bad. You have to be putting out those good vibes to bring the good stuff back. Like frequencies connect. It's pure and simple. But some people taking this out for a spin for the first few times equate "good" with being a good person by society's standards. The only way you will generate "good" energy by adhering strictly to society's standards is by abiding by those standards that make you feel good. It's all about feeeeelings.

This feeling thing goes a long way toward explaining why bad things happen to good people and vice versa, especially in the world of work. Some poor woman who's worked her tail off for 20 years doing all of the right things ends up looking for work at age 55 because the company CEO had cooked the books and her pension plan is stuffed with company stocks that are worth zero. The woman who's rebuilding at age 55 would probably say she had a very normal life, and she was good. She went to work, went to church, raised a family. But she was also putting out just enough negative energy to stay connected to a company that was little more than a veil for thieves. Oh, you might be saying she wasn't doing so, that she was just like you, a loyal person working at a company that appeared to be a Wall Street darling. But energy is smarter than logic. Energy connects with like energy; it has no other option. So folks who are connected to these companies are on some level sending out just enough of the wrong stuff to stay connected. Oh, they aren't thieves, but they are vibrating at a level that keeps them connected to thieves. If, at some point, that same person had sent out something other than the frequency that was keeping her connected, she would have disconnected and moved on to another employer.

On the flip side, a high-school dropout lands a leading role in a Disney flick and adds a few million to his substantial fortune. When he left high school to become a rock star, he found himself pumping gas. Throughout the decades, his career has had twists and turns because his energy is at a very creative frequency. His style makes studio executives toss down TUMS and have sleepless nights. But his performances connect with audiences that are willing to plunk down hard-earned cash to be entertained by creative souls. His frequency keeps him employed with a multimillion-dollar price tag. These are both real-world examples. And although most people don't think of these events as the norm, they are every bit as much a function of energy as so-called "normal" lives.

Although what appears in our lives is dictated strictly by frequency, we often ignore our own inner compass of good and bad, our guts, and opt instead to attach ourselves to societal standards. Oh, there's nothing wrong with following the rules. Without some rules, total chaos would prevail. But it's wise to look at the rules and morals for what they truly are to be able to figure out why obeying some feels so good and obeying others feels downright lousy.

Throughout the eons, humans have worked hard at drawing lines in the sand between right and wrong. Every family, every clan, every tribe, every township, every country has spent eons developing rules, laws, and defining morals. So far, it isn't working out very well. First, people never agree on what is right and wrong, or what is good and bad. Even on big things, like killing humans, we say one thing and do another. We say killing humans is wrong, mostly out of self-preservation, but humans kill humans every day. Some day another life form may arrive on planet Earth and dig up the truth that we are a pretty violent species.

In the United States, we find it acceptable for a powerful gun lobby to have a say in the molding and crafting of the laws of the land on gun usage. We claim we need guns for sport and self-protection, but guns seem to get an awful lot of use in the killing of humans that have nothing to do with self-protection. On top of the run-of-the-mill random killings associated with a robbery gone bad or a domestic battle escalating to the point of no return, we also advocate wars. Oh, we don't say we advocate them, but our actions say otherwise. And in the United States, we even advocate our government to function as an executioner. But ask just about any rational person if killing a human is right or wrong, and that person will say wrong without hesitation.

Morals, Laws, and Rules

Some moral decisions have little to do with morals. They are driven by economics. During the potato famine in Ireland, the Catholic Church was able to recruit new priests with little effort. It's highly unlikely that young men as a group were more holy at the time, but it's a pretty sure bet they were more hungry. The Catholic Church meant food in the bellies and no chance of ten kids to feed over the next decade. Some of those men took an economic decision and turned it into a moral one.

There's also an entire set of morals that aren't really morals. They are conveniences. Prior to the 1960s, respectable women didn't live with their boyfriends. They lived with their parents or in women's dorms until they got married. Women were virgins (or supposed to be virgins) until they wed. Oh, it sounds so moral, but the truth was, if they got pregnant before they married, getting a well-paying job was close to impossible. Pregnancy prior to marriage was a one-way ticket to poverty. Morals be damned—society demanded women be virgins for convenience. It was more convenient to have women stay at home and be virgins than it was to supply an avenue to allow women to take care of themselves and their offspring.

Then two things happened that turned this "moral" issue all topsy-turvy. The birth control pill was invented and became readily available at a reasonable cost. The risk of pregnancy dropped dramatically. Sex without babies opened up a whole new world to women. For the first time ever, women could experience sexual freedom. This created havoc for the finger-pointers of the world because nobody could tell who was and wasn't "doing it." Of course, without pregnancy, "doing it" became easy to hide. Once a tipping point was reached and it was assumed that pretty much everybody was "doing it," the finger-pointers had to pretty much give up. Without the active finger–pointers, and with no concrete evidence to determine who was and wasn't "doing it," it became impossible to stop people from "doing it." "Doing it" became the norm. Women didn't HAVE to be virgins.

But the Pill wasn't the only impetus behind the shift in this social norm and moral. Title VII was passed, making discrimination against women in the workplace illegal. Actually, women were tacked onto Title VII at the eleventh hour with the hopes that by doing so the bill would be killed off, but much to the surprise and dismay of some, the bill passed. Women got equal rights and protection in the workplace. It took a few decades to figure out what that meant. I started my working life in the seventies, and to tell the truth there weren't a lot of female lawyers available. In those early years, requesting a promotion to a job that had always been held by a man seldom raised little more than eyebrows. And I can honestly say I recall when bored men would sit in their offices and read *Penthouse* in full view of us "girls" in the office. But as time passed and the lower courts started hearing cases and setting precedents, women began to be elevated in the workplace. With this elevation came the financial resources to maintain a child without a husband if a woman so desired. That pretty much ended the "must be a virgin" thing. In less than 50 years, a moral had been reduced to nothing more than a family wish. It was simply inconvenient for women to live with men prior to the changes of the 1960s, and now it is convenient for women to try it before they buy it. Premarital sex was once cloaked in morals, but now there is very little moral ground to be explored.

Want Fries with That?

Obviously, morals aren't etched in stone. When it comes to moral decisions, some folks take them a la carte. One guy may decide he'd never park in a handicapped space or cheat on his taxes, but he has an ongoing extramarital affair for years. Another guy would never consider straying from his marriage, but he sees nothing wrong with knocking off work early every Friday afternoon and cheating his employer out of thousands of dollars of compensation annually. Another might go to church every Sunday, but gamble away his kids' college funds at his weekly poker game. And yet another would never miss church or cheat on his wife, but he makes a bundle from renting run-down properties to the poor without thinking of his tenants' well-being. From the outside, these guys all look like men with moral compasses slightly out of whack, but the truth is they simply pick and choose which of society's morals they choose to follow and which ones they choose to ignore. And if these men had lived in a different time or place, what they are doing might even be considered right or the norm.

Alongside morals and laws are another set of rules that apply to a small group of people, such as a community or a family. I live in a high-rise building. We have a dozen or so shopping carts in our garage for our use. The routine is pretty simple. We drive in the garage, put our parcels in the carts, take the carts to our units, unpack, and place the carts in the laundry room. The doorman comes around several times a day and collects the carts from the laundry rooms and puts them back in the garage. A new guy just moved in this past week. He keeps dragging stuff to his place in carts and leaving the carts outside his door. It's making me nuts. It looks tacky. It's a fire hazard. His behavior has been playing havoc with my energy. It took several days to dawn on me that he has no idea what else to do with the carts. It's the unspoken rule of this building. He's blissfully enjoying his new home, and I am getting myself all flustered over the damned carts. Although he's doing the "wrong" thing, I am getting the "bad" feelings.

Here Comes the Judge

Here's the real doozy about morals and rules and norms: The people who are busy judging others are causing energetic chaos in their own worlds. Judging people creates massive clouds of negative energy—oceans of it. You only need to look around at the tight faces of some judges to see there's no joy in judging. Energy lacking joy is slow. On the frequency scale, it's probably lower than a snake's belly. Such energy brings back all sorts of stuff and creates some pretty miserable lives for the judges.

People who judge usually aren't looking for the good in their victims. Oh, it might sound like they are eking out some good. "Oh, you can't blame the way so and so drives. If I had to drive that beater, I wouldn't care about an occasional fender bender either." The judge simply wants to demonstrate she has more money than the poor slob driving the beater. In the process, she's messing with her own energy. Perhaps she was raised dirt poor and wants to remind herself that her days of poverty are behind her, but from an energy perspective she's taking a trip down the lane of lack via the Law of Attraction. Perhaps she just got a spanking new luxury car and wants somebody to take notice. Perhaps she simply wants others to notice the state of lack in which her victim resides. Whatever her reason, the result is the same low-frequency energy. It's the kind of energy that almost guarantees her a fender bender or an auto thief.

Have you ever noticed how folks who are being judged often don't know they are being judged? As children, we learned how to pick out a judge at 20 paces. They made us feel miserable, so we did whatever we could to avoid them. When physical distance wasn't possible, we opted for ignoring them. The same is true with adults. Sometimes adults ignore the judge. Other times, they just plain don't care. Those being judged have better things to do with their time and energy than to buy into the self-appointed judge. So who loses? The judge!

Also, most judges are actually judging themselves. In the final analysis, they are more harsh on themselves than those they chatter about. There are no happy vibes floating around them and nobody to let them off the hook.

The Right Thing for the Wrong Reason

Doing something just because it's the right thing to do doesn't mean it's going to make you feel good. I belonged to a group that does volunteer work for other organizations. I joined because I wanted to meet new people and do something good for my community at the same time. When I first joined, I had a ball. Everybody I met was new to me. Each of the events I selected to work at was of interest. My first event was passing out water to runners at a marathon. It was a gorgeous fall day. The runners seemed delighted to see our outstretched hands with paper cups of water. The other volunteers were chatty and entertaining. My next several events were galas. I think every hospital, charity, and theater had a gala to raise money that year. I went to them all as a volunteer to assist with seating or work the silent auction tables. I loved getting dressed in evening gowns. I loved knowing I was going to have a group of people to hang around with all evening. I planned on being involved with this group for a long time.

But that's not how things turned out. By the second year, the novelty had worn off. Unlike other volunteer work I had performed in the past, this group lacked a passionate common thread—to beat some illness, or save the ecology, or get somebody into Congress. This was a group of good-hearted, well-meaning people, but there just wasn't any passion in being good-hearted and well-meaning. And though many of the people I met through the group were wonderful, I never seemed to connect with them on a social level.

There was also a lot going on in my life at the time. Whenever there's a lot of stress in my world, I end up on my bicycle to clear my head. On the day I have in mind, I needed a good ride. I had a volunteer event on my calendar for the evening, but plenty of time for a ride before the event. While cycling, I got into the zone, and ideas were coming to me fast. It was wonderful. Time passed rapidly, and I failed to show up at the volunteer event. Now I had been doing this volunteer stuff for over a year. I knew well that we often had "no shows." The next day I got a not-so-pleasant e-mail asking about my whereabouts the night of the event from a group member. It was like playing hooky from work and having the boss call to check up. Throughout my entire working years, I only had one boss call me on a sick day, and that call was to make sure I had medicine, not to check up on me. Although the e-mail pretty much turned me off, I kept my commitment to the next event the following week. It was a disaster. My duty was to guard an egress so runners could exit the area. I was doing so against all odds with arrogant coaches and well-meaning family members all trying to get to runners, when one of the walkie-talkie-carrying honchos of the event physically pushed me aside. Not only did I not feel appreciated, but I felt downright assaulted. These were not good vibes.

Volunteering for socially beneficial causes is supposed to make a person feel good. For all of the "good" work I was doing for free, I was getting nothing but bad energy. I was feeling like an unpaid servant. Because the Law of Attraction never fails, it's needless to say I was getting more of the same in all facets of my life. One person needed a free babysitter, another a free résumé, and the energy just spread like an infection. I felt like an unpaid servant, and regardless of my good work, I was just churning out bad energy.

Wheat from the Chaff

Fortunately, we don't really have to think about good and bad. We know when things are good or bad, right or wrong. Our Higher Self communicates to us all the time via our gut. We get a secure feeling when we know without a doubt we are right. We experience a peaceful, warm feeling when we do something right on a small scale. And there's a wonderful, exhilarating feeling way up there on the frequency scale when we do something right on a grand scale. It makes us want to do it again, and again, and again . . . Conversely, we get a certain feeling when we are doing something wrong or bad. It's that sinking I-wish-I-were-anyplace-else-than-here feeling right in the gut. We've all experienced the feelings associated with doing something really bad or really good. We've all experienced the extremes because it's hard to miss the extremes. But it's not the only time our Higher Self communicates.

We have also all had the I-know-when-it's-right feeling when we've done some pretty ordinary thing while connected to good energy. When I was young and married, I decided to take up cake decorating as a hobby. I was really into being the perfect wife and had these visions of topping dinners with fancy cakes. I bought enough cake decorating supplies to make the local Wilton rep a happy camper. I spent hours poring over photos of cakes. I'd play in the kitchen, piping out drop flowers in my spare time. I found cake decorating to be enjoyable. I looked forward to being called upon to bring my cakes to special events. Although my cake decorating was never going to make a hill of beans' difference to anybody in the long run, it made me feel good.

The only part of cake decorating that I found tricky was making butter-cream roses. Butter-cream icing is made from real butter, Crisco, confectioner's sugar, vanilla, and milk. It's extremely temperature-sensitive. If it's too cold, it won't move smoothly through a pastry tube. If the icing is too warm, it breaks down. But it wasn't the temperature of the icing or the pressure I applied to the pastry bag that made the perfect butter-cream rose. It was my energy. I could just feel that first rose being created in my hands. If I got the first rose perfect, the rest of the spray of roses would come to me like child's play. If the first rose failed, I'd spend an hour trying to get enough roses to finish a cake that would never quite look right to me.

I knew in my gut, I just felt it, when the roses were right. When I wasn't on the right frequency, no amount of redoing them worked. I either was on the right frequency or I wasn't. It felt right or it didn't feel right. There was no middle ground.

Line in the Sand

The gut is always the best indicator if something is right or wrong. It never fails. Regardless if your action is small or large, significant or insignificant, public or private, the gut always knows if your action is good or bad, right or wrong, and it lets you know. It's how our Higher Self communicates to us on a very regular basis. If we were always in touch with our Higher Self, our lives would be quite different. The world would be quite different. We would be full of joy. We would have no interest in harming others or the world around us. A person filled with joy knows the world is a grand place with unlimited opportunities. A person filled with joy doesn't need society to draw a line in the sand. But most of us feel joy in limited quantities at limited times. We aren't tuned into the Higher Self. We look to the outside world for guidance.

For the most part, it's highly advisable to abide by the rules, laws, and morals of society. Doing otherwise will only lead to others feeling violated. In turn, the violated will violate, and the entire process will escalate into an enormous negative energy cyclone. That is how wars start. But within the rules, it's possible to follow your heart and do things that make you feel good. Just don't expect that following the rules will give you extra brownie points toward the good things in life. Only your energy can bring those things.

And don't expect that doing good things for the wrong reasons will open doors. Your energy won't be tricked. Feelings bring the goodies into your world. Your feelings! Doing the right things for the wrong reasons will only bring back victim mentality. It works against you in the energy game. Be a good person from the gut and watch your world turn into a good place.

So if you've been pumping out résumés, plastering on a smile, and doing little things that you believe should make you feel good, and the good jobs are still out of reach, it's time to take a personal inventory. You might be doing things that you *think* will make you feel good, instead of doing things that *actually* make you feel good. Take the necessary steps to feel good, not just be good. Let yourself off the hook. Let yourself do some things that get you back onto the feel-good express.

Chapter 19

Timing

When's the best time to look for employment? When you desire employment. That might sound oversimplified, but contrary to popular belief, employers hire year-round. I once listened to a headhunter who told me I'd have to wait for a job because corporations only hire after the first of the year and then only after they have time to review their new budgets and determine how many folks they can bring on board. The truth was his limited corporate clients had a limited number of positions opening after the first of the year, and he wanted me to wait so he could place me and collect the tidy fee. I was a fresh college graduate at the time with enough years of work experience to make me a fairly easy placement. Had I known about this energy stuff way back then, I would not have taken his words at face value.

Happy Holidays

I was beating the bushes to find a good candidate for an opening in December. Although the jobs are there, people just don't look for work in December. They wait until after the holidays when the job market is flooded with other procrasti-nators. My challenge was twofold: Candidates were scarce, and the job was poorly defined. All department heads agreed that we needed somebody to sort out the tool room and monitor inventories, but nobody could determine if this person was to report to the plant manager, the maintenance manager, or the facilities engineer. Without a responsible department, it was impossible to determine duties and design a compensation package. My dilemma was compounded because I was also in the process of seeking a new facilities engineer, and the plant manager was a recent transfer from a sister company. Add to the mix my pending departure. I honestly thought the next per-son to sit in my chair would inherit the problem. Then one night I was making wreaths for Christmas with a friend's daughter. This bright young woman had just become engaged and was chattering about making ends meet, completing her degree, and planning her upcoming wedding. I knew she had a great work ethic, so I told her to apply for the open position. At first, she was hesitant, but I told her it would be more money than she could earn elsewhere, and the company paid for tuition.

In the next few days, I did some internal politicking at the office. I had to convince the maintenance manager that a woman could do the job—yeah, even in 2000s this was an issue. I had to convince the general manager that a woman working on an engineering degree would bring more to the table than just some kid seeking a paycheck. The plant manager agreed with me from the get-go. It took several more weeks, but I was finally able to hire this woman. I never posted the job anywhere after the first of the year.

Five years later, she's still with the company. The lion's share of the costs of her education were picked up by the com-pany. She and her husband have purchased their first house. All of the goodies came her way because she was putting out energy that she desired a job with benefits. Had she not been spinning that energy, she would not have connected with me that snowy December night. So for people who say jobs aren't out there until after the first of the year, or after summer vacation, or after the 12th of the month, or after any other arbitrary date they concoct, I can only say that jobs might not be abundant, but they are out there for people who are serious about getting a job and working their energy.

Seasonal

I must admit, though, that even though it's possible to get work anytime, it's easier to get it during specific times. Obviously, seasonal work is only available during given seasons. When I say "seasonal," that covers a broad range of occupations. In fact, many companies have "seasons" that are not considered seasonal positions. My first HR management position was in automotive manufacturing. I thought that was pretty much a year-round operation, especially in my white-collar capacity. Such was not the case. Under just-in-time (JIT), we only made parts when cars were selling. When they stopped selling, I handed out pink slips to 40 percent of the workforce, then got one myself two weeks later. When I worked as a human resource manager at a string of car dealerships, I was quick to learn that cars sell year-round, but the market for new cars is strongest in good weather and when new models are rolling off the lines. I spent three months out of the year recruiting car salespeople. Some of those folks earn well into six figures with only a high-school diploma and two or three years' experience. Retailing starts beefing up in October. I worked for a company that produced calendars and school yearbooks. We were busy in February, March, April, September, October, and November. The rest of the year, I was passing out pink slips.

Now, you may be saying that's true for the guys on the shop floor, but you're white collar. But white-collar workers fail to see their connection to the blue-collar environment. The e-bubble burst because there were start-ups all over the Web, but very few of those start-ups were producing anything. Only e-companies, such as eBay, that produced a delivery system for other people's stuff withstood the crash. When it comes to commerce, somewhere along the line somebody has to produce a product or a service for a company to survive. If that isn't happening, then even the white-collar folks are in jeopardy. Never forget the bottom line is a number that represents the value added to something somewhere.

Value has to be added to have jobs remain solvent. Even in environments that are almost entirely white-collar, such as banking, something has to add value. If loan officers aren't closing deals, and merchant bankers aren't bringing in the merchant accounts, and the branches aren't bringing in the mixed bag of neighborhood dollars, the bank will close or be swallowed up by a larger institution that wants an instant position in a geographic market. All jobs in all companies are dependent on added value.

In fact, adding value is more apparent in the professions than in any other occupations. Lawyers don't get paid for showing up; they get paid because they have enough billable hours at the end of the month to earn their keep. Professional athletes get nice fat contracts as long as they are productive.

So with my little lecture on the ABCs of business behind me, the best time to seek employment is when the industry you are stepping into is going into its busy season. The higher up the corporate chain, the earlier you need to begin your search.

But let's say you've missed this window of opportunity—should you wait until the following season? Some industries pick up faster or stronger than expected, creating more jobs than were initially slotted. These shifts lead to unforeseen openings throughout the season. Also, some new recruits are not good hires. Some quit. Some are fired, leaving open positions into the busy season.

College Daze

Colleges and universities are in the education business, not the job-placement industry. More of them are now offering help in job placement, but they are still educators. If you are in college, it's your responsibility to get a job. Internships are so incredibly important in the real world, but this importance is often overlooked by college counselors. If you can get an internship, take it! Internships connect you with a company that you may want to consider after college. If you perform well during your internship, you have a history with the company when you knock on its door later. Internships allow you to test-drive your career choice before you take the keys in hand. If you take on an internship in the summer between your junior and senior year and discover you will never connect with that line of work, you have a year to transfer as many credits as possible into another degree. Internships connect you with the energy of the working world. Lots of college kids go back for more and more degrees simply because they fail to connect with the energy of the real world. If you think more and more degrees are the answer, you may want to think again. College is great. I had a ball in college. I know I never could have held the positions I've held without my education. I'm an advocate of college through and though. But from an employer's perspective, I have to accept that the educational system in the United States is generally around ten years behind industry and business. Business sets the trends; education follows them. If employment is your goal, get as much education as necessary to break into your given field. Then wrap your energy around working and leave the college green behind.

Attend every job fair on campus. Even if graduation is three years away, if the job fair is open to you, attend to see what companies are interested in your degree from your school. Generally, the companies that attend those fairs have a limited number of positions that they desire to fill per visit. From the human resource desk, it is a numbers game. College recruiters are sent to selected colleges to return with their quotas filled. Landing one of those entry-level professional jobs is easy when hungry campus recruiters have goals. Landing that same job without the help of the hungry college recruiter several months later is another story.

When I worked for a Fortune 100 company, I was amazed at the frustration the early recruiters endured. They went out early in search of top recruits, only to return with a long list of folks who were thinking things over. Most people continued to mull the idea of working for this company far too long. By the time their résumés crossed my desk for the second or third time, it was well into the end of the school year, and the college entry-level positions had been filled by folks who weren't at the top of their classes, but were certainly at the top of the energy game. They had connected.

So, where's the energy in all of this college recruiting stuff? It's still a major component of the process. Your energy will have to connect with the company representative responsible for campus recruiting. You will have to be feeling the connection between yourself and the world of work. In fact, it's that very desire that will put you head and shoulders above classmates who are showing up because they are checking things out or putting out minimal effort to appease parents who are anxiously waiting for the school experience to end and their college dollars to reap some financial rewards.

When I was in graduate school, PCs were expensive, and few kids had access to any computer other than those in the labs. The Internet was in its infancy, so job seekers had to rely on paper résumés. One night I was in the computer lab late. The guy at the next computer had a pile of classifieds cut out of the paper and was sitting at the computer changing wallpaper. After an hour or so, he decided he was finished for the night. Being older, and more than ticked over his waste of time and resources, I asked him why he was leaving. He told me he couldn't think of a cover letter. I took the top classified ad from his pile and started to dictate a cover letter. He looked at me. I told him to start typing. He did. When he finished, I told him I was a human resource manager during the day, and I'd never hired anybody who failed to apply. When I left, he was still busy responding to ads.

Delays

As the saying goes, timing is everything, and there are times when energy just doesn't connect. There will be times when you are so sure you have the job, then smack, it's not yours. It's really hard to take these blows, especially when you are churning out what you believe to be the best energy possible. The good news is that if you are indeed putting out the best energy possible, things will work out. Oh, it may not be according to your timetable, and perhaps not with the employer you had in mind, but you'll find an employer with higher vibes. Sometimes the really good stuff takes additional time because more energy has to connect. It's fairly easy to connect with a lousy employer. The better stuff is more rare. It takes a little more effort. It's hard to see the big picture when your energy doesn't connect. Don't despair. Keep pumping out the good energy. If you drop your energy, you might miss out on the job that is best for you. That's why so many folks who are close to landing a job lose the opportunity and don't see another one for months. Another old saying tells us that "the darkest hour is just before dawn." If things look dark, illuminate your world with your good energy. Give it time to connect with the best job for you. It works. Get your thoughts and feelings away from lack and start spinning energy back into the world of work. Get your frequency fine-tuned. Start looking for the synchronistic events that show you a job is on its way.

Chapter 20

Reinvention

I grew up in a little town that was metamorphosing from a sleepy farm town to a full-blown suburb, complete with subdivisions, a country club, and other such trappings. The school system was hard-pressed to keep up with the growth, and I was pretty much bounced around into makeshift classrooms. Kindergarten was spent in the basement of a church on one side of town. First grade was spent in the basement of a church on the other side of town. For second grade, I thought I was going to the new school on the wrong side of town, but was transferred at the last minute to the old elementary on the good side of town. I spent the rest of that year dealing with a bus driver who smelled of alcohol and tried to dump me at the wrong building. Ahhh, such is the life of a kid whose home happens to fall on the track that separates the good side of town from the bad side of town. None of this really bothered me much. I was young and unaware of much to do with social status. I took baton lessons and played Barbie with friends on both sides of town.

No, none of these social issues seemed to impact me until Craig's dad built a house that was the talk of the town.

Honestly, that house wouldn't have mattered had it not been built when I was in middle school and had this humongous crush on Craig. So, just about the time that the girls in school were talking more about where they purchased their clothes, the guy I was absolutely ga ga over moved into the town's first mansion.

And, oh, what a mansion. It was on acres and acres of land. A long driveway lit by wrought-iron lights curved its way from the road to the front entrance of the Georgia-style mansion. The land was park-like, perfectly manicured, and home to a variety of flora and fauna. Stables in the back held horses. I'd love to tell you what the inside of this house looked like, but I declined my only invitation—oh, to be young and stupid.

Now, Craig's dad didn't just breeze into town one day and build a grand home. Quite the contrary. He had been a resident for years prior to the building of his pretentious home. Craig and I had been together in the same goofy school pageant in elementary school, so I never thought of Craig as being anything other than just like the rest of us until that house was erected.

That house was so ostentatious that people had extreme opinions about it. One left-leaning, fresh-out-of-college teacher made it clear he thought the man who built that house should be doing more for the poor. Although I didn't have much of an opinion of what the owner should or should not do with his money, the house was problematic to me because Craig and I were no longer equals. Things had changed; Craig was rich, or at least his dad was, and I was far from rich. My teenage grief was only worsened by the fact that I was probably the shyest girl in my class. If our yearbook had had a page for the person most likely to drop dead from any public exposure, my name would have been smack dab in the middle of the page without a photo. Had I been a little less shy, and had Craig not lived in a mansion, perhaps, just perhaps, I would have let him know I was interested. Or perhaps, just perhaps, I would have caught on that he was a tad interested in me. See, even back then, even with all of my shyness, the Law of Attraction was working. I focused on Craig, and eventually he did ask me to come to his house after school and assured me his driver would take me home whenever I wanted to leave. I declined—not out of lack of desire, but out of that damned shyness. He got the vibes; I got cold feet.

Since I gushed around the house mentioning Craig's name more often than I thought, my mother knew I had a crush on Craig. Mom couldn't see any reason why Craig wouldn't eventually ask me out except for my shyness and a few tacky outfits that I noticed went into the wash and never came out. Oh, Mom was clever. But I was very concerned that he lived in the biggest house in town, while I lived in a little house that was hard to tell apart from just about every other little house built in the 1950s. Whenever I fretted about the financial variance between our two families, my parents were quick to point out that Craig's dad had filed bankruptcy in the fifties. The way they mentioned it spoke volumes. It was not an "Oh, WOW, he filed bankruptcy in the fifties and REBOUNDED," but more like "he filed bankruptcy, and that's that." End of story. He was a failure, and he would always be a failure.

I had a hard time understanding my parents' perception. The man had filed bankruptcy—so what? Apparently he was doing something now that was shoveling a lot of money into his coffers. The past was the past. It was over. Unfortunately, a lot of folks get stuck in the past or with a label that's no longer relevant. They get stuck in jobs they hate. They get stuck with friends who suck the energy out of them. They end up in long, drawn-out job searches only to get some job they despise when the search ceases. They hear a label so many times that they simply accept it.

On the flip side, plenty of successful folks reinvent themselves all the time. There's a California governor who went from bodybuilder to actor to governor and he wasn't even an American! Think of how different his life would be if he had decided he would be a bodybuilder forever. What would have happened had he not reinvented himself? Okay, that's a famous guy, but a lot of everyday folks reinvent themselves. Some do it to survive. His job had been shipped to China. Her spouse took a hike and left her with a legacy of debt. But instead of focusing on their lack, they take an inventory of their likes, their dislikes, their talents, their skills and experiences, and they go within to find their value to society. They look around and determine a market for themselves, and they re-package themselves accordingly. They unload the labels, they look at failures as learning experiences, they honestly believe they have something of value that can better society, and they move forward. They reinvent themselves. They think and act like the man in my hometown who went from flat broke, bankrupt, to a successful businessman with the biggest house in town. He didn't sit around worrying about his next job. He created it. He had a company in a brand-new building within two decades from his low point. Although my parents and a lot of other local people couldn't get beyond his bankruptcy, this man got way beyond it. He certainly didn't let "broke" define him.

Reinventing oneself might sound like a daunting task. The truth is that reinventing oneself is less painful than allowing an irrelevant title to serve as a prison, with well-meaning friends and family as the prison guards. To reinvent yourself, go back to your "root want" and begin walking toward it. Yes, it involves leaving your comfort zone, but you will soon find greater comfort in your journey to a new life.

New Is Fun!

The Higher Self is always game for a new experience. In fact, the Higher Self thrives on new experiences because they create joy. When the mind gets wrapped around something new, the Higher Self wakes up and is ready to jump right in. Without new experiences the Higher Self doesn't really have much to do other than hang around and wait for you to get sick and tired of low-frequency crap. But, get a new idea, get a new goal, get a new vision, and your energy starts to soar. When I decided to open my own company, ideas began to overtake me. I went from living from paycheck to paycheck to not thinking about money at all. Oh, the money wasn't rolling in at the time, and my accountant was still worried about me, but the ideas just kept flowing. I had ideas for the services I wanted to offer. I had marketing ideas. I had a vision of my new Web site running through my head. I recall one day telling a friend to get out of my way because I was on a roll. He thought I had completely flipped. He tried to rein me in, but I was operating at such a high frequency that things were happening too fast for me to listen to his fear-filled words. I had to move forward.

Most people, employed or unemployed, are afraid to let things get to "spin mode." To avoid it, they fill their days, and nights, and weekends with stuff. They see the same friends, eat at the same restaurants, play the same courses. If you ask them how they feel, they use words like tired, busy, bored. They race from commitment to commitment, but they long for something new and exciting, but they can't put their finger on it.

Marketing firms earn their keep by trying to tap into our need for excitement. Just look at what cruise lines spend a fortune marketing: a million things to do on a floating resort. Automobile companies want to sell us a free, open road. And the ad that currently tickles my funny bone is the razor ad that equates shaving with becoming goddesses in paradise. I shave my legs daily and have yet to reach my inner goddess, although there have been times I've inadvertently reached an inner layer of skin. We may not find a million things to excite us on a cruise, or an open road with a new car, or an inner goddess with a razor, but we will continue to search for things to feed the need for newness within us.

Too often, we are conditioned to think that "something new" is mountain climbing, or finding a new lover, or skydiving—something spectacular. But the Higher Self only needs to experience something new, not something outrageous. It could be as simple as taking up gardening or finding a new friend. But because we think doing something new must involve an activity like mountain climbing, our logical left brain looks at new experiences with trepidation. If we can't mountain climb, we don't see the point in taking on something new that will just eat up more valuable time.

Ironically, successful folks don't take unnecessary risks, and they don't accept boredom as a part of life. In fact, they detest boredom. They find boredom to be a waste of time, and they can't stand to waste time. They try to jam as much into a finite lifetime as possible. At work, they become more efficient to squeeze out boredom. They listen intently when a new concept hits their radar. They listen to old toads with experience, and they listen to the young up-and-comers who are setting the trends. They listen to their peers. They listen to the clerks at the bank and the CEOs. Their Higher Self is always alert to any concept that might be worth a spin. They question just about everything—the locations of buildings, the shift in demographics, the economy, the ecology, the business model a colleague has decided to adopt. They read, they learn, and they know they will never know everything.

On the contrary, folks who accept the status quo claim to know everything. They are fearful of new ideas. They have no desire to learn anything new. They work in the same field, industry, or job for decades even if they hate it. They find reading to be a waste of time. They pretty much talk about the same thing, time and time and time again. They think they are interesting, even the life of the party, but most others would not agree.

If people fail to see the value in new ideas, or new concepts, they become stagnant. They hang onto their own small world and outdated titles. If they have a label, good or bad, they are glued to it for life. So, they stay in the same job year in and year out, and refrain from taking any risks that might improve their lot in life.

Injured Workers

Outdated labels and titles are truly harmful for people who have failed in the past or have been harmed in an accident. Those who have failed may hold onto their failure title, and energy, for life. It becomes impossible for them to lift themselves to a higher mode of thinking or high frequency. This is true for people who have suffered a workplace injury as well. If they are unable to return to their former positions, and if they are unable to feel themselves as anything other than an injured worker, they become a victim of not only their accident, but also their thinking and energy. As they try in vain to hold onto their former identity, they may become consumed in anger at their former employer, at themselves, at the world in general. This anger becomes the station they are always tuned into, regardless of its message. Once plugged into this station, it becomes difficult, if not impossible, to get a clear message from the Higher Self. Higher Self is standing by, ready and willing to assist in the reinvention process. It wants new experiences and is downright bored with the angry routine. It's ready to try something new, rewarding, and lucrative. It just needs its message to be received.

Tingle

Then there are the times when there is a "tingling." A message from the Higher Self is getting through. At first, it's exhilarating. All sorts of things start to happen. Folks who start to get the message develop a mission, they have a goal, and they have energy on their side. They start to get pumped up to reach their new goal. They start looking into the education that's needed for their new job. Or they start to polish up a résumé to shift career paths. If they are looking into opening their own company, they start looking at getting a loan, or building an office in their garage, or going to a couple of Chamber of Commerce meetings. A little synchronicity starts happening. Yep, the energy starts connecting. They bump into somebody who knows somebody who can open a few doors. They get a piece of junk mail that gets them thinking about where to send those résumés. They run into a buddy whose company is seeking a consultant. Things are moving along. Of course, there are a few bumps in the road and a few missed signals, but that's part of doing something new.

Then, for whatever reason, they get a little shiver of fear. Perhaps the schooling is costly or lengthy. It may be the market is a little slow at the moment. They soon forget the synchronicity, and they buy into that shiver of fear. The energy machine that's been bringing in the good stuff starts twiddling its thumbs, waiting for the next request. Nothing happens. The energy shifts from high-frequency flowing to a lower vibration, to pretty much choked-up. And nothing happens.

Pickin' Friends

There are times when somebody, I'll call him Buddy, is so tuned into his Higher Self and has so much synchronicity going on that things are on full-speed-ahead. Oh, there are still a few bumps at times, but those are just bumps. Then, just as things look like they are going to work out, some well-meaning family member or friend decides to talk some "sense" into Buddy. It goes something like this: That well-meaning friend is quick to point out that Buddy has a good job—it sucks, but he has a 401k and it's only 17 years until retirement. Those years are going to breeze by, so why would Buddy want to take a risk now? For what? Buddy could fail and have nothing. The big zero.

So, Buddy goes from being gung-ho to a little fearful. Then another well-meaning bloke joins in the fear choir. Now the fear frequency is pulling in more and more fear from friends, family, and the clerk at the gas station. The synchronicity stops. The energy has gone from high-frequency, get-things-going energy to low-frequency, fearful energy. Soon, the vision is dimming. Six months down the road, the light is extinguished altogether. Buddy is sitting at the bar with his choir mates having a pint and congratulating himself on not being a damned fool who risked his pension on a dream. So, instead of going for the extra education, or taking out that small business loan, or going for a job that holds some allure, Buddy is back onto the safe path—back to the little house, the taco chips, and the Honda Civic.

The old saying that "birds of a feather flock together" rings true in the world of energy. Folks who know everything flock together. They cook wienies together, watch football on TV together, may even know the best plays of their favorite players by heart. But they aren't doing anything to broaden their worlds. After all, what more is there? And risk, well, with a mortgage, and kids, and a wife to feed, there simply isn't time to think of something other than bringing home a paycheck. So they tune out the Higher Self and hang out with birds of a feather. They don't look at the world around them and find the opportunities.

As I mentioned before, if you're like most people, your friends earn the same as you, give or take 20 percent. Oh, you might say you know a couple of rich folks, but do you hang around with these acquaintances and watch the game week in and week out together? Probably not. Your rich "friend" is probably looking into something more interesting than the same old, same old. Oh, this isn't to say he hates sports. He probably loves sports—like skiing, preferably in the Alps. She likes sports, too, and is at the polo field on occasion. If you see him at the ballpark, it's probably in the high-priced seats with a couple of business associates. They didn't learn to ski and ride by sitting on the sidelines watching somebody else get paid big bucks to kick a ball.

To increase your earnings, start hanging out with people who have great jobs and are tuned into their Higher Self. Oh, they probably don't call it Higher Self. They probably call it their "gut," those feelings they get when a deal feels right or wrong. Call it whatever you like, once you tune into it, you too can have the best jobs, the best caves, the best food, and, of course, the hottest babes. Friends matter. Birds of a feather flock together.

Remember back in middle school or high school when you had a friend or two that your parents detested? They would dissuade you from keeping company with that character, worried about the influence he might have on you, and they would threaten you with being grounded until you were an old toad if you were caught with that character. They went to all of these extremes because they wanted good things for you. The friends you hang with today have just as much influence on you as the characters you hung with as a teenager. You are connecting with their energy, you are accepting their visions, you are accepting their limitations, and you are finding yourself living within their means.

Now you might be thinking that it's hard to make new friends. Bull. I had the same problem, so I hung out with a bunch of folks who were getting more and more broke and worse and worse jobs. Here's the kicker: I was blaming it all on a concept that I learned in graduate school. I assumed women over a certain age weren't marketable so we end up going from good jobs to bad jobs to no jobs. And I accepted it. As soon as

I embraced this belief, I found a whole bunch of women struggling with employment and money. As more and more of these women came into my life, I never thought that maybe I had an energy problem. No sireee.

Then I got tired of being old and broke. I just woke up and decided enough was enough. My Higher Self had a field day. I had good idea after good idea. I was meeting people left and right. My old friends starting melting away like April snow. Oh, it's not that I've abandoned them, or that I don't care about them, it's just that a 20-minute talk with any of them is like being around an energy vampire.

Once I plugged into good energy and began to reinvent myself, I went from a burned-out HR manager to a laid-off HR manager, to a self-employed consultant. It took some time and a lot of work, but it was a process that put me on top of my game. Along the way, I met wonderful people and have made some wonderful friends. Some are married, some are young, some are older, but they are all great people, and I enjoy the company of each and every one of them. They are my new friends.

Reinvention vs. Lying

Reinvention is not the same thing as lying. Lying about your past will catch up with you at some point in time. It's not worth the risk. If you are seeking employment, someone somewhere made a mistake. We tend to label mistakes as bad things, but mistakes are learning tools. You may have picked the wrong occupation, or the wrong company, or the wrong job. You may have done this several times. You may have chosen to stay in a region in which all economic indicators say it's time to pack up and move onto greener pastures. Or the company you worked for overstaffed and then downsized. Or it may have decided to use contract labor. Or it may have found a world economy too tough for survival. So, what can you do? Start again, reinvent. Reinventing takes the good and the bad, reaps the marketable stuff, skill-sets, education, experiences, and repackages them into something that holds value for society. It's positive energy. It's high-frequency stuff that pulls in more high-frequency stuff. On the flip side, lying is low frequency and can only bring in more garbage.

When reinventing, don't waste time with finger-pointing, finding fault, or other negative activities that will serve no purpose toward your goals. It's easy enough to say that your former boss was a jerk, or the stupid company moved overseas, but what will all this negativity get you? Another jerk of a boss or another company just chomping at the bit to move to China. You are above all of that nonsense. Focus on the new you—the brand-new you. Focus on the you that has taken a lifetime of experiences and repackaged them into something of great value.

Your Higher Self wants to start anew. It thrives on new experiences. Once you get those good vibes out, the synchronicity will kick in. You just need to make up your mind, focus, get it all together, and let go of the old you. Travel light. Travel on high-frequency energy.

Chapter 21

Make Something Happen

If you want to get a job, you have to make something happen. From an energy perspective, get your energy tuned into the energies of the productive folks who pass out the good jobs in society. From the more traditional job-search side of the equation, if you don't ferret out jobs, if you don't fine-tune your selling tools, if you don't make the calls, if you don't get yourself in front of hiring folks, somebody else will get the jobs. You have to make something happen. It's impossible to play the employment game from the sidelines. You have to jump into the arena wholeheartedly.

As a human resource person, I've coached lots of people looking for work. They've asked me to write their résumés, help them determine their markets, and assist them in the job-search process. For the most part, I've been able to help. But there are times when somebody will ask me for help and it becomes rapidly apparent they don't want help; they want sympathy. They only come to me to pacify a family member who feels their unemployment is becoming a lifestyle. Don't get me wrong—they never call me whining. Quite the contrary, they call or show up all gung-ho, telling me exactly what job they want. They may even have the name of a company they'd like to work for in mind. They have me spend a day or two fine-tuning their résumé. They send out a résumé to their prospective employer of choice. Then the process stops. If they don't get *the* job, or they don't get hired at *the* company, they simply do nothing. They don't make any phone calls. They don't look at other employment avenues. They do absolutely nothing. In one case, I spent two days creating a résumé for a woman who had been a housewife for more than a decade, pulling out her skill-set, presenting it in a manner that would make it sellable in the marketplace. She sent it out to one employer, and when she didn't get the job, all movement stopped. From an energy perspective, she implied that if something fell into her hands, she'd take it; from a traditional job-search perspective, she was a hard sell lacking tenacity.

Tenacity means knowing your want and being willing to continue to pump out good energy when you'd rather call a friend and whine for an afternoon. Tenacity is moving forward when you want to give up. Tenacity is making something happen.

When it comes to seeking employment, there is only one specification you must keep in mind when making something happen: Do something that addresses the root of your primary goal or want. If your goal is to be in management at a company in order to earn a lot of money to generate a lot of income, then your root goal is earning a lot of money. Therefore, to prime the pump and get your energy attached to your root desire, you need to get into a line of work that either generates income rapidly or has the capacity to generate large quantities of income such as sales. If your goal is to work at a given company because of the company's environmental record, then your root goal is to work for an environmentally responsible company, not necessarily any given company. So you must find an avenue into an environmentally responsible company. Your goal may be to work in a given capacity in a specific industry or company. Then your root goal is employment in that industry or company. By doing something that moves you toward your root desire, or want, you get your energy wrapped around that want.

Ring around the Posie

Say you love flowers. You don't just love flowers; you have an obsession with flowers. When you flushed out all of your wants, you decided that if you could be anything in the world, you'd have your own little flower shop. If you don't have the funds to open your own, then get a job at a flower shop. In this case, even a bottom-of-the-rung job would do. Although I am not usually an advocate of starting at the bottom, in this case you wouldn't be starting at the bottom—you'd be getting paid to learn your craft. There's a really big difference. Starting at the bottom means stuck at the bottom. Getting paid to learn your craft might start you at the bottom, but eventually put you at the top.

So, you get a job with a local florist. What do you actually get? You get knowledge of the industry as an insider. Although you may just be bloomin' to open your own shop, you probably don't know one thing about suppliers, distribution models, the impact of the big box grocer on profit margins, or how to become established with Internet companies such as flowers.com. You need to learn which bridal shows bring in the bucks and which drain your wallet. A florist needs to accept major credit cards. You might as well learn all about merchant accounts on somebody else's nickel. Your knowledge of flowers is, of course, important, but there's a lot more to running a flower shop than flowers. It's true of any industry.

With good energy, synchronicity will kick in, and it could play out in several ways. You could take the job and love it. As in industry insider, you'd hear about the competition prior to the outside world, and you'd end up purchasing an old mom-and-pop shop that's looking for a new owner.

Or, you might end up becoming a landscape designer for the shop.

Or, after a few months at the local florist, you realize that you love flowers, but you certainly don't have much enthusiasm for the floral industry. It's nothing like what you expected. Instead of playing with flowers, you are dealing with demanding brides and flower distributors. So, what happens? Since you were learning the industry on somebody else's nickel, you can walk away and not lose a dime. Due to synchronicity, one of the customers picks up on your sense of style prior to your departure and asks you to help decorate his place. So, your love of flowers got you into one place, and your sense of style took you onto another path. Had you not taken that job at the flower shop, you'd never have met that guy who took your career on another path.

The scenarios are infinite because you took your good energy and ran with it. You let synchronicity kick in. Most importantly, you kept your mind open to new opportunities.

Management Training

Say your root goal is to work in management in a given industry or company. Get your foot in the door by getting a job with the company, but make absolutely sure it's a position that helps you. Lots of positions will get you in the door, but only a few will get you onto the elevator going up. Make sure the position you take will give you recognition and knowledge. This position should get the powers-that-be to consider you for the next several steps on the corporate ladder. The only, and I mean only, time I'd advocate taking an entry-level position is if it were an entry-level managerial position that gives you a broad base of knowledge about the company and has avenues to actually put you on the fast track to an actual career with the company.

Although any human resource rep who has the responsibility of filling such positions will gladly tell you they are the fast track to management, lots of the folks who take those positions end up departing a few years later once they have a couple of years of managerial experience on their résumés. There are only so many top jobs at any company, and the last two decades of weeding out the middle have shed thousands of mid-management jobs. So, if you are going in through the entry-level management-training program, make sure you have everybody on board. Let the human resource person know your goals. Make sure your boss is secure enough to let you grow. Don't kid yourself—many bosses are more stuck than anybody. They're stuck in a job they don't like. They're stuck with a mortgage. They're stuck in life. Those folks get bitter and end up keeping those below them below them for as long as possible. They spew out lots of bad vibes.

If you take an entry-level management job, get noticed. If the company rag doesn't send around somebody to interview you as a new hire, search them out and get your mug on their rag. Attend any and all meetings for face time. Look for the quickest way make your mark and hit your target.

Back Door Is Open

If you absolutely must work for a given company and you can't get your foot in the front door, knock on the back door— their competitor's door. Many times it's easier to get a good job in a company by starting with its competitor than it is to go through the given company's management-training program. Just look at the movement of CEOs. Many of the top folks are lured away from competitors, not groomed from within the mammoth corporations.

I like to think of corporations as small children. If you give little Joey a toy, he may or may not want it. But give that same toy to little Jimmy in front of little Joey, and you have a fight on your hands, complete with screaming and grabbing. Corporations are pretty much the same. The last people they tend to look at when it comes to filling positions of power are the unemployed. They perceive folks without employment to be in some way flawed. After all, if the unemployed had any marketable skills, they'd be working. Of course, in the age of downsizing, right-sizing, and off-shoring, this is downright ridiculous. Still, most hiring folks look at gaps before they look at skill-sets. They look at the skill-set from the competition with the most interest. Just like little Joey who had no interest in the toy until little Jimmy found some value in it, then little Joey not only wanted the toy, he *really* wanted it.

Another backdoor route is to get a job with a company that does business with your employer of choice, as long as you can do so without signing a confidentiality agreement. Companies hire from their suppliers all the time. Oh, they don't admit it, but you only need to look at the confidentiality agreements used by many to see there's a real concern about such move-ment of employees between companies. If you are seeking a job in the advertising department of a large company and can't seem to get anybody to look at your portfolio, then get a job at the company that does the printing and make sure you become the key person between their jobs and the little print shop. Once you build the relationship, you will be able to start your campaign to get in their door.

Only by making something happen can you move your energy into the world you desire. Make something happen, get your good energy wrapped around working in a given field, or for a certain amount of money, or whatever your root desire encompasses. And do so with an open mind. You might think you desire to work at a given company and find yourself at home with its competitor.

Get Creative

Sometimes getting a job takes a little creativity. The degree of creativity is a function of the type of job you are seeking. Skydiving onto the top of a bank to get a job in a bank might just land you in jail—not advisable. But purchasing a mailing list to get the name, address, and contact name of every company in a given industry is a great idea. A mailing list will cost around $500 for the first list. It's easy to buy lists on the Internet. Internet transactions are quick, and the list is in your possession generally within 24 hours. Once you are a customer, you may get offers and price breaks if you purchase additional lists.

The hardest part about ordering a list is determining the parameters. Start with your major parameters. For most people, type of company, industry, or geography are the primary parameters. It's a good idea to include the credit rating of a company. It's senseless to get a job for a company that doesn't pay its bills. There are laws that state companies have to pay their employees, but there are companies out there that don't hold those laws in the highest regard.

List companies offer several formats for the data, so make sure you order it in a format that makes it easy for you to manipulate. I've purchased lists and had them e-mailed to me in Excel since I am proficient in the program. You will probably have to buy 5,000 names. Make sure you have the capability to sort the data once it's yours.

The contact name should be the name of the department head or the head of the company. Don't send your letters to human resources. They generally file such letters for one year. Send it to the top banana, who will forward it with some little scribbled note to human resources.

So what do you do with a list? Craft the best letter of your life. Set it aside for a day or two. Read it. Then fix it. Set it aside for a day or two, read it, then fix it. In about a week or two, you will have a letter that will tell any prospective employer what you can do and why you want to do it for them. Print the letters on fine business stationery. Print each envelope to go with the letter. This isn't a time to think of labels. Personalize each letter.

Statistics vary on this type of cold calling. Depending on your letter, your audience, and your skill-set, you should get around three interested responses for every 100 letters mailed. Of course, with really great energy, the numbers mean very little. It only takes one letter to move you from unemployed to employed. I've personally found that the rejections come in quickly, and the offers start coming in within 45 days. Also, although most list companies guarantee their lists to be 90 percent accurate, I've found they are closer to 80 percent accurate. Don't be surprised when some of your letters are returned.

One of the side effects of getting creative about your job search is that creativity will soon be flowing throughout your entire life. I'd been working day and night on this manuscript. I barely had time to maintain the two clients I'd decided to hold onto throughout this writing process. So, what happened? My home needed some major repairs, and I had some off-the-wall idea to put my own photography on the wall that would soon be going up in my home. Now this idea wouldn't be so unusual had I not put down my camera a decade ago and pretty much decided that my photography days were over. Digital cameras didn't interest me. My old 35mm camera is of the heavy-metal variety that produces excellent photographs, but weighs two-and-a-half pounds before special lenses. Now that I've picked up my camera again, my thoughts are clearer. When I am seeking just the right light, I am getting flooded with ideas for this book. The Higher Self is on overdrive. Creative ideas are productive ideas.

Presentation

A few companies at some levels request a PowerPoint presentation about you. Most job seekers will never need to use one, but putting one together is a great experience to raise your energy and see how you present yourself and your skills to prospective employers. They are great for extracting your talents and values.

As technology shifts, it's safe to say that HR folks will find more and more creative ways of requesting information and weeding out candidates. Stay abreast of technology. Keep your creative juices flowing.

Chapter 22

Flying Solo

Throughout this book, I often mention the concept of value. Value is far more than taking an inventory of what you can do. Skill-set inventories tend to be restrictive and constrict a job seeker's options and energy. Unearthing your value expands your opportunities and energy. To unearth your value, simply look at yourself as an entire person instead of just a limited skill-set. Your skill-set, of course, is still part of you, but it's just a part, not the only thing you have to offer the world. Your skill-set might be what you've done for a decade, your degree, or what your parents wanted you to be when you grew up. Your value includes your skill-set, your talents, your likes, your desires, your daydreams, and your personality. It's far greater than a degree or a decade of work experience. I heard that the multimillion-dollar Cirque du Soleil was the brainchild of a talented juggler. Most people wouldn't consider juggling to be a real moneymaker in the real world. But when juggling was expanded to its optimal value in the realm of entertainment, it certainly exceeded a minuscule skill-set.

Once you start to focus on your value, all sorts of things bubble to the surface. You start to look around and discover things that other people can't do, don't want to do, or don't have time to do that you can do better, quicker, more efficiently. Expanding your perception also allows you to look in new directions and at new opportunities. You may decide an entire career change is in order, or you may discover something you love has the potential to generate income. What you love to do may make you rich, or it may only make you happy, but both are rewarding. You may also decide that the best way to do what you want to do for a living is to do it on your own.

There was a time when self-employment was considered something for the risk-loving entrepreneur. Now it's more for the risk-averse types. They see more security in spreading their employment over several "employers" instead of working for one company and hoping it lasts. The glue that once held employees to employers is being dissolved. Companies used to pay for pension plans and health insurance, along with a variety of other perks. In the past two decades, employer-funded pension plans have been replaced with employee-funded 401k plans. Health insurance premiums are now the responsibility of the employee. Downsizing has become a word that equates to lack of employer loyalty. Companies now look for legal ways to off load old toads. This erosion of the employee/employer relationship has made self-employment a viable option with several perks.

The Pros

The self-employed have flexibility. They can take a day off when necessary and move work around to fit their schedule. I'm self-employed. I've found myself taking long bike rides on beautiful days and writing employee handbooks at 3 A.M. when a case of insomnia hits. Self-employed folks don't have to worry about being laid off. They work for several employers instead of one. When one client no longer needs their services, they move on to another one while maintaining an income stream from a variety of other clients simultaneously.

Working for oneself is liberating. The self-employed person is not fenced in by employee handbooks or time clocks. Of course, the self-employed need to have discipline. It takes discipline to be forever prospecting. It takes discipline to work through a weekend to accommodate a client's schedule. It takes discipline to set aside a portion of each payment for lean times, taxes, and to grow the business. But for those with the drive and desire to make it work, self-employment is an entirely freeing experience.

The financial rewards have the potential to far exceed the earning potential in a corporate position, and tax laws are in favor of the self-employed. Oh, that's not to say if you take the route of self-employment that you are going to set up a Web site and immediately become rich. Most self-employed folks have a few lean years. To make a success of self-employment, you need to have a plan, commitment, perseverance, and, of course, energy.

High Energy Equals Success

Your energy as a self-employed person will bring in clients or push them away. Good energy will bring the right people into your world at the right time. Bad energy will have you standing at that station as your train pulls out. All of life is energy, and for the self-employed, energy keeps their coffers filled. The self-employed need a lot of good energy flowing to keep the synchronicity in motion. And, as you know by now, your energy is a function of your feelings. So, how do you feel about self-employment? Does the concept turn you on? Do you get all jazzed up just thinking about working for yourself? Or does it leave you shaking in your boots? Are you envious of other self-employed folks, or do you wonder how they manage to sleep at night? Do you feel that you can develop an income stream in rapid order, or do you feel you will be scraping by for years? All of these feelings need to be considered before you set up your Web site, hang out your shingle, or put that first ad in the local paper.

I am self-employed and an advocate of the lifestyle. I've had hard times and good times, and I know firsthand that energy plays an enormous role in the success of my business. When I feel something good is coming my way, it does. But there are still times when I feel there's going to be a drought. Yep, even in writing this stuff, I occasionally toss everything I know about energy out the window and watch the hard times come my way. I go into panic mode and send out letters, make phone calls, listen to negative friends. I flounder. In time, I just get tired of the struggle and do things that pump up my energy. I get away from the negative crowd and reconnect with the positive people in my life, and lo and behold a random client or two comes my way from an unexpected avenue. Therefore, it's not surprising that businesses go in cycles. It's human nature to fall into the clutches of fear every now and then. Fear thinking happens a lot in the first five years of self-employment. It's a primary factor in the closure of so many infant businesses. Fear thinking is time–consuming, and for the self-employed it's money-consuming as well.

Garnering Support

If you are planning on flying solo, make sure you have the support of your significant other, family, and friends. Your feelings and your family's feelings are key to your success. Therefore, it's important to know how your family members feel, really feel, about you going solo before you take flight. Sit down and talk honestly. Discuss money. Then discuss it again. Since your income may be sporadic initially, and you will have to put some of your income aside for taxes, expenses, advertising, and to grow the business, it may take several months for you to be earning enough to feel like you are contributing financially to the family. How does your family feel about supporting you? How do you feel about them supporting you? Be honest. It's not just feelings about money that need to be discussed. Your hours may be flexible, or they may be long, depending on the type of work you are considering. Discuss how things will get done around the house and how you will be available to take on additional chores or no chores at all. Don't assume your loving family will love you working 24/7 to get your venture off the ground and be thrilled with cooking, cleaning, and attending to your every need. Even the most loving of families want to know they are working for a concrete result. Airing out feelings from the start can make the transition to self-employment smooth.

Examine Your Feelings

Address all of your own feelings as well. Some people are just chomping at the bit to get into the realm of the self-employed. These people prefer to put together two or three income streams over a "real job" any day. They want to expand their earning potential. But some people just can't get a comfortable feeling about self-employment with all of its perks. By taking an honest inventory of your feelings prior to setting up shop, you will save yourself a lot of emotional and financial pain. Although I am an advocate of self-employment, I am currently working with a woman who's dead set against it. She's a prime candidate for self-employment. She has a skill-set that's in demand at a lot of places. She's too costly for most small and mid-sized companies to consider for a full-time job. She's outgoing, friendly, and gregarious, the type of person who doesn't fade away at Chamber of Commerce meetings and other networking events. She has a significant other who is on board with her becoming self-employed and a passel of kids who'd love to have Mommy's schedule a little more flexible. As I've assisted her in her job-search process, I've watched her turn away contract work on several occasions. Considering she's a prime candidate for self-employment, it took a little digging to unearth her disdain for the idea. A long history emerged, one in which she was always at the mercy of others until she landed a position at a top company with a comfortable compensation package, benefits, and a title. Her identity and strength come from her employment. She's terrified that without a real job she will lose her power. Self-employment is not for her at this time, although I hate to have her not even take a peek at it because occasionally there are cases when a person takes the plunge into self-employment only to be offered a full-time position with a client after a few weeks or months.

Taking Flight

It takes both kinds of people to make our economy run well—those who want the corporate cover and those who want to be liberated from corporate chains. If you are just chomping at the bit to have the liberation of self-employment, if you have a skill-set, talent, or product that is marketable, if you have the support of family and friends, then by all means start doing your homework. Check out your market. Read books specifically written for those who want to work for themselves. Write a comprehensive business plan. Draft a realistic budget and tuck in an extra 15 percent or more for unexpected expenses. Talk with an attorney about incorporating. Hire a good accountant.

Once you have all of the business stuff under your belt, get your energy up. Focus on the value you will be bringing to your clients or customers. Feel yourself getting your first client. Feel your first day on the job as a self-employed person. Feel yourself selling your services, getting excited about your company, getting more and more clients. Visualize your first check! Feel yourself buying something wonderful. Now feel it happening over and over again . . .

Chapter 23

The World around You

There's no denying we are physical beings on a physical planet. Oh, yes, we are made of energy, and our energy connects with other like energy, but we still need to know what's going on around us, especially when we are job searching. The trick is being in touch enough with events to be current without getting sucked into negative energy vortexes.

The Ground Floor

The media is a mixed blessing. Job searchers need to know the trends—what industries are moving out and what industries are moving in. If you are seeking employment, you need to know who is building a new facility in your community when the foundation is being poured, not after the name is on the door. By the time the name is on the door, the hiring is pretty well complete, especially at the higher-end positions. When it comes to jobs, the ground floor means getting the goods on the new industries when the ground is being broken.

Any business transaction has opportunity for somebody. If a company is sold, there will be a change of some personnel.

There might be some layoffs, there might be some restructuring, but there will also be a contingent of people who simply don't want to hang around with the changes the new management is proposing. They move on quickly, leaving their jobs ripe for the picking.

Even small business transactions can have a big impact if you are the person who gets the new job. If some mom-and-pop restaurant was just left to some out-of-towner who knows just enough about the local market to go belly-up, and you happen to write restaurant reviews on the side, you can present yourself as a one-person marketing guru for the new guy. Every business transaction employs somebody, somewhere, somehow. A new housing development will need contractors, from the sewer to the roofers. A new hotel will need an interior decorator, a landscape architect, a chef, and the list goes on and on. A new charter school will need teachers. A new church will need a secretary. Even little one-person businesses need a lawyer and an accountant. The time to go for these jobs is the beginning. Find out who's overseeing the projects. Get in on the ground floor.

Trends

A job seeker also needs to be aware of trends in industries outside of a given region. If jobs are moving out of your region, you either have to pack your bags or shift your skill-set and energy to align with incoming industries. With new types of industries sprouting up, the demand for labor will be shifting faster than ever. People who are in the know about industries will be able to get their résumés out early, have the most information to present to the human resource person, and have the highest probability of landing a job.

The types of companies that will be hiring over the next several years are expected to be small start-ups. Start-ups are created by visionaries. These people have ideas. They have their entire life savings on the line. Some are mortgaged right down to their underwear. They are working 18 hours a day to make their vision a reality. If the company is small enough, you will be sitting across from the owner during an interview. If you are sitting across from a person whose entire life is tied up in the company, you must know every little positive thing that's been put in print about that company and that individual. It's important. Walking into a start-up and telling the owner you didn't read the article about his company in the local paper is an invitation to the exit door.

Government Jobs

When we think of government jobs, we tend to think of haggard people with frowns in buildings either built in the 1950s or erected later under the design of some person whose apparent goal in life was to make the building a work of art, but user-hostile. Lots of folks would prefer a nice trip to the dentist over a trip to see a government employee. There's no way around it, the United States government hires a lot of people, but those aren't the only jobs created by the government.

Most bills—the kinds that are legislated, not those pesky ones that show up in your mailbox—create work for somebody. Granted, a lot of the work they create is for lawyers, but not all of it. As a human resource person, most of my work is a function of some law or another. Oh, there was a time when the personnel lady's biggest day was when she pulled off the company picnic without one employee's kid falling into the lake, but those days are long gone. I work because of FLSA, Title VII, FMLA, and ADA laws that impact employers.

When a law is passed to protect some endangered species, somebody has to be hired by the Department of Natural Resources to make sure that the law is being obeyed. Some scientists have to determine if these critters are repopulating, and if so, how many and where. Some techie is going to have to make some tracking tool to assist the scientist. I think you are getting the picture.

In 1999, the Gramm-Leach-Bliley Act was passed. Quiz time, who knows what the heck this is? Buzzzz, time's up! You might not know the act by name, but it's a fair bet it's impacted you time and time again. It's a banking act that requires financial institutions to protect the privacy of customers. It's the reason you get that too-small-to-read notice from your bank and insurance company once or twice a year. It's the law. And it created a lot of work. IT folks had to be hired to secure systems. Risk assessors had to be hired to determine risks to data. Maintenance folks had to be hired to build physical systems to secure documents that contained sensitive data. All these folks got work because the government passed a law.

So if you think the day-to-day workings of the government are boring, you are probably right, but they also might be inadvertently creating a job for you. Therefore, it's in your best interest to stay abreast of the laws that are being passed.

The government is the biggest employer in the United States. Ironically, the government payrolls swell under administrations that claim they are against big government. It's wise for any job seeker to know what's going on in all levels of government—federal, state, and local. And before I shut the door on government, there's one more topic that has to be addressed briefly. The defense industry is 100-percent dependent on the government. If the government needs Hummers and planes, then those industries are humming. If it looks like peace is coming soon, those industries will be cutting back or scrambling for non-government business.

A friend of mine was one of the first women in the state of California to own a tool-and-die shop. Her major customer was a military supplier. As a minority supplier, she got lots of contracts—until the military work dried up. She might have been a trailblazer as a woman in a man's industry, but she was still dependent on the whims of Uncle Sam.

Of Interest

Interest rates can also create or destroy jobs. Any industry that's dependent on customers who must finance are interest-rate sensitive. A prime example of such an industry is real estate. Real estate as an industry impacts hundreds of thousands of jobs. When we think of real estate, we think of the transfer of a home from one person to another. Even in this simple transaction, a title insurance person needs to be involved, and unless it's a cash transaction, a banker has to be involved. The banker has to rely on the credit-reporting company in order to make a decision, so the credit-reporting industry is involved. Transferring a title from one person to another involves a notary. But most transactions are not this simple. Most involve a Realtor, or two, or three. In order to get a house ready for sale, most sellers have to do some work to the house or property. Some sellers perform the work personally, but many hire painters, masons, gardeners, and an array of other craftspeople to enhance curb appeal and get the house up to local specs. After the sale, there might be plenty of work for yet another set of contractors. All of those off-white walls will need some color. The 15-year-old kitchen might be just fine for frying an egg or two, but who wants to live on fried eggs?

There's a pretty high turnover rate in the real-estate field. The barriers to entry are fairly low. In many states, it only takes around $1,000 and six months to get a real-estate license. Lots of people get into it thinking they can make those big, juicy commissions working part-time on Sunday afternoons. Well, the lucky ones can, but the people who make a lot of money in real estate work it full-time and then some. They know their market. They know what every house has sold for on every street for years and years. They have their smiling faces on bill-boards in neighborhoods that are hot. They have a staff that takes the photos, updates the Web site, puts ads in the local papers, and sits at the open houses on Sunday afternoon from 1–3. They are all smiles when they find a client a perfect home and get some creative financing through the bank. They are all smiles five years later when the balloon payments have bal-looned too far, and the homeowner wants out before the bank kicks them out. They make money when everybody signs on the dotted line regardless of the circumstances. Therefore, they are very knowledgeable when it comes to interest rates. When interest rates are low, they can flip houses all over town. When interest rates creep up on notes tied to the prime rate, they know who might be in need of a Realtor to sell the very same home she sold to them three years earlier. If interest rates go sky high, she knows that she will be issuing some pink slips to those folks she has sitting in houses on Sunday afternoons from 1–3.

Of course, the construction industry is tied as closely to interest rates as the real-estate industry. If houses aren't selling because interest rates are too high, then everybody from the sewer contractor to the roofers will be idle. It's not just the blue-collar workers who take a hit. The architects, bankers, and title-insurance people all lose business, and that means they lose work.

In the 1970s, Mexican restaurants were few and far between in northeast Ohio. Good ones were even rarer. One opened not far from my home in what once had been a seedy bar and grill. From the outside, the place looked like the sort of place my mother told me never to enter. The first time I went to the place with some friends and we pulled in the parking lot, I thought they were kidding. I couldn't believe they would fre-quent such a dive. One bite of the fantastic food changed my mind. It was the best Mexican food I had ever eaten, and it was reasonably priced. On Friday and Saturday nights, the line of customers snaked around the building. The owners were smart enough to know that raising the prices would be a short-term fix to the long lines, but a long-term disaster. In the restaurant business, it's far better to have a large crowd than a small one that may become fickle and go to the first new competitor that opens its doors. They had to do something about the crowds, though. They decided to add onto the building. A friend of mine knew a good thing when he saw one and offered to finance the addition and become a silent partner in the restaurant. He didn't want to design menus, cook, serve, or even be there; he just wanted to put his money in the building in return for a share of the profits. If the restaurant made it, he'd have an income stream. If it failed, he was out a substantial pile of money.

Interest rates back then were hovering around 21 percent. My friend's offer could save the owners a bundle. By taking his money, they would save themselves the 21 cents on the dollar compounded and have the working capital. They looked at those lines and knew they had some good energy going. They told my friend thanks but no thanks and opted for a high-interest loan to keep the business all to themselves. Considering the fickle restaurant industry, it was a very bold move. They could have been saddled with debt compounding for years. But they could feel the energy of those crowds night after night, weighed their options, and went with their energy.

The Government's MasterCard

The national debt will impact some industries. At some point, debt maintenance will be absorbing so much of the government's income (your tax dollars, sweetie) that the government will have to stop purchasing things, just as an individual has to curtail spending until the MasterCard bill is whittled down. When the bulk of the national debt was held within the United States, there was a degree of wiggle room. But the early 2000s has seen more and more U.S. borrowing from other countries. It's hard to say how this will impact the future, but it probably won't be good. Government budgets will be cut, and government spending will be curtailed. Industries dependent on government dollars will be at risk, as well as the employees in those industries.

Bad News Blues

A lot of folks I know who are into energy principles avoid newspapers, the nightly news, and other sources of news because they don't want to pick up the negative energy. I understand wholeheartedly why they avoid the presses. After all, the nightly news is never the nightly *good* news. And if you've ever known a news junkie, they are not the most pleasant of folks to hang out with for long durations of time. I know a few, and all but two are downright negative energy magnets. The two exceptions amaze me. One is a man who finds the news—all news—to be entertaining. The other has a unique way of listening to the news without personalizing it. Most of us form an opinion, and then get pissed. It's not a good energy mode.

Even news that's of interest to job seekers is presented in a way that can raise blood pressure to the max and drop energy to the pits. Job seekers needs to know what bills are being passed, what industries are at risk, and what the interest rate is doing, but they certainly don't need the political party spin that's reported with each decision.

The news industry's sole function seems to be to deliver one dramatic downer story after another. And the bulk of the news isn't of any use to anybody; it's just sensational. Wars are sensational. News reporters never run out of wars. Homicides are sensational. News reporters never run out of homicides. They have a stash of bad news that they regurgitate on slow news days. Yep, when things are slow, another photo of poor Princess Diana will turn up somewhere.

As a job seeker, learn to extract the necessary data without getting sucked into bad news. The information you need includes facts and figures about the economic world around you. You need to know what's going up in that old parking lot. You need to know what industries are moving in and out of town. You need to know what industries are under consideration for the big local tax breaks. You don't need the rest of it. Unless you are a researcher who's going to make the vaccination that will save hundreds of thousands of people from the threat of some new strain of flu, you don't really need to know about it. Knowing about it, fretting about it, will just magnetize it, or something just as bad, into your life. And as far as those news stories about some guy who shot his granny because she didn't approve of his relationship with the twins in the next county, guess what? It's not part of your world. It might be interesting to peep into the lives of the more dysfunctional members of society, but why in the heck would you want to allow that energy to mingle with your good energy? It serves no purpose and just lowers your frequencies.

Energy Zappers

The media is having a field day with the offshoring issue, but it's a decade too late. If the media truly wanted to play a role in keeping jobs in the United States, it should have actively promoted consuming U.S.-produced products years ago. It should have exposed the downside of the big-box delivery line models. It should have exposed how retailers that demand 3 percent price reductions annually are forcing suppliers to move production to regions where labor costs are lower. It never ceases to amaze me how people don't connect the big-box discount prices with the departure of their own occupations. And I am not talking about just manufacturing jobs. I am talking about *all* jobs.

A massotherapist I know has been facing serious financial difficulties for the past several months. When I told her that her purchasing habits, combined with those of other members of her community, were in part to blame for the demise of her business, she could not see my point of view. Who can afford a massotherapist if their job has disappeared? She told me that quite the opposite was happening—if her clients shopped at the discounters, they'd have more money to purchase her services. She had a point in the short run, and she had reaped those benefits a couple of years ago. But she was now in the long run where more and more of her clients were finding their jobs moving to accommodate the supply-chain demands of the big boxes, and her clients could no longer afford her services. I doubt if she ever got the big picture. People feel they are too small in the global economy to make a difference. They may be right. We have probably gone beyond the tipping point, to a place where we are so accustomed to big-box shopping that we are not willing to buy goods made on our shores. And, to tell you the truth, it's hard to find goods made at home.

So what does all of this have to do with you finding a job? After all, this stuff isn't very fun. It's certainly isn't an energy booster by any far stretch of the imagination. No, but it's what one faces when seeking employment, and it's one of the biggest energy drainers to be found.

Even so, the good old days weren't all that good. There's no sense in looking back. People who are going to flourish in the coming months, years, and decades are those who don't look back and don't get sucked into the negative energy around them. Folks who move seamlessly from company to company and occupation to occupation on their great energy are going to be the winners. You can be at the head of that movement with your energy. Just tune into the high-frequency stuff that's within you and watch your world fall into order.

Interpretation

You have the power to interpret the world around you to your advantage if you so choose. Your cup can be half-empty or half-full. Of course, there's a lot of fodder for the half-empty interpretation when searching for work. And one of the best places to find negativity is in the numbers: the Department of Labor's unemployment numbers. Oh, yes, back to the government. It's a little hard to ignore when the topic is employment.

Statistics are great for the government, great for journalists, great for all sorts of number crunchers, but they aren't the best friends for job seekers. When job seekers look at the unemployment numbers, they have a tendency to think, *Oh, my God, I'll never get a job.* Those thoughts cause their energy to drop. The end result of such negativity is they fall into a slump and their job search limps along. So if you absolutely must look at the numbers, then look at them from another perspective when searching for employment. If the government's unemployment rate is 6.5 percent, the true unemployment rate is higher since a lot of people who aren't collecting unemployment benefits are not incorporated in that rate. The real unemployment rate could be 11 percent, so let's start with that number for this demonstration. That number represents an economy in which 11 percent of the population is looking for work. That 11 percent is competition for damned few jobs. That perspective can make a job seeker feel downright ready to crawl into a hole. Don't crawl. Turn it around. Look at the number from a different point of view: The employment rate is 89 percent. Obviously, 89 percent is the much bigger number. Think of how you will be joining the majority in a very short period of time. Feel yourself getting dressed for your next interview. Feel yourself breezing through that interview. Feel yourself shaking hands with the person who just offered you the job. Feel yourself telling your spouse, parents, friends, about your new job. Feel yourself performing a valuable service for substantial compensation. Feel yourself buying that new car (clothes, boat, house) you've been dreaming about with your big fat paycheck. Feel it!

Good News

You have to have some news daily to stay abreast of the world around you, but that doesn't mean you have to plug into the networks' daily dose of blood, death, and fear. Change the station. Get your news from a more balanced source. Most daily newspapers have an on-line edition. It's possible to breeze through the business sections on-line in little time by passing by the headlines of hate.

Seek balanced reporting. When the local NPR station has a fund drive, I volunteer to answer the phones. Most people who call the pledge lines pledge, but there are always a few who call to complain. Some call to say they'd give money if the news weren't so to the right; others call to say they'd give money if the news weren't so to the left. It's obviously a case of listener perception. Folks who look for something in the news will surely find it. You can look for bad news and find plenty, but you can look for good news, too.

Listen to the stories that are insightful. There's a lot of business news in the world around us that doesn't sound like business at all. As I said earlier, NPR had a short piece about a machine that tells people when to take their medications, dispenses the medications, and calls a family member if the medication is not taken. This isn't rocket science. It's a practical invention for an aging population. Look around, see a need, and apply an idea. Listening to news stories such as this one gets your creative juices flowing. They are energy-lifting. They let you know it's a big world that's in need of new ideas, new companies, and new opportunities.

Chapter 24

Energy and Economics

For some readers, this book has been your introduction to the Law of Attraction. Welcome to a wonderful new world! Enjoy life to its fullest. Have a ball. For other readers, the Law of Attraction is old hat, in fact, so much so that you've been visualizing a job for months without sending out one résumé.

Well, my friends, life needs balance. The world is forever moving into a state of equilibrium. We pop holes in Earth's ozone layer, and the excess pollution fills the air, proving to be the filter that protects us from the very same damage we are creating. Amazing. We are part of a universe that's forever striving for balance. Even the most extreme natural occurrences heal themselves. Forest fires create fertile soil for new growth.

Most of us strive for some sort of balance in our lives, too. We want love, but we don't want a lover holding our hand at all times. We want to work, but we want leisure time, too. We want money, but we want to spend it as well. Balance is everywhere.

When seeking employment, it's important to balance the use of energy tools with tried-and-true business tools. If you put too much emphasis on either the energy or the business side, you will prolong the process. Sending out hundreds of uninspired résumés, feeling more like a loser with each one, is pretty much a guarantee of lots of free time on your hands. Conversely, sitting around and feeling a job come in is pretty close to impossible. In order to feel a job on its way, you have to be actively doing something that opens the path for the job, i.e., you have to do something tangible. Most folks who claim to be feeling a job but are putting little effort forth to obtain one are probably feeling a little too much of the TV remote as well.

On the upside, keeping the necessary balance is relatively easy since both sides easily work off one another. The better you feel, the easier it is to send out résumés. The more résumés you send out, the more productive you feel. The more productive you feel, the better you feel . . . and so it goes. Since your productivity makes you feel good, you send out not only more and better résumés, but good energy as well. Ultimately, the good energy connects with a good job or other great opportunity.

Before I had even heard of the Law of Attraction, I experienced it big time. I had been in the level of mid-management that companies find dispensable. The economy had tanked, and the available jobs were being chased by a large number of candidates. My summer that year had been spent with a boyfriend who had a heart of gold and a head full of drugs. After months of trying to clean him up, I left him, his big house, and his nice cars, and went back to my little place. I had a big gap in my heart and an even bigger gap on the top of my résumé. After weeks of crying, I decided to take action. It was time to look for work regardless of the economy. It was time to feel like me again.

My dining room became my workspace. One morning in particular sticks out in my mind. I had spent the night before clipping classifieds from the newspaper. This was before the days of the Internet. When I got up that day, I began writing and printing letters. By late morning, I had a nice stack of cover letters ready to sign. As I sat and signed them, I felt like I was working again. The entire process of writing letters and signing my name felt like many days at my former job. I felt employed, and I *was* employed within a few weeks.

Synchronicity at Work

Oh, you might send out hundreds of résumés, and then get a job while standing in a queue at the bank. That doesn't mean those résumés were useless. Writing and fine-tuning those résumés was an essential piece of your job-search process. Those résumés got your energy wrapped around a job. They kept your energy focused on the job, the right job, for you. Each time you read a posting on Monster.com, or read a classified, or refine your résumé, you put out more and more energy toward employment. Had you sat around for days, weeks, or months thinking about a job, your thoughts may have been wrapped around a job some of the time, but your feelings would have been elsewhere. My feelings are wrapped around the fridge for long periods of time, I've noticed. Yep, I think I have this big head of positive energy all fired up to locate a new client, then I realize I've been thinking about a bowl of ice cream for an hour. I can't feel the client, but I can certainly feel the ice cream. Guess what I get? A double scoop.

Without the exercise of writing and refining the résumé, you might not be able to see the opportunity when it appears. In order to sell something, in this case your labor, you have to have it well designed. Lots of products fail not because they aren't good products, but because they are poorly defined to the end-user. Somebody has to see the value in something before they are willing to buy it. The same is true with labor— an employer has to see your value. Once an employer sees the value in hiring you, she will. That employer can only purchase your labor if you know exactly what you are selling. Writing and rewriting a résumé makes it easy for you to tell anybody who will listen exactly what you can do and want to do.

Opportunity Is Knocking

Opportunity doesn't knock on your front door and announce itself. If it did, everybody would see it. It's trickier. In fact, many opportunities don't look at all like opportunities. Some look downright ugly. When my former boss offered me contract work, I went ballistic. That was an opportunity. I not only missed it, but I pushed it away with both hands and gave it a kick for good measure.

Some folks say they never get a break. Probably not true. They just don't know how to spot an opportunity. They become so caught up with looking for something, somewhere, that they are close-minded when it comes to things that don't at first glance look like an opportunity. Once you get in touch with your gut, your Higher Self, you will be able to spot opportunities. If something looks bad, don't walk away without getting a feel of it. Don't be surprised if it looks bad, but feels pretty good. If it feels good, it's an opportunity trying to sneak into your life. Do some investigating and see if it's an opportunity or something you should allow to slide by. You will feel it when it's right.

Some of those hidden opportunities have the potential to rock your world. Hidden opportunities aren't the same as a hidden job market—a hidden job market doesn't exist. Hidden opportunities are turning a passion into an income stream, or being recommended for a great position through somebody you met while stuck in a long queue. They come when you are reading the business pages and determining a local company needs just your expertise. They come big-time when you turn an idea into gold. Those are hidden opportunities. They only appear when you are ready to see them. And when they appear, you have to be ready to move on them. When an opportunity appears, follow your gut.

Respect

Aside from balancing energy and economics, you need to realize that energy, the very substance of your being, needs to be treated with respect. It is you. Even with the knowledge of how your energy impacts your life, you will have good and bad feelings. It's what humans do. Believe me, even with a great deal of working at it, you are going to have some pretty awful days while job hunting. Therefore, don't expect to feel good about yourself every day, and don't beat yourself up when a smiley face doesn't appear in the mirror. Don't try to force your energy. Respect it. Once you respect yourself, your feelings, and your power, you will become very powerful. The down days will lessen. The good days will become your norm. You will have the power to bring in the best of jobs or any other thing that suits your fancy.

Thinking / Feeling

It's important to recognize that your feelings impact not only your energy, but your reasoning as well. When you are feeling low over a job search, you may become withdrawn. I think of it as pulling a blanket over your head. Once you are in your little world, it's hard to see anything, much less opportunities. Anybody who tries to stick a job posting under your covers becomes the bad guy. Even jobs that would be good if your reasoning were in balance appear to suck.

When your reasoning is off, everything gets jammed-up. Getting your energy up is pretty darned close to impossible, and catching a break from synchronicity isn't an option. You wouldn't be able to see an opportunity under your nose. So, if you get into one of those states where everything looks like it won't work, realize you have lost your balance. Your reasoning is off. Your thinking is a tad toward disaster. Your feelings are in the danger zone.

You won't be thinking about energy if your reasoning is off. Believe me, the last thing you will consider is this energy stuff. You will discard it as nonsense. You will say it's for "woo woo" people. You will never with an unreasoning mind be able to see the merit in energy techniques or anything else for that matter. Give yourself a day or two to suffer through it, enough time to bore yourself silly with your private pity party, then do something to make yourself feel better. Crawl out from under that blanket. It's not a security blanket; it is more of an insecurity blanket. Poke your head out. Go back to chapter 4 and try a few remedies. Have breakfast in your back yard. If your reasoning is off, there's no reason to worry about your neighbors thinking you are a bit kooky. Just do something to get yourself back on the right track.

Once you start to feel better, things will turn around. Oh, you won't call it energy at first, but that's perfectly okay.

The Real Thing

If you are staying positive, putting out good energy, contacting prospective employers, things will work out for you. On the other hand, if you are doing all of this with the true intent of just getting a job then slacking off, the folks who pass out the jobs will sense something is amiss and will turn you away. Oh, you might connect with a person whose radar is off the day you waltz in; you may get the job. But you won't be able to keep it. You have to become genuine in your desire for a good job and to be a good employee. Your good energy has to be real. The value you offer has to be real. If you are trying to con an employer into hiring you, don't be surprised if that employer is just as much of a scam as you.

Of course, faking it until you make it is another story. Faking it until you make it is feeling yourself being hired, feeling yourself in the position, and feeling yourself being an asset. You need to feel you are in the job to connect with the energy of the job. If you don't have it, and need to feel you do have it, then you obviously have to fake it. But instead of faking to just get the job, you need to mimic the feeling of being a great employee and being rewarded grandly for performing grandly. There's a difference between faking to get a job and faking it to become a great employee. One is a self-serving manipulation to simply get something you want in the short run. It's bad energy in disguise, a wolf in sheep's clothing—bottom line, it's still negative energy. The other is the true-blue positive energy that will attract more true-blue positive energy.

Tools

While positive energy goes a long way in attracting a job, the folks who pass out those jobs will still want to see your sales tools. Make sure you have a polished résumé at all times. Things move fast when you have energy on your side. There are plenty of resources dedicated to writing résumés. If you're having trouble with yours, I'd recommend looking at a few. Check out the Internet, books, and even résumé software available. With all of the tools at your disposal, there is no excuse for having a poorly crafted résumé. Think of your résumé as your primary sales tool, not a necessary evil or something thrown together to accommodate the system.

Use cover letters to augment your résumé, and always, always, always send a follow-up letter. These little gems have the potential to clinch the deal for you. Writing them also serves as a barometer if you have some reservations about a job. I've found more than once when I went to write my follow-up letter that I really didn't want the job. There was a nagging feeling in my stomach that got worse with each word I put on paper. I knew those jobs weren't right for me. There have been times when I've allowed jobs that would have seemed good to others slip away, knowing, believing, that the right job would appear when I most needed it. And it has.

Good Intentions

Getting the right job involves doing something about it every day, both on the energy and the economic sides. Know exactly what you intend to have your energy and economic tools do for you each day. Take a few moments of quiet time each morning and put out your intention for the day. Your intention may be for clarity on where to seek employment, or whom to contact, or what changes you need to make on your résumé. Your intention may be something of greater magnitude, such as seeking direction on whether to relocate or not. Your intention can be anything you want it to be, but you need to focus on it, get your energy wrapped around it, and watch for it to manifest as you work through your day.

Believe in Yourself

More than anything else, believe in yourself and the value you bring to society and the world of work. Unless your energy is 100-percent positive 24/7, you will still be putting out enough bad energy in bursts and fits to keep some negative energy flowing your way now and then. You will get rejection letters. You will get human resource folks who aren't interested in what you have to say. You will have people discouraging you from following your dreams. Heck, I once had a headhunter tell me I was unmarketable due to an outstanding gap on the top of my résumé. What he really meant was that he would not be able to turn a quick buck on me. I never bought into the unmarketable nonsense. There are opportunities everywhere, and you may even be able to create a couple of opportunities for yourself. Examine what you want in a job instead of what you're being told you should be doing. Raise the bar for yourself to maximize your utility.

Dream high. The world has enough people willing to do the work at the bottom of the corporate food chain. Once you get pumped up about a new job, a new career, about what you are going to do for a living, you can keep moving forward and put out good energy long after most people would have given up. You will find that you have the drive to get the necessary credentials or write the perfect résumé. Your energy will open doors that others believed were welded shut. You have energy. You have power.

Be conscious of your energy. Use the tools you now have to bring your energy up three or more times a day. Stay up and stay focused. Have fun!

You are a valuable person. You have a lot to offer the world. You have the power to shift your energy. So, with gusto, entrench yourself in the job-search process, stir in a large dose of enthusiasm, get your energy up, and bring the perfect job into your life.

Appendix

Your To-Do List

By now, you know that high-frequency feelings are essential in getting a job. The Law of Attraction never fails. Here are a few pointers to get the Law of Attraction working for you.

- Get up early and meditate. Get the message from your Higher Self. If you aren't working, you'll be able to take a nap later in the day. The best insight comes in those really early, quiet hours.

- Set a schedule each day. Long days make for long job searches. Get your mind and body on a timetable. Make a to-do list that incorporates how you are going to contact employers, where you are going to search for employment, whom you are going to call, how and when you are going to cold call.

- Follow a point system:

One résumé sent in response to a classified or job posting	1 point
Ten résumés sent cold calling	1 point
One contact made (networking)	5 points

| One follow-up call made | 5 points |
| One interview | 10 points |

Aim for 60 points per week. Remember, when sending out résumés they must include all of the buzzwords, or they will be filed for one year. Getting out ten résumés will take more time than a few clicks of a mouse. It's better to get 12 points per day than to procrastinate and get 60 points on Friday. Although you may find this point system to be aggressive, it will keep your energy wrapped around job searching and keep you feeling productive, which is essential.

- Go from "needing" a job to "wanting" a job. Needing is loaded with bad vibes. Needs suck. Wanting is light and lofty—the kind of energy that gets you connected to other light energy.

- Walk for 30 minutes every other day. Notice the changes in your neighborhood. Seek them out. This will not only get your blood flowing, but it will get your energy attaching to change.

- Schedule leisure. Just like any working soul, you need time to have fun. Play is very important to the human experience and helps connect you to the whispers of your Higher Self.

- Find two things that make you feel great. Do them. Keep those vibes up!

Three or more times a day feel yourself getting that great opportunity. Feel yourself breezing through that interview. Feel yourself shaking hands with the person who just offered you the job. Feel yourself telling your spouse, parents, and friends about your new job. Feel yourself performing a valuable service for substantial compensation. Feel yourself buying that new car (clothes, boat, house) you've been dreaming about with your big fat paycheck. Feel it!

Index

About the Author

Laura George began her human resource management career in 1989. Her "gut" feelings have prompted her to give further consideration to less-than-stellar candidates while bypassing candidates whose presentations looked good. She's also learned all the tricks of the trade, such as how HR departments weed out résumés with software, how they flush out incorrect data, and what kinds of companies advertise globally and hire locally.

Laura's job-search knowledge comes from both sides of the human resource desk. She is, as Barbara Ehrenreich terms it, a disposable white-collar worker—a professional who has found the world of work to be a revolving door more than once due to downsizing. Therefore, her job-search advice comes from her own employment searches, as well as from her experience in helping many colleagues find employment.

Laura has worked in several industries, at both small and mid-sized companies, as well as at a Fortune 100 company with thousands of employees worldwide. She currently owns her own consulting company, LHG Consulting, Inc., which provides human resource expertise to small businesses in northeast Ohio (see www.lhgconsultinginc.com). She holds a Bachelor of Science degree in labor economics, and has completed work toward a master's in the same field. Laura lives in Ohio and enjoys cycling and exploring her spiritual side.

HAMPTON ROADS
PUBLISHING COMPANY, INC.

Thank you for reading *Excuse Me, Your Job Is Waiting*, the first book in a new Excuse Me series that applies the successful "Law of Attraction" principle to specific aspects of our daily lives. In 2000, Hampton Roads published Lynn Grabhorn's *Excuse Me, Your Life Is Waiting*, which became a *New York Times* bestseller. Hundreds of thousands of readers have felt their lives transformed by Lynn's message. Lynn's book has brought us positive energy that has attracted other authors whose lives are guided by the principles she espoused.

Excuse Me, Your Life Is Waiting
The Astonishing Power of Feelings
Lynn Grabhorn

Ready to get what you want? Half a million readers have answered with an enthusiastic "yes" and have embraced Lynn's principles for achieving the life of their dreams. This upbeat yet down-to-earth book reveals how our true feelings work to "magnetize" and create the reality we experience. Part coach, part cheerleader, Lynn lays out the nuts and bolts of harnessing the raw power of your feelings. Once you become aware of what you're feeling, you'll turn the negatives into positives and literally draw all those good things to you like a magnet, creating the life you know you were meant to have—right now!

Discover the secrets that have made *Excuse Me* a *New York Times* bestseller!

Paperback • 328 pages • ISBN 978-1-57174-381-7 • $16.95

www.hrpub.com · 1-800-766-8009

The Excuse Me, Your Life Is Waiting *Playbook*
With the Twelve Tenets of Awakening
Lynn Grabhorn

Human beings have evolved physically, socially, and technologically but are unable to take the next step toward spiritual evolution because of self-defeating habits and conditioning—in short, we are our own victims. Lynn Grabhorn has taken the concepts that made *Excuse Me, Your Life Is Waiting* a bestseller and transformed them into a complete workbook for empowerment. The clearly focused explanations, discussion material, meditations, and exercises are essential building blocks to a new way of being.

Trade paper • 288 pages • ISBN 978-1-57174-270-4 • $22.95

Excuse Me, Your Life Is Now
Mastering the Law of Attraction
Doreen Banaszak

Lynn Grabhorn's wildly popular book, *Excuse Me, Your Life Is Waiting,* offered four fundamental principles for attracting what we desire most in life. Now Doreen Banaszak has created a sequel that not only presents a convenient review of Grabhorn's four basic tenets—identifying what we don't want, naming what we do want, getting into the feeling of what we want, and, finally, allowing what we want to flow into our lives—but also offers overwhelming evidence, including dozens of first-person accounts, that these principles really work!

Paperback • 208 pages • ISBN 978-1-57174-543-9 • $15.95
Available August 2007

ExcuseMeCourse.com

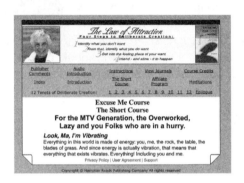

Lynn's unmistakable voice on spoken audio guides you throughout this program as she walks you through the four steps of her life-changing Law of Attraction. **ExcuseMe Course.com** offers powerful, guided meditations to take you to that next level of understanding. Plus, an interactive online journal allows you to catch your insights as they happen so you won't miss any opportunity to turn your new knowledge into real-world value. **ExcuseMeCourse.com** offers multiple ordering options and a **free ten-day trial period** to navigate and use any element of the course you'd like.